P9-AFI-088

Crosscurrents / Modern Critiques / New Series

Edited by Matthew J. Bruccoli

Robert Coover

The Universal Fictionmaking Process

Lois Gordon

Southern Illinois University Press
Carbondale and Evansville

For Alan and Robert

Printed in the United States of America
Edited by Teresa White
Designed by Gary Gore
Production supervised by John DeBacher

Library of Congress Cataloging in Publication Data

Gordon, Lois G.
  Robert Coover : the universal fictionmaking process.

  Bibliography: p.
  Includes Index.
  1. Coover, Robert—Criticism and interpretation.
I. Title.
PS3553.0633Z67   1983   813'.54   82–10337
ISBN 0–8093–1092–9

82   83   84   85   5   4   3   2   1

Contents

Acknowledgments

I am grateful to several people who kindly offered advice, information, and support: Richard Seaver and Fred Jordan, who furnished useful material about Coover's publishing career; Theodore Beardsley, who extended generous assistance in acquiring biographical and bibliographical data; Albert Soletsky, who provided thoughtful translations of Coover's Spanish in the *Pricksongs and Descants*; Melissa Montimurro, who listened to me think through some early ideas; and Lois Spatz, who provided some helpful discussion on comedy and tragedy. I also wish to thank Mary McMahon for her energetic and conscientious acquisition of library materials, and the staff at the New York Public Library for granting me the privilege of working in the Frederick Allen Memorial Room. I am especially grateful to Bernard Dick for suggesting that I contact Southern Illinois University Press with my idea for a book and to Matthew J. Bruccoli, who endorsed my project and encouraged its publication. I wish to make special mention of Gene Barnett who, here and in former work, carefully pondered my grammar and logic. For the sustained interest of old friends, Warren French, Ricardo Quintana, and Donald Hall, I am appreciative. My greatest debt is once again to my husband, Alan, for his indefatigable patience and optimism. He offered intelligent suggestions at every stage of this book. Finally, I must thank my young son, Robert, for his magnetic cheer and great forbearance on many a Sunday when my need to work restricted the family options.

New York City   Lois Gordon
1982

1

The Universal Fictionmaking Process
An Introduction to Robert Coover
and the Avant-Garde

While an impressive number of contemporary authors like Saul Bellow, Alexander Solzhenitsyn, and Heinrich Böll continue to publish traditional fiction—with linear plot, recognizable character, definable theme, and the unities of time and space—a growing number of writers have turned away from what Erich Auerbach termed mimetic fiction and created an entirely new form. Whatever its name—metafiction, postmodernism, postcontemporary fiction, surfiction, parafiction, fabulation[1]—it shares a number of specific stylistic characteristics and the notion that the old fictional devices are no longer appropriate to the modern world. Literature, it is implied, can no longer reflect a stable reality of fixed values, because the very existence of that reality and/or the possibility of accurately reflecting it are questionable.

John Barth, in a much-discussed *Atlantic Monthly* essay (August 1967), described the demise or exhaustion of the modern novel and the dilemma of the writer working in a form whose plots, characters, and themes had all been tried and used up. For Barth, the only course left to the writer lay in extending the boundaries of form through radical changes in structure and statement, in writing about the only thing left to write about, the act of writing itself.[2] His *Notes from the Funhouse* (1968), like some of his earlier work, exemplified this new direction, for its subject was exactly this, the difficulties of writing fiction. Samuel Beckett's earlier trilogy, *Molloy, Malone Dies*, and especially *The Unnamable*, and the fictions of the already well

1

regarded Jorge Luis Borges, Vladimir Nabokov, Gabriel García-
Márquez, and Thomas Pynchon were similarly innovative.

Following these writers (and also publishing since the mid sixties),
an international avant-garde emerged which included Julio Cortázar, Robert Pinget, Italo Calvino, Claude Simon, Philippe Sollers,
Jean Ricardou, J. M. G. Le Clézio, and the Americans Robert
Coover, Donald Barthelme, William Gass, John Hawkes, Gilbert
Sorrentino, Ronald Sukenick, Ishmael Reed, and Raymond Federman. In addition to rejecting teleological forms, such as conventional plot, character, and theme, these writers frequently take as
their subject the problems of using language to refer to a reality that
is largely unknowable, unfixed, and incapable of linguistic
documentation. The act of writing becomes an existential act of
reacting to and "reading" the events, people, and "meaning" of the
universe.

Robert Coover has frequently been asked if he and Barth (also
author of the now famous dictum "The [traditional] novel is dead")
have discussed their views, since they appear to be working in the
same direction. Coover's response that they have never even met
suggests that many artists working independently are responding
similarly to significant changes in the contemporary *Zeitgeist* (to
"something in the air," as he put it)[3] and to the changing demands
and function of art. In fact, like many in the avant-garde, Coover has
commented on the need to pursue an innovative fiction in order to
better serve the radically new perceptions of reality: "I felt we had to
loosen fiction up and reinvest it with some of its old authority as a
self-aware artifact, a kind of self-revealing mode, as it were, for the
universal fictionmaking process." All "conceptualizing," he asserts,
is "a kind of fictionmaking." Coover also remarks: "What I read in
physics, psychology, sociology, what I saw happening in all the arts,
all seemed to suggest a basic shift . . . to a less conveniently ordered
view of the world in which everything seemed random and relative,
and . . . all the old isolated disciplines found themselves flowing into
each other."[4]

Despite the dangers of generalizing, it is interesting to note how
the concepts of "randomness" and "relativity" characterize many of
the contemporary descriptions of reality. One can perhaps then
better understand why so much contemporary art in every form
(especially painting, sculpture, music, and literature) has aban-
doned the conventional pieties. One might also speculate upon the

ironic possibility that the avant-garde rejection of "finalized" event, personality, and morality, and the subsequent construction of open-ended collagelike forms, have given birth to an entirely new form of mimesis.

Contemporary physics, for example, demolished the idea of a fixed and stable reality and demonstrated instead the relativity of space, time, matter, and energy—both to their environment and to the very instruments that measured them. Einstein, Planck, Heisenberg, Wilson, and Penzias established the reality of the universe's physical entropy, the merging of space and time, and the fact that mass and energy are interchangeable. Physicists after Weinberg, Salam, and Glashow, pursuing mathematical derivations rather than empirical proofs, now speculate that the smallest observable particles of the universe consist of even smaller, *forever unobservable* units (quarks). Science continues to demonstrate that reality may consist of the unseen (like atoms, quasars, quarks) or of data that contradict the senses and traditional logic.

The social sciences, especially psychology and the work from Freud and Jung through Deleuze, Goffman, and Laing, have also radically altered traditional notions of reality, specifically in the areas of human behavior and thought process. What had been called "human nature" or behavior "common" or "natural" to all, was subjected to intense investigation in the light of radically new methods and theories. The study of personality extended to the unseen, to that part of the mind that defies time, space, and logic (the unconscious). Motivation and personality were no longer identified simply through intention and act, and definitions of normality and aberrance became blurred. Once again, appearance and reality, the real and the fantastic, and, more specifically, the normal and abnormal were redefined. Identity, like mass, could not longer be considered a fixed or measurable entity observable to the senses. In addition, the observing instrument could be subject to subtle but possibly uncorrectable distortion.

Contemporary philosophy argued the arbitrariness of moral values and questioned the implicit difficulties of using language as a tool in apprehending and explaining the world. The existentialists, such as Heidegger, Sartre, and Camus (in the line of Pascal, Kierkegaard, and Nietzsche)—contending with the fundamental notion that God is missing, absent or "dead"—pursued the speculation that the moral beliefs by which one asserts his values and identity are

similarly relative. The demise of absolute good and evil precipitated
the breakdown of absolute standards—like (Aristotelian) responsibility, courage, and heroism.

   Students of phenomenology (Husserl, Heidegger, Merleau-
Ponty, Bachelard) and linguistics and semiotics (Saussure, Todo-
rov, Jakobson, Barthes, Derrida) have more recently theorized
about the relativity of language—a metaphor or translation of experience, in itself indefinable and beyond words and logic. Cultural
anthropologists (like Lévi-Strauss) and psychologists (like Piaget and
Lacan) raise questions about the mind's a priori structures which
universally impose a set of patterned responses upon a foreign and
disordered reality. Following Wittgenstein, analytical philosophy,
like these newly related fields, has been preoccupied with meth-
odological difficulties imposed by the nature of language and
thought. Indeed, in all areas of study, redefinition has been
pervasive—from such diverse manifestations as the biologists' ex-
pansion of evolutionary theory and animal observation into the
theories of sociobiology to the historical speculations of Foucault
and the microhistorians following Braudel. Poincaré's categorical
denial of empiricism—his proof that $2 = 2 - 11$—may be the last
word in what was once called simple math.

   Considering all of this, even in the most general of terms, it is
understandable that this vast and pervasive intellectual migration
away from absolutes toward an awareness of the relative, complex,
and random nature of things should be reflected in literature. The
rejection of one-point perspective, the breakdown of linearity for
multiple renderings of time, place, and character, and the interpenetration of interior and exterior reality were all tendencies that
marked the modernist movement.

   What is innovative in the new fiction is the extent to which these
techniques have been utilized and the unique function that fragmentation now assumes. No longer an end in itself (chaos reflecting
chaos—e.g., the Dadaists, like Tristan Tzara), or a method of mirror-
ing the unconscious (e.g., the surrealists), or a technique toward
reestablishing value (a counterpoint against traditional religious,
mythic, or historical values, as James Joyce, William Faulkner, and
T. S. Eliot used it), fragmentation now functions as a means through
which both author and reader assert meaningful, albeit tentative
patterns regarding human experience.

   The reshuffling of fragments and the act of giving oneself to the
"flow" of a story (or a literary style) which then expands or dissolves

through shifting and alternating tones and techniques (or through distracting or contradictory materials) which frequently merge into multivalenced ironies—all function to dissolve centrality of focus and to force one into the creative task of organizing meaning. As in viewing collage, one's perception of design or meaning depends upon his temporarily staying the shifting surfaces of his subject and then evaluating them within their own dynamic relationships to time and space. The artistic rendering of multitextured and open-ended event and identity thus evokes the richness of experience, and the act of reading (like that of writing)—of participating in these "readerly" texts—becomes the creative endeavor of designing meaning in an infinitely rich and irreducible universe. Art and life imitate one another.

It is perhaps then not surprising that, with shifting surfaces behind both method and critical response, this literature should frequently look at the mechanics of form and meaning as its very subject. "Metafiction" (fiction on fiction) well describes a literature that assumes a definition of reality as one's fictionalized articulation of nonrational sense experience. That is to say, if the experiential life is one of the senses, obviously outside language and thought, and if that life is comprehended only through its translation into the artifices of language, then the very conceptualization of life— precisely because it is in the translated terms of language (with causality, plot, and characterization its major components)—is an act of fictionmaking.

Evocations of relativity and flux obviously vary from writer to writer, but again, some generalizations may be useful. Many of the avant-garde authors, for example, dissolve plot linearity (time and space) and the traditional components of genre (and sometimes even grammar); most incorporate into their forms entirely new elements—the use of counterpointed linear textures or perhaps spatial, typographical, or other pictorial designs. Relationships between people, things, and events are generally viewed from multiple merging objective/subjective) or dissolving points of view, or within shifting ironies. Fixed point of view is noticeably absent, and any implied moral judgments are qualified through additional layers of irony. A new, spatial, collagelike form emerges, where character, place, event, and point of view reflect the plasticity of ordinary experience.

Interestingly enough, despite Robert Coover's fascination with the randomness and richness of event and despite his preoccupation with the destructive ways in which human values and behavior become fixed, he frequently retains a strong narrative line. Not at all inconsistent with the stylistic tendencies mentioned above, Coover's retention of plot, like his fascination with design, is actually illustrative of the unique uses to which irony has been put by the avant-garde. It is, in Coover's case, the means toward accomplishing a nondidactic art. "The writer's experience is paradoxical," he comments, "the imposing of order on a disordered reality.[5] We *are* turning back to design," he continues, for it is "useful . . . to express the ironies of our condition."[6]

Coover's method, more specifically, is this: at the same time that he maintains a strong narrative line he counterpoints it (his musical term is "descants") with numerous mythic, legendary, or symbolic levels (in painterly terms, "washes"), which serve to explode any final meaning or resting point. One is continuously distracted by the diatonic strands which simultaneously qualify or dramatically alter what one assumed to be fixed descriptions of personality, event, or human values. In such highly structured forms, not unlike those of cubist art, film montage, or even symbolist poetry, Coover creates fluid and metamorphic designs that reflect the nonfixed nature of both external reality and human potential. His subject is always process—and the perfection of process, flux, and possibility.

An important effect of this sort of design, also typical of the avant-garde, is that it never "finishes." In *The Universal Baseball Association*, for example, after the reader is offered, in eight chapters, a concatenation of varied responses to a series of human dilemmas, he is left to his own devices to provide the essential and concluding chapter 9, like the final inning of a baseball game. Even in *The Public Burning*, Coover daringly incorporates the reported "facts" surrounding the Rosenbergs' espionage trial, sentence, and execution, but one ends the book convinced only of the profoundly complex issues of the time, totally uncertain of the Rosenbergs' "guilt" or "innocence." While history, like traditional art, religion, or science, proffers its own conclusions, Coover does not. He can only suggest the complex and ambiguous nature of reality and truth.

Also typical of this nonteleological literature, which never "finishes," is the fact that each novel, play, or short story "reads" differently each time one goes through it. While one could say this about all great literature, here, as in collage, the entirely metamorphic or transformational quality of images, characters, events, and vision resists conclusions and more closely mirrors the existential universe. Process is once again subject, and each new reading accomplishes a new mimesis. We have come a long way from, say, Sir Philip Sidney's pronouncement that literature serve a morally utilitarian function; nevertheless, Coover's metafiction, like that of the other experimentalists, observes its own pragmatic and perhaps social and educative function. It reengages and reminds one of his daily and urgent task to discover fresh meanings in an endlessly rich and contingent world.

Coover has developed a style unique among his contemporaries, mixing so-called fact and fiction with realism and surrealism, merging narrative line with adjacent and "descanting" poetic or fragmentary evocations of moral, mythic, historical, philosophical, and psychological dimensions. He writes in virtually every form, including short story, poetry, fairy tale, filmscript, drama, and novel. Within each, he demonstrates a remarkable diversity of styles and manipulates the trappings of every conventional literary form from old comedy to theater of the absurd; he also translates or transposes techniques associated with other art forms—e.g., film montage and operatic interludes. Any of these might then be transformed into the most extreme forms of parody. Coover has the uncanny ability to reproduce or mimic verbally the written, spoken, or even kinesthetic styles of literally hundreds of historical or popular figures. He can also arouse the emotions traditionally associated with tragedy. Regardless of length—and he has published noticeably long and short fiction—his work is always rich and difficult. Throughout, one would have a hard time finding an ill-chosen word or awkward phrase.

Within this dazzling variety of forms and styles, and fitting for the new spatial designs, is Coover's insistent focus on the need people have to organize their lives in arbitrarily created rituals which inevitably carry with them destructive value systems and role models. Repeatedly, Coover illustrates the human need for structure and order and yet the constrictions (and sometimes catastrophe) they bring. Religion (*The Origin of the Brunists, A Theological Position*), politics (*A Political Fable, The Public Burning*), art (*Love Scene*), personal "games" or systems (*The Universal Baseball Association, Spanking the Maid*), and even the moral lessons one might absorb from the Bible, fairy tale, myth (*Pricksongs and Descants, The Kid, After Lazarus, Hair O'The Chine*), or, perhaps most revered of all, from Hollywood films (*The Public Burning, Charlie in the House of Rue*) both define and usually destroy.

This is, to modify Rousseau and Freud, a new type of social/psychological/religious contract designed to barter inner disorder — psychological and sexual needs, as well as more conscious pride needs — and external disorder — the fear, rage, and helplessness one feels with the knowledge of death's ubiquitousness. The Coover man, with all his political, social, and moral schemes, exists within a vast and benignly indifferent, cosmic universe. But he struggles as well against an equally enigmatic and sometimes more purposive inner one. Survival, it would appear, depends upon achieving an equilibrium between the inner and outer worlds through the construction of rituals — and this one achieves through the mediation of his controlling imagination. To paraphrase Dylan Thomas: the force that through the imagination quiets the spirit is one's redeemer; but it may also be one's destroyer.

Coover's eye is always upon human neediness, upon one's yearning for significance in both concrete and metaphysical terms. Throughout, his protagonists face eternal predicaments: how to deal with the need for power, control, significance, and immortality within the realities of personal and human limitations (time and fate) and how to deal with personal failure, sexual longings, and the wish for control over chance and morality.

Although his writing has been citicized for its emphasis upon bodily functions and its religious irreverence,[7] body and soul frequently complement one another in Coover. As in much seventeenth-century metaphysical poetry, his evocations of sexuality often portray human strivings for more permanent significance, just as his depictions of religious experience are often the compensatory expressions of very basic sexual drives. One cannot separate body and soul in much of this earthy and religious literature. Coover examines the sexual/metaphysical roots of imaginative creation, as he chronicles the destructive mythologies and behavior that mark human history.

In Beckett's and Pinter's worlds, the individual is ruled by inner and outer forces that defy his best efforts to construct games or stratagems to endure time. While this may also be true of *Origin* and *The Public Burning*, in works like *Pricksongs and Descants*, *The Universal Baseball Association*, and *A Theological Position*, Coover is closer to Yeats, Woolf, and Joyce in restoring to man the redemptive imagination — and, in a unique sense, the games that it constructs — as the means toward comfort or despair. Coover is significant among the postmoderns in these works, in returning to man his own destiny, for neither external forces, like fate and chance, nor character and the psyche—and certainly not the media or highly technological society—define and drive so much as imagination. Granting the capriciousness of chance and the power of unconscious drives, one has a certain amount of freedom or choice in determining his fate. Unfortunately, as Coover goes on to portray, most people tend to retain credos or games that have outlived their usefulness, or they invent others that inhibit rather than release. At times, one even constructs myths with the same machinery as the reality against which he is fortifying himself.

Although this might suggest a new terminology regarding the tragic condition, Coover's implicit belief in man's near limitless potential for transcending circumstance accounts for his comic orientation. "The higher truth," he remarks, "is a comic response. . . . There *is* a kind of humor extremity which is even more mature than the tragic response"; "great ironic, comic fiction can . . . be equal to the same kind of strange emotion you get out of tragedy because your emotions can be mixed."[8]

Irony, as already noted, marks much of this work, and if Coover's is a comic art, it belongs to the ironic mode, though again, in a unique sense. Coover is fully aware that if he explodes historical documents or traditional religion or other mythic forms that have frozen the human spirit, his fictional replacement may ultimately do the same. (One does not destroy the old and absolute in order to substitute the new and absolute.) He is, however, a responsible and empathic artist, and although he does not destroy the old without replenishing the void, the open-ended quality of his fiction resists, to an unusual degree, unambiguous interpretation.

Since he realizes that myths are man's "necessary" means of "navigating through life,"[9] and that "the world itself . . . [is] a construct of fictions," he accepts the "fiction maker's function" to "furnish better fictions *with which we can re-form our notion of things* [italics mine]."[10] His designs thus serve less as ends in themselves than as stimuli to the reader's greater freedom within normal experience. One questions his commitments to the rituals that define his life. "The writer's [and reader's] experience is paradoxical. Like life itself," Coover further explains. One must impose "order on a disordered reality"—but with continuous self-consciousness; as a result, fiction must always be "self-aware about what it's doing, exposing its own activity as it goes along."[11] This strangely tentative mythifying, at once ambitious and humble, also characterizes Coover's work. We are back to defining a uniquely mimetic art.

A general introduction to Coover would be incomplete without some attention to his comprehensive erudition and the broad scope of his work. In his complex investigations into history Coover frequently writes of historical forces that repeat through civilization, and he focuses upon the arbitrariness with which they are evaluated; once again, he would open up to his reader not only his present reality but also his heritage and the manifest complexities eternally present in human affairs. Challenging the narrow perspectives of legend, history, the Bible, and art, Coover educates in many areas. One gains an entirely new understanding of biblical and American history (*Pricksongs*, *Public Burning*, *After Lazarus*), but Coover is also a master sociologist and psychologist, detailing those complex and unresolvable psychic drives and pride needs that both necessitate and maintain not only historical, religious, and literary myths but also the specific sociological patterns that recur in culture (*Origin*).

Most recently, Coover has published, in limited editions, filmscripts and novelettes which retain earlier themes but which are, in addition, remarkable *tours de force*. *Hair O' The Chine* (1979), for example, is one of his most challenging, funny, and ambitious works as it treats the "Three Little Pigs" not only as fairy tale but also as etching (one by Robin McDonald is included in the text) and as several other interpolated art forms like painting, drama, collage, and cartoon. These are then set against a scenario involving a young maiden and man which dramatize their meanings; all of these strands are then juxtaposed against a narrative voice that interprets the several modes of storytelling according to a variety of scholarly disciplines (literary, historical, psychological, anthropological, religious, etc.). *Charlie [Chaplin] in the House of Rue* (1980), delves into the recesses of the human psyche in a strikingly original way. It explores—in a verbal equivalent of Chaplin's silent film techniques —the underside of comedy with its eternal transformational possibilities for sadness and hostility.

After Lazarus (1980), in its poetic transcription of archetypal dream images, reminds one of a de Chirico painting. Once again Coover illustrates his belief that myths are useful because they tell us something about ourselves, and he reads the Lazarus myth against a series of mirrors. He begins in dramatized linguistic terms, with diachronic and synchronic levels of language; the narrative, another filmscript, then expands to evoke the artist and his eternal striving after linguistic authenticity; it then suggests the natural divisions within the human mind and the eternal needs of the human spirit; finally, it deals with the human resistance and need for structure—for myths—and it approaches, with atypical sobriety, a definition of the tragic. *Spanking the Maid* (1981), with its "Bolero"-like intensification of repeated motifs, reminds one of the metafictional, linguistic, and metaphysical exercises in *A Theological Position*. It deals with the metaphysical/erotic struggle for authenticity and freedom in daily life and the creative task of dealing with the Word/word, the abstract and concrete dimensions of experience and language. All of these, in one way or another, once again deal with the human need for significance within an absurd reality.

Robert Coover was born in Charles City, Iowa, in 1932. When he was nine, the family "drifted away" to the Midwest, first to Bedford, Indiana, and then to Herrin, Illinois, but it was "never very far away from Iowa."[12] The young Coover was well rounded, especially interested in dramatics, civics, and writing. He was high-school class president, a member of Quill and Scroll, the National Honor Society, and the school band. As "Scoop" Coover, he edited various school papers (he also had a column "Koover's Korner") and wrote short stories and poems; he is said to have entertained dreams of travel and of becoming a foreign correspondent.[13] Among other hobbies, such as watching the Cincinnati Reds practice in nearby French Lick, Indiana, he belonged to a coed cheering group (the Pep Club) for the local basketball team. He also enjoyed parlor baseball games, popular at the time.

Coover worked for his father when he became managing editor of the Herrin *Daily Journal*, and he entered Southern Illinois University, near Herrin, in 1949, where he was once again active in school activities—e.g., he was a reporter on the newspaper, the *Egyptian*. He remained there until 1951; from 1951 to 1953, he attended Indiana University, where he received his bachelor of arts degree with a major in Slavic studies. A mining disaster occurred on one of his trips home in 1951, and this, along with his newspaper experience, may have inspired two central details of his first novel, *The Origin of the Brunists* (1966). One might also relate Coover's parlor baseball games to the subject of his second novel, *The Universal Baseball Association* (1968).

The day Coover received his college degree, he also received a draft notice. He joined the navy, attended Officer Candidate School and spent the next three years in Europe. (He has actually lived most of the past twenty years there.) On an early Mediterannean tour, he met his future wife, Maria del Pilar Sans-Mallafré, a student at the University of Barcelona.

Coover has referred to the following period as the turning point of his life. During the summer of 1957, he spent a month at Rainy Lake, Minnesota (mentioned in "The Magic Poker), and began his innovative fictions, many of which appear in *Pricksongs and Descants*. Once at the University of Chicago, which he attended from 1958 to 1961 (he received his master's degree in 1965), and having read Kafka, Henry Miller, García Lorca, Sartre, Dylan Thomas, Dostoevsky, and Shakespeare, he discovered Samuel Beckett.

Beckett, Coover has written in an important essay "The Last Quixote,"[14] became a sort of artistic-spiritual father; for years he "held up the walls of my studies," and offered "a way of going on, of making art, without affirmation." Beckett was Coover's literary model in his "odd abrupt transition between different fictional levels," his "ironic echoes and parallels, funny games with numbers, numbers and logographs . . . the inconsonance between words and their referents . . . academic gags, abstruse puns, rhetorical parody . . . virtuosity." Through Beckett Coover also arrived at Joyce, Dante, Proust, Swift, and even Cervantes. Above all, Coover concludes, "he helped scrub the canvas clean."

At the University of Chicago Coover came to some important insights regarding the changing descriptions of the universe and the limitations of traditional fictional form. He recalls conversations with the philosopher Richard McKeon on "the history of ordered discourse" and how "the fashion of the world was indeed changing. Not only were we about to leave behind the recent age of expression, of analysis, of words and deeds, for another frantic go at the strange instable [*sic*] stuff we stood on, more *Weltanschauung* explorations, but in fact a whole cycle of innocence and experience, begun in the Enlightenment, was drawing to an exhausted—even frightened—close."[15]

Even as an undergraduate, Coover was a serious student, "attracted to courses in theology and the philosophy of religion," while unorthodox in traditional religious commitment: "The problem of Christian belief bothered me: it wouldn't leave me alone and yet I couldn't solve it. Then I found a vibrant way to understand the matter: I imagined a character like Jesus, created him in my own mind, and carried this thing on with him. Rather than try to discuss the historical arguments for his existence or non-existence, or to investigate what had happened to the Gospel texts and how much we could depend on the various parts, I merely took the story itself, and, involving myself in it, considered various variations."[16]

At the same time he also encountered the argument between the theologian Rodolf Bultmann and the philosopher Karl Jaspers. Bultmann insisted that Christianity should demythologize itself: "One should go to the Noah story, Adam and Eve, the Virgin Birth, all those things that looked ridiculous to the modern eye—but not the Resurrection. The Resurrection had to be saved, because it was that moment in which God's finger touched history." For Jaspers, on the other hand, whose argument was imminently more comfortable to Coover, "if you throw the rest out, you've got to throw the Resurrection out too." Coover actually took Jasper's argument further and set forth his own methodology: "But, why throw any of it out? Why not accept it all as story; not as literal truth but simply as a story that tells us something, metaphorically, about ourselves and the world?" Jasper's conclusion—"the only way to stuggle against myth is on myth's own ground"—Coover repeats, was the "verification of what I had been writing clumsy notes to myself about."[17]

In addition to Jaspers, Coover has cited as influential Freud, Lévi-Strauss, and especially, Emile Durkheim. Durkheim appealed to his religious instincts and through him Coover found an "excuse to make fictions instead of doing something more 'serious'"[18]—support, perhaps for his own artistic obsession with America's civic religion and the spiritual forces behind organized society.

In addition to the writers already mentioned (and obviously the authors of ancient, classical, and biblical literature), Coover made early researches into Ovid and *The Arabian Nights* because of their fascination with metamorphosis. Change, or metamorphosis, as Coover sees it, is the inevitable life process which man most resists. ("The basic, constant struggle for all of us is against metamorphosis.")[19] Coover has also singled out Melville, Washington Irving, Poe, and Hawthorne (for their "far out stories"), and "of course, Mark Twain."[20] He once listed as the contemporary writers of special interest to him Stanley Elkin, Sol Yurick, Thomas Pynchon, John Hawkes, Günter Grass, John Barth, William Gass, and the Latin Americans Miguel Asturias, Julio Cortázar, Jorge Luis Borges, Carlos Fuentes, and Gabriel García-Márquez.[21] (He is fluent in Spanish.) His debt to Cervantes he acknowledges extensively.

Cervantes, he explains in *Pricksongs and Descants* (discussed in chapter 5),[22] responded to the changes of his time in revolutionary artistic terms. He rejected the exhausted romance tradition and created the novel; he united the disparates of human experience and synthesized "poetic analogy and literal history (not to mention reality and illusion, sanity and madness, the erotic and the ludicrous, the visionary and the scatological)." He provided for his readers a new vehicle of games—in today's parlance, "les jeux" (*donde cada uno pueda llegar a entretenerse*: "where everyone may be able to enjoy himself"). He gave his audience entertainment, design, and morality, a reaffirmation of human possibility through concrete and realistic experience. Throughout Coover, the concept of game—the combination of rules and pleasure—is associated with both the high function of literature and one's adaptation to the exigencies of the absurd universe.

Beckett then labored with Cervantes's form in its death throes and illustrated the difficult if not impossible process of dealing with a dead language, feeble logic, and the "incoercible absence of relation . . . between the artist and his occasion." At the same time, Beckett affirmed the need, indeed the "'obligation'" to write. Although Coover never uses the word "metafiction," he defines Beckett's work as a "lifelong parable on what writing itself is all about." Quoting Beckett's remarkable *The Unnamable*, he repeats: "'To name, no, nothing is namable, to speak, nothing is speakable, what then, I don't know. . . . I shouldn't have started . . . strange pain, strange sin, you must go on . . . I can't go on, I'll go on.'"[23]

One might parenthetically note the interesting and shifting triangular relationships here. Although Coover pays tribute to Beckett for inspiring his work, he, in fact, picks up Cervantes's fictional form and redirects his syntheses of disparate experience. He transforms what he calls Cervantes's "sword"-become-Beckett's-"crutch"-and-"pencil stub" into his own redesigned magic poker or golden pen. On the one hand, it seems true that for Coover, like Beckett, words remain "'my only loves'" and that he has also been "obsessed by mystery, by the impossible Self and the tyrant Other, by paradox and flux." On the other hand, where Beckett's concern with process and the inefficacy of the old fictional structures have produced what Coover calls "painting absences, [like] white on white,"[24] Coover's textures are less "abstract expressionist" than, as we have said, multitextured and multicolored collage.

There are additional ironies and coincidences. Coover's essay on Beckett, published in 1971, though clearly composed during his

Chicago days, is one of the most lucid essays written about Beckett. Similarly, Beckett's 1931 essay on Proust remains one of the best (and first) essays published on his spiritual mentor. Yet, as Beckett lauds Proust for his remarkable evocation of time's bounty through recollection, his own treatment of both voluntary and involuntary memory portrays time as the "monster." Analogically, although Coover apotheosizes Beckett for singing the death knell of words, he himself uses words for their generative possibilities.

Finally, in so far as ironies, paradoxes, and the use of language and vision are concerned, as Beckett is to Joyce, so, up to a point, is Coover to both Beckett and Joyce. Although Beckett and Joyce are exiles from their native countries, and religious exiles as well, they both create a very religious literature about an always deeply loved homeland. Coover is also (as shall be discussed shortly) a self-imposed exile, and he writes a very American fiction about a very religious nation—as he views it in political and social terms; he too remains religious in spirit. But where Joyce evokes a linguistic universe full of possibility and infinite subtlety, and Beckett draws a stark world through pruned and negated language, Coover's infinitely rich linguistic universe challenges the fixed and stable material world and the continuing historical, mythic, and religious values that underlie Joyce's world.

Coover's publication history is interesting, because (1) it belies the true chronology of his works, (2) many of these publications (e.g., each of the novels) were initially conceived in other forms, and (3) Coover always seems to be working on numerous projects simultaneously.

Although his first full-length publication, the prizewinning *The Origin of the Brunists* (1966), was a novel, Coover at that time really considered himself a short-story writer. Written over four years, *Origin* grew out of a mine disaster story "Blackdamp," published in *The Noble Savage* (1961). Coover had been concentrating on his short, innovative fictions since 1957, and although they were virtually finished when he published *Origin*, they did not appear until 1969. In addition, at the same time that he was doing the major work on *Origin*, he was also completing the first draft of *The Universal Baseball Association*. Coover admits that the reasons he began *Origin* were several: friends, agents, and editors suggested he write a novel; "Blackdamp," his first published story, had been well received; but most importantly, he felt obliged to "pay his dues" before gaining "the right to move into more presumptuous fictions." ("The trip down into the mine was my submerging of myself into the novel experience.")[25]

The short story "The Second Son" (1962) contained the kernel of *The Universal Baseball Association* and actually became its second chapter. (Coover intended it to be part of his collection, *The Unhappy Cosmos of J. Henry Waugh*.) Coover has called the novel "a book about the art of writing," although he has qualified that this is "not necessarily as it ought to be read."[26] *The Public Burning* began as a play, but because it seemed awkward in that form, Coover transformed it into a short story, "The Public Burning of Ethel and Julius Rosenberg: An Historical Romance" (1974). The novel took ten years to complete.

During these years, among other things, he also revised "The Cat in the Hat" as *A Political Fable* and worked on several short works including the plays in *A Theological Position* and the novella, *Whatever Happened to Gloomy Gus of the Chicago Bears?* It took two and a half years for *The Public Burning* (about the Rosenberg executions with Richard Nixon one of its major figures) to get published, since at least four publishers refused it for fear of litigation.

Coover is obviously a man of prodigious energy who, in addition to writing in virtually every fictional form, also publishes translations, book reviews, and literary criticism.[27] He has even written, directed, and produced a film, *On a Confrontation in Iowa City* (1969). He has contributed to a variety of publications including *Evergreen Review, Cavalier, Argosy, Noble Savage, TriQuarterly, Antaeus, Playboy, Penthouse, Iowa Review, Harper's, Quarterly Review of Literature, Panache, New American Review, and Fiddlehead*. One of his plays, *The Kid*, was nominated for an Obie Award.

He has lived most of his professional life in Europe, mostly in England (Kent) and Spain, for the ostensible reason that this has been the best way of surviving financially. He has remarked, however, that it is easier to assert and create your life without all the "familiar vibrations. . . . Almost everything I've written has been done out of the country—and after midnight."[28] It has been said that in "an uncharacteristic note of rancor," Coover is angered by the "dictatorship" of the American "marketplace": " 'You make a million or you don't even get printed.' "[29]

To be sure, the popularity (and profit) Coover enjoys in America is not commensurate with either the high praise his books have earned among respected readers or the enormously high esteem with which they are held by the literary and intellectual establishments. Although *Origin*, for example, won the William Faulkner Award in 1966 for the best first novel, Coover earned little, if anything, from it. Saul Bellow calls Coover a "small audience writer";[30] he has frequently been called a writer's writer. Although many people thought *The Public Burning* would have made him more accessible to a larger public, because of its subject, Coover's name is still far from a household, or even classroom, word. Coover's editors, nevertheless, similarly describe his artistic integrity and their conviction that he is among the most significant authors of the century. Richard Seaver, champion of *The Public Burning*, responds to the "small audience" remark by saying "That is accurate only in the short term. In the long haul, when we look back over the end of the century, he [Coover] will have sold more books than his contemporaries. Like any good writer, he's not necessarily in tune with his time or catering to his time."[31] Fred Jordan, who also knew Coover at *Evergreen Review*, remarks: "Most writers are torn between the marketplace and their vision. I've never encountered that in him. The marketplace is immaterial to him."[32]

Coover returns to the United States, it would appear, for both practical and artistic reasons — not just to take on teaching jobs for necessary income but also "to touch base with home and not lose the idiom; he is, after all, very much in the American tradition."[33] Gaining a teaching job was at one time even difficult. Only after applying to two hundred schools in the New York area was he finally hired at Bard College (1966–67) where he had to prepare seven different courses the first term. Over the years he has also taught at or been invited as writer-in-residence to the University of Iowa, Wisconsin State University, Washington University, Columbia, Virginia Military Institute, Princeton, and Brown. Most recently, he has been at Brandeis.

Contributing to his financial and professional support over the years, he has won, in addition to the Faulkner Award (1966), the Brandeis Creative Arts Award (1969), a Rockefeller Foundation grant (1969), the Guggenheim Award (1971 and 1974), and the American Academy of Arts and Letters Award in Literature (1976).

Coover is a very private man, intensely devoted to his work. Geoffrey Woolf, who interviewed him for the *New Times*, also observes: "More than any writer, more than any man I have met, he is invincibly self-assured and secure in his professional self-esteem. This he expresses not through stridency or arrogance but through a relentlessness of purpose; he knows what he means to do, and does neither less nor more. He has outlined sufficient work to occupy himself for the next 200 years."[34]

Perhaps a fitting conclusion to this introduction might consist of a few of Coover's remarks regarding his purposes in writing and what he considers to be the high calling of the artist:

> Serious writers always tell the truth, and that truth has to do with the metaphors or clusters of metaphors they've chosen to work with . . . to penetrate reality. . . . [Fiction] wrestles with the shapeshifting universe. That, for me, is a moral act. . . . [This] intransigent penetration of a metaphor [is] . . . a little like chasing a vision.[35]

> Any pursuit or attempt to unravel or discover or understand the basic underlying assumptions about the world is a religious experience . . . [a] religious quest.[36]

> [I'm] particularly . . . interested in the American civil religion [and] . . . the roots . . . of this heresy of Western Christianity.[37]

> [The main responsibility of the artist is] revelation. . . . [He must] reach the emotions. . . . The whole organism is a sentient being. . . . The writer's role [is] priestly, [as Joyce describes] this in *Portrait*. He's torn between . . . entering the priesthood . . . and entering political life. . . . This leads to a vocation in which he sees the synthesis of the two, the synthesis of life, the world . . . and the religious or meditative life. . . . He becomes monkish at times.[38]

2

The Origin of the Brunists
The Origins of a Vision

The Origin of the Brunists (1966) has the rich texture of prose styles one associates with the mature Coover and is a *tour de force* of subtle and diverse characterization. It represents Coover's self-imposed apprenticeship to conventional form, as at the same time it demonstrates his precocious mastery of that form. It even contains, in its last pages, the unique blending of realistic, fantastic, and mythic materials that one associates with Coover's most original work. Perhaps in the very writing of *Origin*, Coover exhausted the limits of traditional characterization and plot to his own satisfaction and then felt free to pursue his innovative fictions.

In this epic narrative Coover portrays the sexual, religious, and pride needs at the heart of human nature, and his vision reaches every extreme: it is tragic, bawdy, bitter, condemnatory; it is also wildly jubilant, lyrical, and comic. The human mind, Coover seems to be saying, in its bouts with human suffering, personal failure, and sexual desire, is capable of infinitely inventive and destructive possibilities. One yearns for a sustaining sense of self-importance and for control over chance and mortality, while the most one can ever really attain is a vision of the illusory and indeed ridiculous claims of such quests. In the meantime, one constructs fictions or metaphors (religious, political, philosophical systems) as though these could stop time, the process of change, and the inevitable humiliations of body and spirit. Pleasure in the sensual present remains, and this, as ever in Coover, is a recompense not to be valued lightly.

Coover's specific focus in *Origin* is the individual and his society's need for religion as an ordering system in a world of violence, death, failure, and boredom. *Origin* exposes the brutal, eccentric, and sexual origins of a modern day "Christian" religion. Ignorance, lust, pride, and paranoia are channeled into the new faith, which suddenly materializes as a lifeline to a drowning society. Coover takes the basic Christian story and, as though placing it in a centrifuge, precipitates out the variety of imaginative, concrete, historical, sociological, philosophical, and psychological possibilities implicit in the myth both intrinsically and extrinsically. These form the weltanschauung of the new Brunist cult.

The human mind is eminently creative as it projects its unfulfilled passions into the new faith, which is then cultivated and celebrated with zeal and even euphoria. Religion, at least in this early work, functions less as a rationalization for death and a palliative for cosmic loneliness than as an outlet for aggression and the need for power. It assures one of victory over the projected forces of darkness. As one of the novel's main characters Justin Miller might put it, religion is an arbitrarily structured system that organizes the flux; like politics or literature, it is another "game" that makes life tolerable. Miller's comments could preface any of Coover's books: "Games were what kept [him] . . . going. Games, and the pacifying of mind and organs. Miller perceived existence as a loose concatenation of separate and ultimately inconsequential instants, each colored by the actions that preceded it, but each possessed of a small wanton freedom of its own. Life, then, was a series of adjustments to these actions and, if one kept his sense of humor and produced as many of these actions himself as possible, adjustment was easier" (pp. 141–42).

While Coover is compassionate toward the human need for such "adjustment" and belief systems ("games"), he also warns against the purposive and destructive power they impose over the mythmaker. One can too easily be swept up into his own metaphor and lose the world in return. Morality, Coover insists here and throughout, must remain living and individualized, rather than dogmatic and generalized. Ironically, in his own search for truth, the novelist creates his own (artistic) metaphors and mythology, which, of course, face the same dangers he warns against.

The skeletal plot (later elaborated in the discussion of structure) is this: the strange and schizoid Giovanni Bruno has survived a mine disaster in the small midwestern town of West Condon. His rescue, interpreted as miraculous, inspires the birth of a religious cult loosely based on the vocabulary of Christianity. Central to the new sect is the prediction of an imminent apocalypse, and it is toward this event that preparations are made by the Bruno worshipers (all the local eccentrics and religious zealots) and their opposition, the old-time evangelists (equally neurotic and demonstrably more violent). Although the Last Judgment fails to materialize exactly as expected and the leader, Bruno, is carted off to a mental institution, the power of the cult has grown secure and is even spreading abroad, succored both by the indefiniteness of the prophecy, with its endless possibilities for new interpretation, and by the insatiable media. Near the end, the newly named religion, the Brunists, is born—with the local newspaperman Justin Miller, the cult's initial publicist-defiler, literally sacrificed to it. In the fantastic and surprising conclusion, Miller is resurrected and united with his ministering nurse. He affirms a pagan embrace of life—the second but true religion—and the book ends on the final words of affirmation: *"Come and have breakfast"* (p. 441).

Miller's sudden reappearance is the novel's most puzzling aspect, necessary, one might speculate, for Coover's contemporary and, in many ways, whimsical version of the Resurrection story. If, that is to say, Christ's generally *unobserved* resurrection inspired a new religion, Miller's literal and also sexual "rebirth"—his "erection"—might do the same, at least existentially, so far as his sensuous "bride" and he are concerned. Miller's "resurrection," however, also introduces the novel's metafictional dimension.

Coover's defiance of the realistic material thus far—in over four hundred pages—draws the reader's attention to the artifice before him, to the author's self-conscious manipulation of his fictional materials. Implied is the idea that literature does *not* mirror a stable and fixed reality (if such even exists) and that *any* rational ordering of experience is fictional. In a somewhat recondite irony, if the journalist Miller, through selective distortion, has spread the Brunist gospel (media can accomplish in days what it took the apostles and their spiritual descendants hundreds of years to effect), Coover, the literary historian, can similarly author a gospel of their gospel though, as he explains in *The Water Pourer*, art's translation of experience is always idiosyncratic.[1] Finally, Miller's fantastic resurrection draws the reader into the creative partnership of completing the novel, of working through its intentionally unresolved ambiguities and contradictions of imagery and characterization.

The major characteristics of Coover's later work are here: (1) his focus on man's need for personal and cosmic significance in a world of chance and personal frustration; (2) his depiction of the genesis

and grammar—the evolution—of myth (morality) in contemporary
society; (3) his vision of sensuality as uniquely redemptive; (4) his
creation of an "open-ended" novel in the metafictional mode (he will
later raise questions about the fictional nature of reality and the
difficulties in the use of language); (5) his use of ever-expanding
symbolic levels—Bruno as Christ, Job, John Brown, Giordano Bruno,
Saint Stephen; Miller as Christ, Adonis, Osiris, Justinian, John of
Patmos, the Christian apostle; and even man as beast; (6) his
incorporation of a variety of styles; (7) his treatment of recurrent
themes, such as the power of media in distorting and historicizing
reality and the dialectical nature of moral alternatives; and (8) his
Tolstoyan vision of history as flux which cannot be explained despite
all efforts to describe and understand causality.

   Origin is also unique in many ways, especially in its detailed characterization of a large and diverse midwestern population. Although
in the later work Coover creates as many as four or five major
figures, here he draws in copious detail at least twenty.[2] Their
individualized perspectives of a presumably common experience
form the substance of the novel. In effect, Coover portrays the
panorama of conscious thought processes, the variety of phenomenological apperceptions, and the unconscious needs and dreams
that comprise a culture.

   The novel consists of six major sections with varying subdivisions.
These can further be broken down into monologues, streams of
consciousness, pop songs and spirituals, satirical epistles, and
poems, along with the more realistic descriptive and dialogue materials. Coover moves the plot either through his separate characters'
first-person perceptions and descriptions, or he writes in the third
person, incorporating the vocabulary and cadences of each figure's
unique "style."[3] To Coover's credit, despite the book's density and
complexity, its syntax is always lucid, and there is always a clarity of
plot and character.

   In these sections, which vary in length from short paragraphs to
thirty-five-page sequences, each person is directly or peripherally
involved with the religious movement or with other prominent
figures and the life of the town; sometimes Coover captures a
character within the solipsism of his own mental world. This is a
brilliant display of personality depiction in the technique Virginia
Woolf mastered by holding time still and moving within as many as
five or six contiguous and peripherally related minds (or by holding
personality still and moving through time). In Coover's case, the

number is multiplied four or five times. The reader thus encounters an enormous range of perceptions and language styles, all counterpointed with historical and legendary imagery. He lives through, and participates in, the communal birth of a religion.

Coover's panorama of the ways in which people cope with disaster also provides a sort of psychosociological version of the *Origin of Species*. Until the mine accident, life in West Condon, for the most part, was stable and peaceful, a place of "wearisome monotony" (p. 29). The explosion, much like the random mutations that impel evolution, radically disrupts the precarious balance of forces. It evokes throughout the population a combination of despairing helplessness and immense excitement. Everyone now shares an awareness of mortality and contingency. At the same time, each unearths buried longings for rebirth.

The catastrophe arouses and serves a variety of needs. Those who require an explanation for their sudden despair also thrive on a new excitement brought into their otherwise drab and empty lives. Disaster also appeals to everyone's pride needs—to the yearning to feel important—and it prompts opportunism and untapped creative energy in the least likely corners. An aging faceboss of the recently closed mine (Bonali), for example, latches on to the dream of rebirth as a grassroots political figure. A repeatedly displaced and perverse schoolteacher (Eleanor Norton) seizes the moment to gain prominence as a mystic; a meanspirited evangelist (Abner Baxter) schemes his way to replace his revered predecessor (Ely Collins), a courageous and saintly leader who dies in the mines.

Catastrophe gives life to both the individual and to all the groups that form in response to it. The cynical intellectual and small-town journalist, Miller, finds a fresh game to play by joining the newly formed cultists. Since he believes life is meaningless, he continuously seeks out short-term projects (games) with beginnings, middles, and ends. (He, of course, designs the rules.) His scheme is to use the Brunists both for the game of it and as a means to gain national prominence as he publicizes their story. Newly formed religious organizations similarly afford each member special powers to explain and conquer the inexplicable.

Everyone has the need to be the protagonist in this drama and as such, requires an antagonist or "force of darkness." For the Brunists, the entire uncomprehending world which would short-circuit their common communion with the infinite is the potential enemy. For the opposing, traditional evangelists, the Brunists are threatening because of their special claims to knowledge. For the wealthy and prominent, the chaotic spectacle of medieval, internecine religious warfare imperils the community's reputation as stable, sane, and God-fearing.

At the other end of the socioeconomic spectrum, the miners are intent upon proving that the inadequacy of their bosses' safety precautions caused the accident in the first place—i.e., insufficient rock dusting. (The mine management, in the meantime, contends that worker negligence was responsible: miners smoked where prohibited.) As to which group has the best, or worst, hold on things, it is perhaps ironic but obvious that the wealthy and respected are the most threatened. Although powerful and prominent, they continuously fear that everything will be taken away from them, and they thus maintain a constant vigilance over the status quo. In a strange way, the wealthy do have most to lose, because of all the people in this well-stratified society, they have had the most control over their destinies.

Everyone is thus everyone else's potential adversary, competing for the same power, sense of importance, access to sexual goods, recognition, and greater control over his life by virtue of these things. It is a great achievement that Coover takes a seemingly quiet community with an apparently stable sense of religious and political values and, in minute detail, illustrates how in a time of crisis everyone becomes acutely aware of the ambiguous and precarious nature of existence.

The structure of the novel is fascinating. Like classical epic which begins *in medias res* (as Milton, for example, introduces the already fallen angels), Coover begins, so to speak, in the middle of things—at the penultimate "Gathering" scene two days before the anticipated apocalypse. This is a tryout, they believe, for the coming time when they may well face persecution, suffering, and death. Now, in what Coover calls a "Prologue," the West Condonites and many newcomers, who have traveled from afar dressed in white tunics, meet at the site of the mine disaster, the Mount of Redemption (also called Cunt Hill) for the end of the world and the Last Judgment. Automobile lights suddenly appear, and Bruno's sister, Marcella, is fatally struck by a car. As to what follows, Coover merely speculates: "Some seemed to remember a luminous white bird . . . a heart-shaped bloodstain . . . [Marcella pointing] to the heavens." Coover concludes: "This death in the ditch, the Sacrifice, became in the years that followed a popular theme for religious art, and the painters never failed to exploit this legend of the heavenward gesture . . . the bubble of blood" (p. 24). Most of what follows is Coover's speculation, *his* book of Genesis, regarding the birth of a religion. We are back to the beginning of things. (The novel's last few pages are an epilogue, which Coover labels "Return," thus challenging linear time and reinforcing the circularity of the book.)

It is (a Holy?) Thursday when Number Nine, Deepwater mine explodes and ninety-seven men are killed. Three days later, Bruno, properly "gashed," is carried out. Perhaps through fear, Bruno had remained on a ledge, apart from the others. An outcast even before the accident, he was always an "*inter*-verted type," a renegade Catholic, and schizoid poet, disliked and mocked by his coworkers: "He'd jis stare . . . at you . . . a funny bird" (p. 101).

A small group of local eccentrics interpret Bruno's survival as divinely ordained. They project onto his weird comments—about a white bird, the coming of light, and the gathering on a hill—the truth of religious revelation. It just so happens, in addition, that the local preacher, Ely Collins, killed in the disaster after a grotesque leg amputation, scribbled a few words on paper which has also survived: "I dissobayed and I know I must Die. Listen allways to the Holy Spirit in your Harts Abide in Grace. We will stand Together befor Our Lord the 8th of" (p. 96). These words, and the fact that Collins apparently saw a white bird in the mine, seem to coincide with the strange messages of the saved Bruno. It is as though the West Condonites have in Ely a witness to the resurrected Bruno who is, in fact, nearly catatonic and probably brain damaged by overexposure to carbon monoxide.

Coover's characterization of the lunatic fringe that comprises the cult is subtle and complex. The new religion, which begins with a few widows and relatives of the mine victims, as well as the local spiritualist and her husband, eventually attracts other local spiritualists, theosophites, proselytizers, astrologers, fallen Catholics, deviant Protestants, and rebellious adolescents. It is also a magnet for the emotionally disturbed and sexually frustrated.[4] Bruno, truly a life-in-death figure—mute and hollow-eyed—is a virtual tabula rasa, to be read as anyone wishes. For someone interested in numerology, for example, and the number seven and its multiples, Bruno's mystical identity is indisputable. He was, after all, the ninety-eighth man to come out of the mine and the seventh in his assigned area.

The lawyer Ralph Himebaugh (as in *Golden Bough?*) is one of the group's numerologists. Described as nature's "victim . . . sacrifice . . . [and] outcast (p. 184), he surrounds himself with cats, instead of people. Many of his efforts are devoted to collecting newspaper disaster reports. Himebaugh sees the world in terms of mathematical clues to a higher reality, and he believes, like the dead preacher's wife, Clara, that it is moving on an irreversible course toward cataclysm. Later called Rahim, Himebaugh has constructed an elaborate and objective system regarding the supreme, ruling mathematical force, and through it, he predicts events. Although he is contemptuous of most people, his fascination with the number ninety-seven draws him to Bruno, and once at his house he shares a "spiritual" affair with the more intuitive and equally mad Eleanor Norton.

Eleanor, wife of the veterinarian, Dr. Wylie Norton, is in many ways the novel's most villainous character. A high-school teacher who has been chased out of eight towns in the past fifteen years for consorting with young males, Eleanor has a vicious quality about her. She has an affair with a local boy which drives him insane, and at the end, she literally tries to castrate Miller. Yet for all her destructiveness, there is a radical innocence about her as she absolutely believes in the other world and her communications with it.

Eleanor actually becomes nationally recognized as an important spiritualist. She is an occultist, a "practicing medium" and "automatist" (p. 141), an old-style sibyl in touch with her spirit "Domiron." In her feverish trances, she reads the "emergent design of revelation" (p. 119). Despite Eleanor's snobbish attitude toward the cultists with their "stale dream" of a Last Judgment and especially toward the déclassé Italian Bruno, her worship of numerology and astrology eventually attract her to Bruno; his astrological sign is also propitious. Eleanor visits Bruno, believing his body to be invaded by the higher spirit and calls him the chosen, "immortal one."

In fierce competition with her is the more sympathetic Clara Collins, the preacher's (Ely's) widow. Before Ely's death, Clara lived in "that great man's shadow" (p. 15). Now, bereft of him, she is "as though possessed by the Holy Spirit itself." She rushes to Bruno's side with her husband's note and shares with him the visionary prophecy of the white bird. Clara is the word of Ely now conferred upon Bruno, the necessary male vessel to continue the faith. She too shares the belief that the apocalypse is at hand.

If these people see signs as wonders, Coover characterizes them with "signs" from a variety of sources. Their symbolic identities, however, are as misleading as their false reading of events. The

Nazarene preacher, Ely Collins, whose note prophesizes the apocalypse, is a case in point. Although his message, like his name, suggests his divine powers (Eli, Eli lama . . . : My God, my God, why hast thou forsaken me?), since the event does not materialize, he is, like his name, "a lie"—in fact, both deliverer and betrayer. The same is true of Justin ("Tiger") Miller—not quite John of Patmos, Justinian, or any of the negative symbolic associations one brings to him.

Of special interest in the group is Giovanni's sister, Marcella, the girl killed on the hill, the "Sacrifice." Marcella often feels dissociated from herself and, like Eleanor Norton, she hears voices. Darkly "turned into herself, and yet somehow radiant," Marcella is often draped in a blanket and allusively associated with the Virgin Mary (p. 78). She carries the spirit of her brother, as Clara carries Ely's word, and delivers it to the newspaperman Miller ("Giovanni was visited by the Virgin"), who publishes and sensationalizes the purported gospel.

Despite Marcella's madness, she yearns for order in her life. The cynical Miller finds her mysticism ridiculous, but he has fallen in love with her and would marry her. Marcella, however, is torn between her religious and sensual impulses. When she discovers Miller's bad faith, she starves herself in deference to her own faith and in denial of her body. Justin has defiled the purity of her vision.

Appropriately nicknamed "Tiger," Miller both fits into and is a loner among the Brunists. On the one hand, he is granted special privileges as the cult's publicist because, among other things, he is associated with "grace," with the magical number seven: he was the successful "14" on the West Condon high school teams, and he worked for the paper fourteen years. Now he not only chronicles the group's activities (like Saint John?), but he also authors the apocalypse (John of Patmos?). On the other hand, Miller is the cult's gravest opposition—cunning and manipulative, while forcefully attractive sexually and intellectually.

At one time Miller was more optimistic and honest, but he has grown disillusioned, "the prince become a frog . . . drowned in debt, sick to death of the disenchanted forest, and knowing no way out" (p. 69). He clearly sees things as they are, but a good story is always his first priority. Although he initially views Bruno as a "browbeaten child turned egocentered adult psychopath" (p. 140), because Bruno will sell papers, Miller feigns friendship and support.

Miller's main problem, or really Marcella's—with his attitude that survival demands game playing—is that he fails to announce his rules. Though he truly cares for Marcella and becomes repentent of his opportunism (later returning incriminating photos and copy), he has gone too far in his revelations about the Brunists. Not only has he historicized and institutionalized their insanity, but he has also been responsible for the marketing of it. There are scripts, records, and texts for sale.

Despite Miller's personal appeal and clever mind, one dislikes him—both for knowingly exploiting these people, whatever their failings, and for his own maniacal worship of news, the "proverbial lotus" (p. 151). If Bruno is the silent rock of the church (a complement to the illiterate Ely with his scribbled note), the newsman Tiger is, ironically, its verbal proponent. He has as much to do with its founding as the others; in fact, its global popularity is due to him. Yet, as Miller himself says, if he is their Judas, it is ultimately through them that he finds his own salvation; in his own more earthy religion, he becomes both "savior" and "church."

Like any political organization, the cultists provoke an opposition which similarly channels its own frustration, envy, power needs, and lust. Stirred first by Miller and then by the mass media, each side typically condemns the other as the force of darkness. Prominent among the anti-Brunists is Abner Baxter, husband of the ever-tearful, ever-pregnant Sarah and father of five regularly whipped and subsequently sinister children. Baxter, with his red beard and fiery temper, arrogates the Nazarene pulpit after Ely's death. Now, although he despises most people, there is a fiery radiance about his preaching, which grows increasingly more impassioned as he grows ever more fearful of losing his newfound hegemony. His pride, jealousy, and possessiveness parallel the cult's popularity. Eventually, he too gets caught up with the Brunists.

As both the cult and the opposition evolve, it becomes clear that not only is morality a matter of convenience but so is ritual. Any word or sign (personal or social) is significant: catastrophe is "assurance in the contest with doubt"; anything can be rationalized into their religious frame. Meanwhile, their greed and frustrations grow, with everyone increasingly obsessed with details.

Everything is symbolic: "The Spirit is manifest by signs" (p. 214), they all believe, and through the novel, black crucifixes, the theft of a window, snowstorms, and even poor television reception are turned into omens of "positive eventualities." Anorexia caused by illness is distorted into an act of religious fasting; dead cats, dogs, and even chicken feathers are relics; a charred, scabby, black hand from a dead miner becomes sacred. Teenage vandalism is the devil's hand-iwork. Everyone's speech is also filled with the language of "illumi-nation," "mystical fascination," "transformation," and numerology. In one lengthy sequence (pp. 295–96), Coover summarizes the community's recycling of traditional symbolism even in the details of its clothing. All of this, of course, adds a heightened sense of apocalyptic foreboding to the daily procedings.

In maintaining their normal piety and everyday life-styles, the townspeople sublimate their frustrations and lust, and this is appar-ent in their most ordinary activities, from snacking on pecan waffles to playing cards. Violence and sexuality—repressed, restrained, or overt—is everywhere. A novice miner of eighteen is nearly sodomized by the older miners as an initiation rite. Teenage banter and backseat foreplay are suffused with ignorance and macho pre-tensions. Parental discipline is regularly applied to vividly bare but-tocks. A respectable bachelor lawyer sleeps chastely beside a nude, beautiful, and by-then demented woman. The well-to-do lunch to the enthralling tales of a local pressman's "best [and savage] lay ever." A local prostitute provides secret, sexual services to seemingly everyone in the town.

For such people the most banal or violent event is easily trans-formed into religious experience. Scapegoating seems a way of life, and Coover demonstrates its insidious chain reaction effect. The local evangelical minister tortures his children who then, in the form of the Black Hand and Black Peter, vandalize the neighborhoods, stealing and putting "poop on porches" (p. 164) and strangling cats or burning birds they have shot in gasoline.

The faithful apostles, in the midst of all of this, gather around the crazed Bruno, the unlikely candidate for martyrdom. His patent emptiness makes him an ideal vessel for their needs and enables them to develop an entire history, creed, ritual, and political system—a religion of "light"—based on fear and death, rather than on love or grace. Ironically, as they bastardize and then exhaust the vital and original forms of traditional religion, they assume the pagan names associated with its origins—Womwom, Elan, Karmin, Ko-ei, Mana. Indeed, as they exploit Bruno and use his house for their own personal needs, Bruno becomes less and less important to them. His eventual disappearance—like Damon's or Henry's in the *UBA*, or even Christ's in history—is irrelevant to the religion's sub-sequent growth.

To set things right amidst the warring zealots, a Common Sense

Committee is organized among the "respectable" members of the community, led by Cavanaugh, the banker; Whipple, the mayor; and some of the prominent shopkeepers and clerics, including Wes Edwards, a liberal, urbane ecclesiastic. The group also enlists the help of Vince Bonali in order to gain popular support among the miners and their families. There is an implicit promise to Bonali of a political future.

Despite their manipulative qualities, the Common Sense Committee is basically well intentioned but unequal to its task. The Brunists' fame has already stirred powerful and irresistible, irrational forces in everyone, and the national and international media are already on the march to West Condon. In fact, some of the Common Sense members are no longer acting sensibly. Bonali, entrapped by the businessmen Robbins and Castle, is put up to a prankish and vicious assault on the Brunist Himebaugh's house. This results in a drunken, sexual attack upon the Widow Cravens, a woman who had previously seduced Bonali but who is now enraptured by the Brunists. Cheese Johnson, a hillbilly whom Common Sense had tried to co-opt, becomes an uncontrollably vicious force, as he tries to initiate a gang rape of the widow. When the police finally capture him, he successfully bribes them. Bonali, who, despite his drunken state, had finally tried to protect the woman, is nevertheless undone by media attention to the ruckus.

The plot has now reached the point where the prologue began. Both religious groups have been attending a preliminary demonstration on the Mount where, two days hence, they expect redemption. In an ensuing traffic jam, Marcella, long since deranged by Miller's betrayal, wanders aimlessly on the road and is accidentally run down by the archenemy Baxter. Her "sacrifice" reconciles the antagonistic religious groups and is the initial episode of the book's denouement which occurs two days later on the hill.

At the climax, the Brunists hold aloft Marcella's mortified body and march on the Mount, exalting in sermons, prayer, and song. They are followed by converts from near and far, numerous reporters, and hundreds of curiosity seekers. The hotelkeeper Fisher, with typical entrepreneurial ingenuity, has rented, for the day, the hill, a previously worthless piece of property. This legally entitles him to charge admission as well as to promote various concessions, including alcohol and gambling. A thunderstorm occurs, perhaps an analogue to the "eclipse" at the Crucifixion, and mayhem follows. A child is accidentally killed, and several other people are injured.

Miller, suddenly compelled to be involved in the ultimate moment, whose dubious grandeur he has helped create, charges the hill and is ritually attacked and whipped. As he "dies," Eleanor Norton, the sanguine mystic, prepares to wield an ax to his genitals (an analogue to the wounded Bruno?). Also part of the final scene, Clara's plain-Jane daughter, Elaine Collins, renounces the sincere, romantic Carl Palmeres, and she engages in mutual flaggelation with Junior Baxter, the unsavory offspring of an abusive father.

Although the book is not yet over, one cannot help but pause at the wild carnival scene which, like a Roman spectacle, everyone seems to welcome, enjoy, and indeed need. Later, Happy recalls that even though there is no Last Judgment, if the machinery for it is set in motion, people welcome the excitement of the process. As Coover repeatedly portrays these spectacles (*A Political Fable*, *The Public Burning*), he would seem to agree. These circuses are theaters in which one can satisfy his craving to court disaster. They are socially condoned forums that permit the exorcism of aggression and guilt. One can even pretend—at least at this sort of spectacle, with a Last Judgment—that there is an "end" to the eternal "beginning" and "middle" of life, a justification, or at least a symmetry (even as Blake portrays it emblematically in his "Tiger"). Life, otherwise, consists of mysterious incidents without cause and effect, and all one can do is accept, with frustration, the legacy of mythic commentary which the prophets, philosophers, newsmen, and artists create in order to perpetuate a sense of order and meaning. In one's indefatigable search for meaning, he might even accept the end of the world.

After this wild carnival scene, despite the violence and chaos and the fact that nothing miraculous transpires, the religion spreads. Its leaders, in the tradition of the great prophets, go on to bigger and more successful ventures as bishops and national television figures. For the ordinary man like Bonali, despair returns. The mine is closed, and the excitement of new possibilities is ended; a vast "emptiness" returns. For a moment, Bonali is hopeful that his daughter may have been impregnated by the mayor's teenage son; but she has merely broken up with the boy, and Bonali has no such luck.

As though Coover were playing upon the transference of epic roles from Satan to Adam in *Paradise Lost*, he now focuses on Miller, his literally reborn epic hero. Actually, Coover leaves it up to the reader to understand Miller's "return." Thus, if one accepts the incarnation and resurrection myths, he might also accept Miller's rebirth. On the other hand, perhaps Miller has just been mistaken for dead, in which case his "recovery" is miraculous in the colloquial sense of surviving the odds. One way or the other, before "passing on to his reward [heavenly or concrete]," Miller had a vision: "[he] amazingly . . . saw, or thought he saw, a woman giving birth: her enormous thighs were spread . . . blood burst out" (p. 410).

Miller's reward is his rescue and hospital reunion with his own impregnated Happy Bottom, the loving, creative, sensual nurse who enjoys her body and who views the supernatural and the Brunists with affectionate mockery. (Her satirical epistles of the Last Judgment are some of the funniest sequences in the book.)

Reality and religion, to be sure, are in the eye of the beholder. If the townspeople find comfort or meaning on their "Redemption" Hill, so does Miller on his "Cunt" Hill. The miners have descended to their deaths in cars or "shafts," and the mine which was once their womb, their life support, has become their tomb. For Miller, the mine/hill becomes life, and its vernacular name reconciles all paradoxes, much like Kubla Khan's caves of ice and dome of sun. It may be noteworthy that at the end, Miller and the childbearing Happy will leave West Condon, whose name in abbreviation, W. C., suggests waste.

The end of the book is a *tour de force* of comic bravura, as sex is apostrophized in the language of religion. Happy, Miller's equal in intellect and sensuality, has, throughout, written and phoned him with wry messages concerning the Brunists' misguided behavior. Like one character in *The Universal Baseball Association*, she thinks God is "a nut," and her idea of real communion is good sex. She and Miller have indeed found the true religion, and their sacrament is physical union. That the Word is in the word (to paraphrase Wallace Stevens, in the flesh beauty is immortal) is a theme that recurs virtually throughout Coover.

Tiger's return, his "recognition" and "reversal," involves his embrace of temporal experience as the only reality: "Nailed fast to his torment, he stared out with blind eyes on the impossibility of the cosmos." As he is reborn, he sees "what looked like a cord with a button at the end [the hospital bed intercom]" (p. 431). His resurrection process includes his stigmata (being "pierced" with Happy's healing needles), his "descent" and receiving of "spices" (adjusting the bed and receiving medication), and even being wrapped in a shroud, in clean white "linen," all normal hospital routines. But everything is endowed with the language of joy and exaltation, for indeed his life has been saved. Even the enema he receives during his "recovery" is a "flood," the exultant release of most former despair (p. 435). Happy and Miller discuss their children as the "sons of Noah," a "sign of the covenant" (p. 440).

As they enjoy each other, they discover concretely the promise at the heart of all religion. They feel passion and power— immortality—in the momentary conquest of time and flux. Near the end, the covenant is sealed; Miller is both fallen man and Peter; he will build his church on his sexual passion: "She dipped an index finger into his navel. 'And on this rock . . . ,' she said, and they both watched the church grow" (p. 434). Then they "signed a pact, exchanged gifts, broke a chamberpot, bought Ascension Day airline tickets . . . and, nailed to the old tree of life and knowledge that night, she murmured in his ear one *Last Judgment*" (p. 440).

This is Book XII of Coover's *Divine Comedy*, the postlapsarian Adam and Eve, embracing experience, imperfection, and time. It is in a mood of laughter and jubilation that they affirm: "Yes, there was that. Not the void within and ahead, but the immediate living space between [the] two" (p. 435).

3

The Universal Baseball Association
The Props of Meaning

Perfection wasn't a thing, a closed moment, a static fact, but *process*, yes, and the process was transformation. (P. 212)

Henry Waugh, Coover's protagonist in the *UBA* (1968), faces the eternal human predicament: how to meet the need for power and control, omnipotence and immortality, in the face of one's own particular limitations, as well as the more awesome constraints imposed by time, aging, death, and the vagaries of fate. Coover draws upon a rich panoply of symbolic, historical, political, and social detail in order to characterize both Henry and his world. He manipulates the imagery and machinery of a score of artistic, religious, and social myths which, through the ages, have attempted to deal with the human dilemma. In both form and subject, he illustrates the limitations of the many "answers" construed by man to comfort him in his own temporality. Though one is driven to create them, they can never fully satisfy one's deepest longings, because they can never halt or compensate for the alterations of time. One generation cometh, and another passeth away: such is the only truth, with the corollary truth that each generation retains the need for a sustaining mythology.

Coover subtly weaves through the text myriad, multifaceted allusions to popular and classical mythology. He then modulates, distorts, elaborates, or explodes each to prevent the coalescence of fixed meaning. Damon Rutherford, the novel's ace pitcher whose death transforms Henry's life, invokes the pagan world's reverence for the beautiful and perfect young athlete and its ritual celebration of his death in the Adonis surrogate. But Damon also points to later spiritual, political, and even sports-world messiahs like Jesus, John F. Kennedy, and Babe Ruth.[1]

Exploding fixed associations with single or even multiple referents, Coover demonstrates through artistic example the diversity and precariousness of belief systems devised to handle the tragic condition. In the shifting and blending of characterization, symbolic equivalences, and events, the fiction also rejects traditional concepts of morality and psychology, and terms like good, evil, and normal become inapplicable.

This new and open-ended text obviously demands a unique reading. One may, for example, experience a part of the novel as Christian allegory, but Coover's multiple Christ figures simultaneously transform into antichrists and any number of literary, historical, or political figures. This shifting of "meaning" has led some of Coover's critics to view the *UBA* as pure metafiction, as a story about the exigencies of communicating in language.[2] Structuralists have read it in terms of language's diachronic and synchronic functioning.[3] Others view it, like *Origin*, as a parable of mythmaking in the service of one's savage instincts.[4] Possibly one should consider it with all these views in mind.

Actually, the very subject and structure of the novel, as well as one's complex response to it, reflect both the tragic and existential paradoxes, which assert that in order to live to the fullest and surmount despair, one must balance a sense of boundless potential with a sense of inevitable helplessness. One must see himself as a God, limitless and eternal, in a universe enclosed by death. Thus, the experience of reading the novel, where myth enriches and symbolic variations resist final meaning, where one discovers both power and powerlessness (knowledge and ignorance), becomes paradigmatic of the tenuousness of reconciling the word with experience, and life with contingency. Indeed, even plotwise, the book appears unfinished, for a final denouement is omitted. The reader is asked to supply his own concluding chapter, which will then depend upon his own history and "mythology." The act of reading mirrors and continues the experience of living. Mimesis now extends to a third dimension, from the world and the work to the act of reading, and "subject" and "object" are interchangeable among the three.

J. Henry Waugh, an aging and lonely man who works as an accountant at the firm of Dunkelmann, Zauber and Zifferblatt, finds little pleasure in his work, let alone any real sense of individuality or accomplishment. Although he has an occasional friend or two and from time to time allows himself a night out with a local B-girl, he is isolated and bored. He has tried to divert himself with a variety of hobbies and games, but he has found them all unfulfilling. It is the structure of baseball—and all that that implies—that appeals to Henry: "Real baseball bored him—but rather [he enjoyed] the records, the statistics, the peculiar balances between individual and team, offense and defense, strategy and luck, accident and pattern, power and intelligence. And no other activity in the world had so precise and comprehensive a history, so specific an ethic, and at the same time . . . so much ultimate mystery" (p. 45).

Henry thus constructs his own game, a league of eight teams, whose every game is played out in his head. With the props of three dice and an elaborate superstructure of records and statistics, the game is this: he throws three dice and then consults charts to determine his particular plays—home run, strike, and so on. Henry has carefully authored every person in the Association—in personality, character, physique, and history; as for the game, every contingency has been covered, even the unlikely death of a player. Henry abides by strict rules: everything will be played out fair and square.

The actual climax of his game occurs shortly after the novel begins, an event that catapults him into a consuming absorption with his players.[5] Although Henry has enjoyed his league for years, here too, a certain boredom has begun to set in. Now, a potentially great rookie, Damon Rutherford, appears and pitches a perfect, no-hit game. Elated, Henry discovers new imaginative and sexual energy. He picks up the gap-toothed Hettie Irden, the novel's lusty earth mother and pretends he is Damon: "Hettie . . . how would you like to sleep with . . . Damon Rutherford?" (p. 26). They enjoy a night of sensual merrymaking, and Henry accomplishes wondrous rookie feats. Coover subordinates the language of religion, superstition, primitive ritual, and even linguistics[6] to a lengthy and clever sequence in baseball jargon that describes their night of gala and bonanza scoring. Hettie and Henry, like the athletes on Henry's baseball diamond, defy time through physical pleasure.

Henry realizes that he is growing too involved with private fantasy: "Damon Rutherford meant more to him than any player should" (p. 38). In the next game, knowing that the boy should be rested, Henry nonetheless pitches him. Damon is now about to set a world record, but as he goes up to bat, Henry again rolls three consecutive 1-1-1s. He is horrified to realize that, according to the rules, the *"batter [must be] struck fatally by [a] bean ball"* (p. 70). Damon is indeed killed. From this point on, Henry becomes so distraught that he finds it increasingly more difficult to function in his life in the world. When he does go to work, he makes mathematical errors, or he takes refuge in other imaginative distractions; he even falls asleep. He rejects the well-meaning advice of both his friend and coworker, Lou Angel, and his boss, Mr. Zefferblatt. His several attempts to relate to real people fail.

He experiences Lou's apartment, for example, as a church funeral, with all the UBA players present for the Damon service. He has even gone into a florist's shop to buy flowers for the dead boy. " 'Oh, Lou!' he cried, holding his sides, 'Why do we go on?' " (p. 92). In one of the novel's most moving scenes, Henry imagines all the ballplayers (from the distant past, as well as the present) at his local bar ("Jake's"), now Damon's wake. With everyone expressing a variety of attitudes toward death,[7] or joking, drinking, or smoking cigars, Henry is nearly driven mad. "It was some gathering . . . like they'd all been . . . seeking a transformation, a way of going on with it, some viable essence unaltered by the boy's death that they could start over with" (p. 98).

One of the retired players, Sandy Shaw, now a folk singer, in a ballad that touches on the eternals of sex and death, provides some consolation for the men, who weep and experience some release. Henry is ambivalent about Sandy's commemorative song, with its "dreams and legends that blocked off their perception of truth." Nevertheless, he acknowledges, "What was the truth? Men needed these rituals, after all, that was part of the truth, too" (p. 103). Sandy then sings a bawdy tale of Long Lew and Fanny, after which each of the men plants his seed with a local bar girl. Henry comments: "They'd passed through the dissolutions and descensions and coagulations: what they wanted now was union" (p. 115). Henry lacks any way of transcending time.

He remains inconsolable and becomes so immersed in his fantasy that the ensuing portion of the text consists entirely of Henry's (imaginary) characters' meditations on death. Sycamore Flynn, for example, the Knickerbocker manager, walks around the ball park and utters a sad and poetic elegy on time and life. The next day that Henry returns to work, he pays particular attention to the everyday rituals of hanging up his coat, sorting his ledgers, and sharpening his pencils, but again he can't function. He leaves work to return home and play his game for twenty-four hours. Nothing he does can bring Casey and his team to their knees: "If he didn't know better, he'd suspect the dice of malevolence, rather than mere mindlessness" (p. 152). He goes out to Mitch's restaurant to meet Lou for dinner.[8]

Henry again attempts to step outside time through sex. Now, pretending to Hettie that he is Swanee Law, the opposing pitcher in Damon's perfect game, he fails. Although Law, as pitcher, has "phenomenal staying power," Henry's performance with Hettie lacks "magic"; he can passionately satisfy neither himself nor her on either a real or fantasy level. He even refuses to give Hettie her "benedictive slap" on the bottom, Hettie's own particular ritual when she leaves. Hettie, then entering the real world of time, disappears from his life. At this point, combining the language of both the game and sex, Henry confesses his "self-disgust" and suicidal leanings: he felt "like giving it up, a life misused, an old man playing with a child's toy; he felt somehow like an adolescent caught masturbating." He played "too much, too hard, since Damon died" (p. 171).

Lou's arrival (with a pizza) initiates Henry's recognition and reversal scenes. He tries to share his game with Lou, but "clumsy" Lou (Lucifer? Angel?), who, unlike Henry, has wiped his hands on his pants rather than washed them, spills beer (a "flood"?) all over Henry's papers. "Oh my God," cries Henry ambiguously, after which he dismisses Lou, much as he had Hettie. He then cries, and as he folds his hands and "leans his head upon them," he realizes that it has been Damon's death that has brought him to this state: "That was what did it, it was just . . . too much." But, he goes on, "you *couldn't* quit" (p. 201).

Henry's only way out is to kill Casey. He "picked up the dice, shook them," and as he whispered, "I'm sorry, boy," he turned them over to "6-6-6," the sign of the beast—the first time Henry ever cheated or interfered with the rules of the game. At this moment, Henry is transformed through physical and spiritual orgasm: "A sudden spasm convulsed him with the impact of a smashing line drive and he sprayed a red-and-golden rainbow arc of half-curdled pizza over his Association. . . . And when he'd done with his vomiting, when he'd finished, he went to bed, and there slept a deep deep sleep" (p. 202). A baseball hit, sexual release, vomiting (cf. Sartre's *Nausea*), a covenant with God, the magical rainbow—all commingle before his long and peaceful sleep.

From this point on, Henry seems reborn—at least in his game playing. The season is duly played out, like "ancient yet transformed ritual" (p. 208), and Henry reorganizes the leagues. Barney becomes chancellor; Sycamore takes over Barney's management of the Pioneers, and even Damon's father finds a job with the Knockerbockers. Henry returns to his role as historian-artist, through his character Barney, and he articulates his meditative concerns on history, time, and equilibrium in his book *The UBA in the Balance*. Here he utters what would seem to be the novel's message, that perfection is process (quoted above), an idea expressed earlier in Henry's emotionally felt experience when at the florist's shop he understood that plastic wreaths alone survive time.

Henry, in the last chapter in which we see him, with Jake dead, goes to the bar now run by Trench. All the players there seem to have achieved some sort of equilibrium. Henry has quit his job and decided to get another one, half-time, so he can have more legitimate free time for his game. He has even discovered some uncashed checks from Zefferblatt to help tide him over. From this point on, he disappears entirely from the novel. In the eighth and last chapter, the ancestors of Henry's UBA, one hundred years later, enact what has come to be known as the Damon-Casey duel. Unlike their forbears they express a number of opinions regarding the purpose of life, and they even question the ritual they are about to perform. Although Coover omits a ninth chapter in which one can see if or how the game will be played—and its outcome—one is left with the positive image, near the end, descriptive of both baseball and life: "It's just what it is . . . alive in the sun" (p. 242).

That Coover should portray his hero at "play" is credible to the modern reader, for play has become a popular metaphor or emblem of man's relationship to his universe. Writers like Barth, Beckett, Borges, and Pinter clothe their existential vision in the language of game playing. (Hemingway even literalizes it in his courageous hunters and bullfighters.) Integrity to one's chosen role and to the rules of the game is a reflection of his authenticity and good faith in an absurd universe.

But Coover clarifies his characters at play in very specific terms. He makes clear that the routine banalities of the real world are so consuming that one can pursue freedom, power, and control, only in fantasy. As though to project Beckett's stoical vaudevillians (or Hemingway's code heroes) as literary myths, Coover suggests that real freedom may be sought only in imaginative escape. Henry can never truly be free from his actual nine-to-five routine at Zefferblatt's (whose name means clockface), except in the imaginative construct of his baseball game. Although Coover's plot treats, primarily, Henry's increasing absorption in fantasy—the creation of his private myth—Henry himself explains the need for balance between the constricted everyday world and dreams. Total commitment to either extreme is dangerous: "Over the long haul he needed that balance, that rhythmic shift from . . . [reality to fantasy], and he knew that total one-sided participation in the league would soon grow even more oppressive than his job" (p. 141).

What is fascinating, however, and loaded with multiple levels of irony, is Coover's portrayal of the "game." (One must again approach Coover's fictions like a series of boxes within boxes.) Although the game would seem to allow Henry a control over time (e.g., he can play several seasons in two weeks), it contains, intrinsically, all the ingredients of life. First, it reflects and indeed defines Henry's personal life. Designed to keep him from the brink of loneliness and boredom and to distract him from the full realization of his own limitations and limited possibilities, Henry's baseball satisfies his deepest needs. A game of tremendous excitement, it pits control against chance; each and every move offers its players potential great accomplishment, public adulation, and even immortality. As such, it allows Henry an escape from the frustrations and emptiness of his workaday quotidian. More important, this elaborate fantasy—in which Henry describes the intimate details of his characters' lives—allows him the warmth and comfort of personal and family relationships sharply missing from his real life. Henry's game is an extravagant construction of wishful thinking, a projection of his many selves. Through it he can actualize the various aspects of his personality, of his potential selves, which he cannot (or dare not) enact in ordinary society. He can "be," for example, the legendary Brock Rutherford (both men are the same age as the UBA), proud father of the young, brilliant and beautiful Damon. He can also "be" the cynical, hard-bitten, antisentimental and outspoken Pappy Rooney, whose stomach eats him up but who, like many biblical patriarchs, goes on to lead a vital and sexual life until he is one hundred forty-three. Another possible persona is Fenn McCaffree, the present chancellor of the Association who, like Henry, welcomes the excitement Damon has brought into the league, and who, when Damon dies, suffers his own (political) losses.

Finally, since Henry has a certain control over time and can record and interpret events, his fantasy elevates him to the role of historian and artist. Master of this world, Henry is virtually godlike (and his initials, J. H. W., suggest the Old Testament Yahweh, just as his name sounds like Jehovah).[9] To be sure, in his fantasy he creates the total human family—different "types" or "styles" recorded not only throughout American but throughout human history, and as each interacts and also plays out his own drama, Henry can search for a viable value system. He can create the history of the world and all its belief systems through which all the philosophical, political, and social possibilities have existed, where all the great heroes of the past have coped with the common problem of survival. During the crucial moments of Damon's life and death, the novel reverberates with lines like "[He] tore all the buttons off his shirt" and "[The crowd felt] the moment's ripeness, but that was all" (p. 70), recalling *King Lear*.

Like Adam, Henry names the creatures of his world, and like any artist, he knows that words are mythmaking, that, as Mallarmé put it, "to name is to create."[10] "The dice and charts," he explains, "were only the mechanics of the drama, not the drama itself. Names had to be chosen ... that could bear the whole weight of perpetuity." "Name a man," he continues, "and you make him what he is" (p. 48). Thus, Henry creates a Damon Rutherford, Jock Casey, Barney Bancroft, Fenn McCaffree, and the many others.

The Pythagorean-mathematician-God, Henry may initiate the play through the roll of the dice, and his charts may provide instructions for his hits and outs, but he finds some aspects of his play more interesting than others. Recording the fielding statistics, for example, he finds dull. But once he interprets events, Henry becomes the artist. Utilizing a variety of techniques, he stylizes event and forges a new reality. In the beginning was the word, and the word was with Henry. Another example of the paradox inherent in the existential stance, incidentally (and reiterated in the Art Is Long/Life Short hypothesis), is Henry's "delusion" that his records of human experience—his statistics—can touch those recorded (the dead). Nevertheless, scorekeeping—and baseball thrives upon statistics and records—invites this illusion of immortality. Scorekeeping, Henry comments, is "stirring" and "beautiful," like "doing something heroic" (p. 168).

Henry's game playing is indeed his religion, the baseball stadium "a church" but "more real." "Ball stadiums," he goes on to say, "and not European churches were the American holy places" (p. 166). Indeed, that baseball is an American religion is worthy of some commentary. It is, after all, a game within which one asserts both mental and physical agility (power, control, and grace) against the natural order. Not entirely unlike bullfighting, the human dilemma is, in a sense, crystallized into an intense and brief period of time during which one can both figuratively and literally either win or lose it all. "You're a dead man," cry Henry's players to one another, and their language, like their symbolic game, reflects the human drama. Sports—like sex, eating, and drinking, the other activities that fill the book—are man's way of defying time.

Interestingly, baseball is a game that makes much of Revelation's numerology. The UBA allows Henry (an accountant, after all) to fulfill his particular need for systemetizing, but here, numbers take on a metaphysical quality. The number three, for example, associated with the Trinity, the third day upon which Christ was resurrected, the age of Christ at death, is connected with the all-or-nothing (life or death) three strikes; Damon is killed at the bottom of the third inning; the earthly "four," the four balls that permit "a walk" to the first of the four bases. Their important addition (three and four), associated with the apocalyptic number seven, the day God rested, suggests the maximum seven pitches (three strikes, four balls) allowed each player and the number of fielders; "seven" has even been carried over into baseball's seventh inning stretch (during which, at the beginning of the book, Henry goes out for a pastrami sandwich). Finally, three multiplied by itself, nine (the sign of the antichrist, 6-6-6 inverted), is connected with the nine players of the game, their nine innings, and the nine months of human gestation. In this intricately structured novel, Coover omits the ninth chapter.

With baseball then like a religion (the "paraclete" is a "pair o' cleats"),[11] Henry's game has all the mystery of Christian ritual—along with a variety of trappings from many other myths similarly constructed to deal with time and man's fate. Coover's rich opening combines the language of Christianity and superstition with that of classical mythology and sexuality. This big game (Damon is about to pitch the perfect no-hitter) recalls "the old days all over again." From the "charged" stands, the crowd "leaps up for luck," screams "one! two! three!" and consumes beer and hot dogs. The people "cross" their fingers, kiss their fingertips and knock on wood; they pray for the beautiful, young, "unscratched," and unscarred Damon. With "timeless gestures" at this "eleventh" hour, all are about to "witness" this "event of the first order." Though the sun is "high," this may inaugurate "a long night" (pp. 3–4). To be sure, after Damon's success, he shall be treated as the sacrificial god, and the "frenzied hometown rooters" would "tear him apart out of sheer love." From

above, Henry describes the scene like a "great roiling whirlpool with
Damon afloat in the vortex," the dismembered god now embraced
by a terrible "flood of fans in a wild world that had, literally, for the
moment, blown its top." Women shriek, "arms supplicating," but
"the whirlpool uncoiled." For a moment all have participated in the
"relief and tension" of ritual, a moment of spiritual-sexual ecstasy (p.
17). Damon has defied the natural order and pitched a "perfect
game." "Zero," Henry comments, "the absence of number, an incredible idea! Only infinity compared to it. . . . Perfection was available" (p. 57).

Though the sun may be high in Henry's outdoor fantasy, in
reality, in his room where he is playing the game, "a small warm bulb
[is] unfrosted, its little sallow arc so remote from its fathering force as
to seem more akin to the glowworm" (p. 4). Typically, this rich and
evocative line suggests, in images of light, the natural and artificial,
perfection, fatherhood, death, sexuality, communion, immortality
—subjects of the book.

But baseball is not only an American religion; it is the American
way, representative of activities and a unique psychology wor-
shipped by Americans. In its dogged competition of men set against
one another, it represents the American capitalist system (with jargon like "trading," "property," and even "stealing"); it exemplifies
the Horatio Alger myth, in that anyone, regardless of heritage, can
achieve fame and wealth through application and achievement. In
its stylized version of men combating other men, it satisfies a nation's
lust for (and guilt toward) war and power, but it also fulfills a
primitive power lust, and its teams often have animal names or
generic names of the hunt or conquest (Tigers, Giants, Pirates,
Braves). Baseball also reflects the eternal rivalry between the generations, the cyclical transcendence of the young and vital over the old
and worn. With time still the enemy and success dependent on good
or bad form, baseball reinforces a prominent distinction in American culture between the old and young. A few, elite aged are always
honored as advisers to the now young in their prime, while the rest
are "put out to pasture."

Henry's UBA players are indeed American "aristocrats," socially,
politically, and even spiritually. Speaking of their baseball slumps,
he says: "It was the same when a man fell from class" (p. 39). (In the
novel, absence of grace—i.e., clumsiness—is connected with both
physical and spiritual decline.) Their names, intimately connected
with their fates, remind one of the Kennedy ancestors (especially

Henry's many Irish characters), as well as the Vanderbilts and Rock-efellers, the robber-baron magnates who created American dynasties. The UBA's historical lineage is reminiscent of American history: Swanee Law suggests LBJ, Woody Winthrop, Woodrow Wilson. Henry even began his League, he tells us, with Civil War and Reconstruction teams, and the Association has gone through many new "epochs" with its elaborate political structure, its chancellors elected every four years. Presiding over teams with names like the Pioneers, Knickerbockers, and Bridegrooms, Henry's leagues develop from early (Boggler) principles of "individualism and egocentrism" through the Legalists, to the Guildsmen's moral and philosophical concerns with the very nature of man and society.

When Jock Casey kills Damon and Swanee Law ascends, the reader is thus invited to entertain a multiplicity of historical and mythic allusions. Henry may be reenacting the overthrow of the pagan world by Christianity (*J*ock *C*asey); the violent death of the young hero (JFK and Martin Luther King) and the reassertion of an older, southern law (Swanee Law, LBJ); Henry may be repeating the destruction of natural vitality by the forces of social convention, the child (Babe) (Ruth-erford), subordinated to legend ("Casey at the Bat").

Henry's baseball, then, because it contains the archetypal patterns common to a plethora of myths, finally typifies the oppositional structure that may (if the cultural anthropologists, like Lévi-Strauss, and the linguists, like Saussure, are correct) characterize all relationships, linguistic and otherwise. In its actual play and mystery, it may even typify the pattern of tragedy. Henry sounds like his contemporary tragic prototype, Willy Loman, another aging, dreaming functionary longing for significance, when he poetically describes his life in terms of traveling from North to South, in a image of the (baseball) diamond—the epitome of the American dream (Willy's brother went into the jungle in search of it): "The rovin' gambler. Cowpoke and trainman. A travelin' man always longs for a home, cause a travelin' man is always alone. Out of the east into the north, push out to the west, then march through the south back home again: like a baserunner on the paths, alone in a hostile cosmos, the stars out there in their places, and him trying to dominate the world by stepping on it all" (p. 141).

This is Henry's game—a game that contains all the ingredients of life, the responses to it, and the records of it. His characters are each examples of the individual set against the world of probability and unpredictability, tests of man's prowess in the face of change. But not only is the format of Henry's game a reenactment of men *in extremis*, so is Henry's very play of the game. Coover's conception is ingenious. Since it is *Henry's game* (as any of our fantasies is a construct of our own making), not only must his most private and extravagant fantasies be defined by his conscious and unconscious frames of reference—in the vocabulary of the very experience he seeks to escape—but his role within that game must also be governed by these identical rules.

Thus, although Henry has designed a world of every diverse human interaction within a system where statistical likelihood and biological parameters are still obeyed, the very *human* elements that provide his excitement or comfort ultimately cause his isolation and despair. Perfection is process, and process is time, and time fells all men and their accomplishments. Damon may one day defy chance and pitch a perfect game, but the next day he may die. Death, as Wallace Stevens put it, is the "mother of beauty"; the only paradise Henry can envision is one where ripe fruit must fall, for its fall, like Damon's, gives pungence and poignancy to the game. The drama of life involves man, the protagonist, against time.

The only things, in the end, that Henry would seem to guarantee are the high moments of his game, but these victories can be meaningful to him only in terms of the costs they inevitably exact. The game may temporarily make him feel young, but it is always linked with time. Indeed, this is Henry's story, as well as the story within— the drama of his UBA. Ultimate freedom is illusory; to transform a Yeats image, one cannot resign his part in life's casual comedy. Henry "dreaded, in short, the death blow, yet it was just this rounding off in the Book of each career that gave beauty to all these lives" (p. 214).

That Henry disappears from the last chapter and Coover projects the UBA one hundred years hence raises many questions. Perhaps—at least for the time being—Henry has learned something about life (that perfection is process), which is why he doesn't need, for the moment, the thrill of a game. He has come back to life, in a sense, having gained a sense of "the teamwork of human enterprise" and the balance of accomplishment and loss, life and death. On the other hand, perhaps this chapter is a fantasy within Henry's fantasy, *his* projection of the UBA one hundred years hence, the descendants once again representative of a variety of historical, legendary, personality and philosophical types. Perhaps Coover wishes to suggest the autonomy of the creative fantasy, how once the artist creates, the child of his imagination takes on its own identity and serves others in totally new terms. Or perhaps, in larger, allegorical terms, Coover is portraying how after God created the universe, He simply disappeared from the scene. Whatever his reasons for omitting Henry, it is interesting to consider how this last chapter illustrates the perfection/process theme. Indeed, what *has* happened to Henry? After all the dramatic and linguistic events in which Coover has portrayed Henry's growing absorption in fantasy, why has he suddenly omitted him from the last twenty-four pages of the text? Coover's conception is once again ingenious.

Whatever Damon's and Casey's deaths have meant to Henry—and there are an endless number of possibilities[12]—has been suggested in only the most general and often conflicting of terms. This is because they have been entirely personal to Henry. The only thing the reader can be certain of is their profound significance in Henry's drama: Damon's death has precipitated his spiritual decline (Damon dies on a Friday), Casey's, the reorganization of his life and game (Henry "rises" on Sunday).

Coover communicates Henry's emotional extremes by knitting together the diverse myths upon which he has based his game. Final meaning, however, especially in his killing of Casey, never clarifies, because in this act Henry steps outside all the traditional myths (and rules). He asserts his freedom and takes upon himself, for the moment, the total responsibility for his life; he designs his own destiny. Killing Casey is the truly creative part of his game, the artist's use of a totally private vocabulary and vision, comprehensible to others—to us, the reader—solely in our own language (which must then distort Henry's, the original). Henry, at least for this moment, would seem to have found a balance, although "balance" implies uncertainty (the double meaning of Barney's title *The UBA in the Balance*). The paradox underlying tragic or existential poise is echoed once again in the concept that nothing is final but process; balance, by definition, is change (process). Perfection, as process, is alien to mythology and history.

A last box within the many others (at least to be discussed here) is how and why, with Henry absent from the last chapter, Coover turns his focus to the way private vision evolves into social or cultural myth. The logic of going from Henry's story to the players' enactment of it involves a somewhat difficult transition for the reader, a reshifting of focus.

First, since Henry's "lesson" (his perception of truth) has been a private one—hence *our* multiple hypotheses as to why he kills Casey—there is just so far that Coover can take us with Henry as subject. After a point, he simply must be dismissed. But Coover's "story," or at least the new turn it takes, really begins at this point. (In keeping with the circular and spatial form of the novel, the drama that begins here may well provide the background for any subsequent generation's need for fresh and private "systems"; one could even use chap. 8 as a preface to chap. 1.) Like Pär Lagerkvist in a work like *Barabbas* (or D. H. Lawrence earlier in *Apocalypse*)— indeed, like his own *Origin of the Brunists*—Coover schematizes how civilizations, not only individuals like Henry, survive on myth by picking up on the trappings of someone else's personal experience, ritualizing them, and eventually rewriting and often gutting them of their original poetry and energy.

Henry's "game" is similarly actualized and, as it first appears one hundred years later, diluted and even bastardized. While it serves a necessary function to surviving generations, those enacting it—as they anticipate their ritual—lack any true comprehension of its purpose; they also lack Henry's original and passionate commitment to it.

That anyone engaged in ritual (as opposed to raw, personal experience) truly misunderstands its original function even Henry admits. When he first created his baseball leagues, he too had to rely upon a given structure in the particulars of his game. It was only when the oldest players died—those inherited from the Civil War and Reconstruction eras—that he finally felt in control. There is always an a priori frame for every myth, as there is for every ensuing chapter in human history, a grammar or structure upon which one builds, even though such structures inevitably both constrict as well as construct. "You know, Lou," Henry says, "You can take history or leave it, but if you take it you have to accept certain assumptions or ground rules about what's left in and what's left out" (p. 49). We are back to the same paradox about freedom within limitations, another variation of the existential/tragic pose, or even the concept that perfection is process.

Coover's last chapter concretely dramatizes this perfection/ process theme. If our earlier discussion focused on how Henry's game and his play of it illustrated the contradictions of man's freedom in a limited world, in this last chapter, Henry's great-great-great-grandchildren demonstrate, as well, the alterations, both creative and destructive, that they and time have placed upon Henry's original game. They too act out life in the balance.

Dozens of players stand on the grid, ready to enact the "annual rookie initiation ceremony, the Damonsday reenactment of the Parable of the Duel," an event each has been preparing for through his "childhood programming," his "catechism." Each has, noticeably, at least as he is about to begin, little idea what he is doing; he has little choice regarding not only his scenario but also his role. Hardy, for example, who is to play Damon, is a reluctant sacrificial figure. Though a "renegade" in his own way, he says: "[It] doesn't make sense . . . to knock off your best young talent every season." Yet, he concedes, "if that's the way they want it . . . [I want] to take it like a man." And, in a false comparison with his pure and poised progenitor, the completely unquestioning Damon, he adds: "Like *the* man himself" (p. 220). Hardy is bored and skeptical; he is even contemptuous about the legend he is to enact.

Paul Trench, a company man, "incurious and doltish," will play Ingram, Casey's killer, who was, incidentally, Hardy's own great-great-great grandfather. (Note how their "roles" do not correspond to their names/their ancestors. How far they are from Henry's equation of name and person.) Trench feels "stage fright," but he will act, all the same, as the avenger, Casey's "murderer," in this "Great Atonement Legend."

As one gets further into the chapter, it becomes evident that not only are the characters alien to their original "functions," but they are uncertain if there was an original function—a single, common focus in this ritual. Perhaps, some speculate, Damon never lived; perhaps he was "a perversion and a tyranny." On the other hand, perhaps Damon "had the truth." Once again, depending upon the political perspective from which each speaks (and the Damonites and Caseyites are also radically different now from their founders), it is questionable if they are playing to celebrate Damon's freedom or Casey's "mystery." To be sure, once they begin talking of Casey, there is an equal amount of confusion. Someone even refers to "all that shit" about "Gawky Jock, the Mad Killer." Perhaps they are playing to establish Barney, or even Royce Ingram, as the central figure. "Other theories," writes Coover, "have Brock Rutherford, Sycamore Flynn, Fennimore McCaffree, Chauncey O'Shea, even Flynn's or McCaffree's daughters at the center."

Despite these many uncertainties, the audience to which they are performing is clearly defined. Contemporary society, which now demands blind conformity to the enactment of ritual, has been transformed from Henry's worshiping congregant-fans into a voracious mob, the antichrist, the beast, the "whore of whores" who unmans and devours the young. "Dame society . . . responds, a terrible roar dredged up from the very gut of the beast, a horrendous witless bellowing, that sucks up all their scrotoms, and makes them catch their breath" (p. 237).

As the players persist in discussing their "functions," Coover gives us a replay of the various attitudes toward experience expressed by a variety of Henry's players, though never by Damon and Casey. This is indeed the modern age, the post-Christian era, where belief is relative. Damon's and Casey's surrogates are far more sophisticated, cynical, and less charismatic than their ancestors. Their comments vary from Trench's soliloquy on a kind of "to play or not to play" theme to someone's more concrete suggestion that they "just go diddle themselves and leave." One player calls God "a nut," another, "a 100 Watt" light bulb.

Perhaps, someone says, this play between rookies represents the basic opposition of good (Damon) and evil (Casey). Perhaps life is a dream or grammatical construct, and each act just fulfills its predetermined function: "We have no mothers. . . . The ripening of their wombs is nothing more than a ceremonious parable. We are mere ideas, hatched whole and hapless, here to enact old rituals of resistance and rot" (p. 230). Perhaps this is just another of the "ancient myths of the sun," the victim "slaughtered by the monster or force of darkness." Perhaps it is in fact a perversion of truth. They can be sure of nothing. Nobody understands history. One "can't even be sure about the simple *facts*. . . . In the end you can never prove a thing" (p. 224).

In the midst of all these postreligious issues, the eternally provocative question is prominent: If there is no God, do the rules remain the same? The mystery and affirmation that underscores this conviction once again reflects existential poise and tragic nobility. It may also bespeak the reconciliation at the heart of the comic vision. "I don't know," says one player, "if there's really a record-keeper up there or not. . . . But even if there weren't, . . . we'd have to play the game as though there were. . . . Continuance for its own inscrutable sake" (p. 239).

To live is to play, and to play is to mythologize, to place into contexts the disordered specifics of daily life, to locate design and arbitrarily assign value and then abide by that value as though it were absolute. The baseball league, like any number of constructs for comprehending the world, is a means both of and toward grace, a necessary diversion from the boredom and pain of time.

It is in this spirit of play "for its own inscrutable sake" that Coover's last game is begun. Once on the field, everyone and everything is transformed, the perfection of life once more reflected in its constant change ("process"), the balance of life once again "in the balance." Personal fears or flamboyant and cynical reservations cast aside, detached observers become impassioned participants. This is the only true transsubstantiation to be celebrated in ritual. "The black clouds break up, and the dew springs again to the green grass, and the stands hang on, and . . . [one's] own oppressed heart leaps alive to give it one last try." One has no choice, in answer to the "universal" question raised throughout—"Where is truth?"—but to "Play ball!" (p. 241): "[One] is afraid. Not only of what he must do. But of everything. Beyond each game, he sees another, and yet another, in endless and hopeless succession. . . . What difference, in the terror of eternity, does it make? . . . Why is it better to win than to lose? Each day: the dread. . . . [One] wants to quit—but what does he mean, 'quit'? The game? Life? Could you separate them? . . . [One] tries to speak, but he can find no words. It's terrible, he says; or might have said. It's all there is....'Hey, wait. . . . You *love* this game, don't you?' . . . 'Then don't be afraid.' . . . It doesn't even matter that he's going to die, all that counts is that he is *here*. . . . It's not even a lesson. It's just what it is. . . . hard and white and alive in the sun. . . . 'Hang loose'." (pp. 238–42).

The book ends on this epiphanic note, but the reader's experience is not over. As Henry's personal vision, expressed in the first seven chapters, gives way to the transformations of the "dying generations" which succeed him (chap. 8), so their vision—indeed, the entire book, Coover's "myth"—is passed on to the reader. Like all the artists in the book, beginning with Henry and including not only Barney Bancroft, Sandy Shaw, and Fenn McCaffree but in fact all the characters, the reader is asked to perform his own transformation, and in the act of reading, to undergo his own creative meditation—to balance for himself the concrete and the imaginary, the particular and the ultimate—to create his own last inning, his own ninth chapter.

4

The Public Burning
The Making of the President

The great experience of the twentieth century has been to accept the objective reality of time and thus of process— history does not repeat, the universe is not changeless, masses dissolve and slide through the fingers, there are no precognitions—and out in that flow all such assertions may be true, false, inconsequential, or all at the same time. (P. 195)

What was fact, what intent, what was framework, what was essence? Strange, the impact of History, the grip it had on us, yet it was nothing but words. Accidental accretions for the most part, leaving most of the story out. We have not yet begun to explore the true power of the Word. . . . What if we broke all the rules, played games with the evidence, manipulated language itself, made History a partisan ally?" (P. 136)

The Public Burning (1977) is Coover's most daring book, extraordinary in its mixture of fact and fiction, epic and fantasy. Coover stretches the limits of the historical novel to include any number of literary forms and techniques—from ballad, melodrama, and farce to tragedy and old comedy—and he incorporates, as well, structural devices from several other popular and high arts, like opera, collage, film, and cartoon. The novel is a vivid and bitter panorama of America during the early 1950s, and its major characters range from Richard Nixon and a materialized Uncle Sam to Gary Cooper as the sheriff in *High Noon* and Wild Bill Hickok—countless real and imaginary heroes of American history and their media representations.

The narrative climax centers around the ritual and grotesque

51

public electrocutions of the convicted traitors Ethel and Julius Rosenberg at Times Square, June 19, 1953, the night following their fourteenth wedding anniversary. Equally dramatic is Richard Nixon's passionate lovemaking to Ethel on the floor of her prison cell just minutes before her execution and Uncle Sam's sodomizing the nation's future president. Coover's subject, announced throughout in high-pitched tones and violent imagery, as well as in casual references to fashionable novels, pop songs, or catchy ads, is America's rendezvous with destiny—the victory of light and right, God and country, over the forces of darkness—the evils of atheism, communism, and wanton sexuality.

Beneath this mixture of the real and surreal is Coover's microscopically sharp focus on the nation that blindly cheered the Rosenberg executions and the psychological and political forces that gave rise to such an event. Coover's purpose is not to judge the Rosenbergs as innocent or guilty but to question the American spirit—its psyche, morality, and structures of justice. The novel examines the many conflicts between (1) instinctual and (2) existential freedom and (3) the problematical freedoms promised by the American dream. This is a nation, Coover implies, whose repressed sexuality and aggressiveness are kept in check only through a structured political mythology of good versus evil, through an ideology that not only permits but also designs the ritual exorcism of what are really its own deepest and most menacing drives.

Like all great art that transcends a particular historical focus, The Public Burning contains meditations on more universal philosophical matters. It is a visionary exploration of the human condition. Coover moves from the particular to the abstract, from the concrete, political or psychological event to more subtle and profound epistemological and ontological issues. What are the forces that shape history? he asks. How can one know the truth of human experience? What is the meaning of freedom in a contingent universe organized by arbitrary political, social, and moral laws designed to satisfy the needs of the human psyche?

Coover approaches these questions by scrutinizing the instruments that create and nurture personal and national identity—the various mass media. In his ruthless portrayal of everyone's acts as artifice (each person is linked with a historical character or, more frequently, with a movie or drama script), he challenges those sacraments of contemporary culture that rubber stamp identity and morality. It is the media, after all, which provide society with the heroes to emulate, the ideals to live by, and the jargon to mimic—in everything from Grade B films, pop songs, and tall tales of American folklore to weekly magazines and daily newspapers. These simplifications, addictive tranquilizers for metaphysical uncertainty, are as much Coover's target as the personal and social vocabularies they commercialize.

In his particular emphasis upon literature and its many genres, and in his self-conscious and sometimes sardonic parodies of them, Coover also mocks himself and his profession. Literature is, to be sure, another manifestation of the selective eye that presumes to define and measure human experience and to provide a vocabulary and morality for consumer consumption. Once one synthesizes experience—either in the media or in the more subtle testaments of literature or historical text—distortions are inevitable.

The word, finally, is Coover's subject, not only in itself but as a metaphor for man in the universe. Especially in his Nixon figure, Coover emphasizes how one remains incapable of designing a morality out of what will always remain limited vision and limiting language and personal resources. In the last analysis, despite one's insights into the human condition, he is simply too insecure to stand alone and act freely—to redefine, in his own terms, his place in the scheme of things.

There is a continuity in Coover's vision. As in *Origin*, *The Public Burning* again portrays the fanatical core of American life and how, in the service of one's deepest instincts and fears, one creates political, social, or religious mythologies which then structure and orchestrate his culture and morality. Compared to the *UBA*, *The Public Burning* is more ambitious, a familiar brush engaging a larger canvas.

Henry's harmless baseball game, a distraction from both his boredom and fear of death, is now transformed into the very real and dangerous game of politics. While many of the stakes and goals are similar—e.g., the rags to riches (and to immortality) Horatio Alger dream—American politics, as Coover represents it, is no game or distraction from which one returns to work. It is, instead, a concrete enactment of what Henry's game only symbolizes; there is always a winner and a loser, and the side one is on may literally be a matter of life or death. Further, because one's commitment is arbitrary and issues can at times become murky, one may easily be attracted by the opposition. At times, the line between light and dark may evaporate. If the golden rule of politics is "the ends justify the means"—

otherwise known as political expediency—those with the expedient means, and often the golden tongues, may be (or seem to be) the golden gods of political and historical mythmaking. Certainly more than Henry's baseball (game), American politics is a religion, and one's obedience to its particular sacraments may determine his salvation or damnation.

The subtler and even more interesting connection with the *UBA* involves the protagonist's (Nixon's) game playing within the larger political "game." While Nixon is more sophisticated than Henry in his intelligent and articulate understanding of the arbitrariness of all human values and evaluations, like Henry, he becomes increasingly absorbed by the imaginative life. What is strikingly different is that while Henry's baseball game is originally conceived as independent of his ordinary life (he plays it on the kitchen table), and although its rules are, finally, the rules of his everyday life, Nixon's fantasy as Hollywood leading man and Horatio Alger success not only originates in his external world (which provides its vocabulary and rules) but is played out publicly. Indeed, one of the book's climaxes involves Nixon's total immersion in fantasy which he acts out before an American public which itself functions according to identical fantasies of glamor and success.

A most striking aspect of the novel is its encyclopedic texture, its blend of fact and fiction detailing the early Eisenhower years, specifically the two days that preceded the Rosenbergs' execution. The amount of research Coover must have undertaken for his nearly seven-hundred-page chronicle is dazzling.

He quotes dozens of people and devotes a single chapter to the June 19, 1953, *New York Times*, with information whose "relevance" (if not "import") varies from the most weighty to the most trivial. Major battles in Korea receive attention, as do other historical and political events; one learns that Arlene Riddett won the twenty-eighth girls' marble tournament at Asbury Park; Eleanor Hortense Almond died at age one hundred three; cantaloupe sold for nineteen cents a pound. Rosemary Clooney, Johnnie Ray, and Harry Belefonte serenaded America, as well as Nelson Eddy ("Stout-Hearted Men") and Frankie Laine ("I Believe").

In epic or biblical fashion Coover lists, and often characterizes, virtually everyone closely or peripherally associated with the Rosenbergs—Judge Irving Kaufman; defense lawyer Emanuel Bloch; prosecutor Irving Saypol; Attorney General Herbert Brownell; the president's assistant Sherman Adams; the White House press secretary Jim Hagerty—people as "prominent" as the Supreme Court justices, and as "important" as the Sing Sing executioner, Joseph P. Francel, and its jailkeepers and coroners.

Fictionalized material is mixed with "hard facts," and Coover's blend is at times serious, sarcastic, bitter, or whimsical. Television production was up "70 percent . . . doing even better than pornography and missiles." An "ingenious" America produced "plastic carpets, paper snow fences, blindmen's canes that glow in the dark, cockpit listeners, 3-D movies, propane locomotives, [and] chlorophyll cigarettes" (p. 215). Ethel cost the state $38.60 a day, but Julius cost more because of his dental treatment (although in the spirit of American common sense, temporary dentures were procured).

As one grows increasingly absorbed in the book, he is taken with the range of Coover's details. Is it true that Eisenhower required valet assistance each morning with his underpants? Did Ethel really want to become a singer? At some point, issues escalate and become matters of morality and of life and death. Did Eisenhower really fail to understand the case? In fact, did the Rosenbergs receive a fair trial, and granted they did, did they receive a fair sentence? In these last matters, Coover provides voluminous information on both sides of the question.

The issue regarding Coover's mixture of fact and fantasy led many of his reviewers to indignant rage at what they called his bitter distortion of truth. He had a difficult time publishing the book, and when Richard Seaver accepted it, the possibility of litigation from Nixon, as well as the Rosenberg heirs, remained. Once in print, the book evoked a great deal of controversy, and political and aesthetic issues were often confused. Norman Podhoretz, for example, called it a "cowardly lie," while Pearl Bell, speaking of Coover's "misuse" of historical evidence, described it as "overwrought subversion of reality by polemically inspired fantasy."[1]

One should come to terms with these issues now, although they really anticipate and are integral to any discussion of Coover's vision or technique: What is the fictionist's obligation to so-called fact if he chooses to write about a historical event? May he indulge in "poetic license" at the expense of recorded information? To be sure, with all of Coover's work thus far rejecting teleological, mimetic form, it may have seemed odd that he would write a "factual" novel. Nevertheless, because he utilized historical events, when the book appeared it was compared to the many other nonfiction novels (or even the New

Journalism) popular in both the 1960s and early 1970s—to works as different as E. L. Doctorow's *Ragtime*, Truman Capote's *In Cold Blood*, Norman Mailer's *Armies of the Night*, and Jerome Charyn's *The Franklin Scare*.[2]

These novels, unlike Coover's, were acclaimed for their juxtaposition of imagined dialogue, character detail, and event with real, historical occurrence—e.g., the antiwar march on the Pentagon (Mailer)—for their imaginative heightening of empirically verifiable events. Even Pynchon (in *Gravity's Rainbow*) and Barth (in *The Sot-Weed Factor*), with their more experimental forms, were applauded for their originality within this genre. Their mixture of the absurd, farcical, and grotesque, with high and low brow culture, was praised as an innovative way of conveying the real and hallucinatory, frenetic, or entropic condition of America—as a verifiable, though nonmaterial, reality.

Whether or not one would question these critical assessments, Coover's *particular* balance of fact and fancy ("particular," since all art balances both) was generally overlooked. Actually, like Pynchon and Barth, Coover goes beyond traditional definitions of fact and fiction as he *describes* in verbal form the ontological ambiguity of character and event, indeed history, through the constructive/constrictive vehicle of language.

Once again he suggests that one can only describe rather than reproduce (nonverbal) experience through language, and history is merely one such description. Just as the process of transcribing felt experience into grammatical, pictorial, or musical structures loses something in translation, so does history dissipate and distort in its structuring of selective events within a priori patterns. One must view historical testaments much like biblical literature—with a certain skepticism regarding their relationship to reality.

Historical perspective is thus one "reading," based, in addition, upon political and social bias, although its heroes (sometimes only temporarily distinguished from its despots) provide the moral exempla for future generations. Ultimately, the degree of fact and fiction in Coover's book is irrelevant, because one can never sort out and finalize motivation, event, or truth. Coover's novel, like the news documents of the 1950s, is another arbitrary construct, another metafiction, concerning the Rosenberg event.[3]

What *is* fascinating in Coover's tapestry of so-called fictional and factual details, and what distinguishes him from, say, Capote and Mailer, is his demythification of history. The traditionalist separates history and myth by considering history as the organization of empirically verifiable facts, with the text gaining a mythic autonomy; myth as a combination of the concrete and fantastic. Coover actually demythifies history and concretizes myth; he then goes on to demonstrate that *any* reading of events is an act that is both arbitrary and mythifying: arbitrary because each reading is unique, mythifying because it is a balance of fact and fiction. It is a participation in the external phenomenological world ("fact") and an imaginative interpretation of that raw experience in words. It is an artistic ordering of random events and details, the imposition of linguistic order upon a nonverbal world. Experience, once "explained," is thus fiction. Yet—and once again the irony is noteworthy—in the very act of demythifying history and rearranging details, Coover substitutes his own mythology, although his truth may well be that there is no truth.

The most dramatic example of this is in the first of his narrative voices, in Uncle Sam, the Spirit of God and country, who is personified as a sort of prairie, boondock Zeus, complete with goatee, corncob pipe, and red, white, and blue costume. His "chapters" present the objective voice of America. Frequently with the voice of a newscaster, he evokes the macrocosm of America, the flow of events, the chaotic atmosphere, and the often unclassifiable data of the times.

Uncle Sam proclaims the glory of America, where the power of the individual is considered supreme, as opposed to Russia, where inexorable historical forces are presumed to control human destiny. Nonetheless, he is ever threatened by the "Phantom," especially in the forces of communism. (At last count, the Phantom claimed 800,000,000 people and the U.S. only 540,000,000.) The conclusion reached by "America's top cop," J. Edgar Hoover, was: "It's a spy ring . . . always is. . . . Find the thieves [the Rosenbergs]" (p. 15). Actually, since the Phantom never materializes, or at most is literalized once (as a cabdriver who defines evil as "the Creator of Ambiguity"),[4] the force of darkness may indeed be Uncle Sam's delusion, if not a projected part of him—a necessary complement to his identity as the force of light.

As to the folks at home, Uncle Sam is "dadblame" pleased. His coarse and puritanical offspring have been created in his own image. Both have a postwar mentality of "conform or be killed," a bitter and ironic reflection of America's past and present totalitarian enemies.

As Uncle Sam details the events of the times, a strong personality emerges. He can be corny and sentimental, but he is most often vulgar and boastful, a satiric and bitter amalgam of all the coarse, brutal, self-righteous, and zealous heroes of American folklore. A holier-than-thou braggart, he was "né Sam Slick, that wily Yankee Peddler who, much like that ballsy Greek girl of long ago, popped virgin-born and fully constituted from the shattered seed-poll of the very Enlightenment" (p. 6); he was born out of the heart (or the bowels) of America, at Times Square. At various points, he is described as the "American Autolycus," or in the context of Brer Rabbit, Peter Minuit, John Brown—and a host of American heroes of film or history—e.g., Abe Lincoln or Raymond Massey acting him on the screen.

He believes in the "manifest dust-in-yer-eye [destiny] of America" and Armageddon (America's *"Dominion over the Whole World"*) which, as one unpatriotic observer in the novel described it, he would accomplish through "perverted nationalism and a sort of nostalgia for barbarism" (p. 10)—through "patient extermination of the opposition." Thus, he races around the world mouthing the "glittering generalities" of the Declaration of Independence. To be sure, he could annihilate an entire nation with his special fire.

Needless to say, most everyone worships Uncle Sam, discovering in their "Superhero" all that's "best in themselves." This "hope of the world," this "Great Jehovah," "Thor," the opponent of Mandrake the Magician, can even blow smoke rings that take on the U.S. map outline, although they halo like mushroom clouds with rings that "spread like shock waves." One of his most remarkable attributes is his mammoth phallus, whose waters are likened to Niagara Falls and whose mere exposure can darken the heavens. "There's one thing about criminals and kings, priests and pariahs," he brags; they "generate the universe" (p. 90).

Most magical are Uncle Sam's transformational qualities. He "shazams" himself in and out of the president's body, and when "out," he visits key people involved in the current moral drama— e.g., he meets Nixon at the "Burning Tree Golf Club." His advice is always to follow the right "track," and "God helps them what helps themselves" (p. 7).

Uncle Sam has an extraordinary way of incarnating himself into each American president. "*I want* YOU!" he begins, after which he actually buggers each president-elect, who is obviously aware that this is part of his "manifest destiny." That such an act leaves its physical, as well as political, mark is hilariously reflected in Nixon's musings: "I recalled Hoover's glazed stare, Roosevelt's anguished tics, Ike's silly smile: I should have guessed" (p. 533).

A few last comments about Uncle Sam: like the godheads of classical mythology, he is visible to everyone; "wild," "wooly, and fulla fleas," he acts and speaks in the variety of styles of all his children—from Abe Lincoln to baseball's Country Slaughter. His sentimental platitudes and hokey phrases alternate with more formal and abstract language. Furthermore, what endows him with such power, it would seem, is his awareness of the need for authority in an arbitrary universe and the need for scapegoats. At one point, in typical Yankee lingo, he answers Nixon's speculation that the Rosenberg prosecution testimony was rigged: "Hell, *all* courtroom testimony about the past is . . . a baldface lie. . . . Like history itself. . . . *Opinion* ultimately governs." The Rosenbergs' "guilt" is merely "technological cattle-rustlin'" (pp. 86, 87).

In addition to satirizing the myth of the benevolent Uncle Sam, Coover dispels any glamorous notions of his offspring, the American people. In fact, focusing on an abstract population throughout (Nixon is the only fully realized person in the novel), Coover describes the early Eisenhower years as not so much a time of tranquility as one of anesthetization masking hysteria and vindictiveness. For over half the book, he portrays as the façade of America, a banal, conforming, and empty nation that well reflects its leader, Eisenhower, at one point called "unconscious." This is a country looking for leaders and listening for cues; thus lacking power and identity, it lacks moral responsibility. Its identity is created by film and any variety of tacky and manufactured slogans or junk.

When Coover gets to the execution and everyone is stripped naked, both literally and metaphorically, he reveals a universal vulgarity, cruelty, and paranoia—a combination of fear and greed, bloodthirsty megalomania and loneliness. The public is outraged by the Rosenbergs' treachery (associated with sexual as well as ideological license) and yet, as it projects upon the Rosenbergs its own deepest drives, it is also gleeful at their violent punishment. Indeed, it is the equation between the (Rosenbergs') so-called crime and punishment and America's sin and guilt that is once again Coover's subject.[5] In many ways, the Rosenbergs are America.

One should make clear, regarding this portrait of American society, that Coover makes no political distinctions. He is as savage and satiric in his vision of the Popular Front's maniacal opportunism as he is in his contempt and ridicule of the anti-Communists' pious self-righteousness. That the mob is indistinguishable is treated lightly at one point when Nixon, on the way to his office, makes his way through "a killer mob," presumably the Communists, only to realize "This was my own constituency": "Could I have your autograph?" he is asked (p. 208).

The Rosenbergs, also demythified, are more difficult to discuss. In the fifties, virtually everyone felt strongly one way or the other about them, and not only did one's position define his political stance, but it also contributed to the making of a political era. (For some, the Rosenbergs stood at the opposite pole from Nixon and Joe McCarthy and what were called their "witchhunts.") Coover, interestingly enough, is scrupulously nonjudgmental about their treason, although he does consistently portray them as Horatio Alger types gone astray. His Rosenbergs are people in search of fame, recognition, and glory, their words as hollow and full of rhetoric as those of their judges. They are two unlikely candidates for martyrdom nevertheless committed to martyrdom, *their* manifest destiny.

Coover summons forth enormous amounts of material regarding their innocence or guilt. One can, of course, never "know" if the 1953 data was accurate or complete and if the Rosenbergs received a fair trial. (If Coover's several implications are thus plausible, are they hence possible? Can one ever determine innocence or guilt, especially in life and death terms? How does one reconcile the need for order and justice in the face of such ambiguity?)

Were the Rosenbergs, for example, innocent pawns sacrificed to reinforce the momentum gained from the McCarthy hearings? Were they an expedient way of eliciting patriotism for the boys in Korea and a warning that America would tolerate no more threats? Were they used to facilitate American imperialism abroad, as well as at home?

Were they innocent of—if not all—some of the charges? Were they victimized by an inadequate defense? the suppression of important testimony? a not totally impartial judge?

Or were they guilty—as convicted, or otherwise?

As to their sentence, could they have averted it? Were they too caught up in their need for martyrdom to take advantage of their options? Were they convicted because they acted for moral principle rather than for money? Were they convicted because of their attorney's gross ineptitude? Did Eisenhower truly not understand the trial? Was he himself just part of the bloody tide, unable to recall the die?

Were the Rosenbergs victims of gross legal injustice? Were two witnesses or a confession really necessary for their conviction? If two penal statutes applied to their verdict (and did they?), should the lesser sentence have been imposed? Did a capital sentence necessitate a jury recommendation?[6] Indeed, were the Rosenbergs victims of American fascism, of America's own maniacal need to exterminate all differences and "purify the race"?

Once again, although he presents a mass of information, parts of which could be used to support any of these points of view, the only stand Coover seems to take about these miscast martyrs is that they were compelled to play out their roles. In a strikingly ironic way, they seem psychologically, if not morally, committed to historical process.

The Rosenbergs' innocence or guilt, and the justness of their sentence, is actually less important to the novel than the way in which it is used by all of America. At this point, one must turn to Richard Nixon, Coover's second narrator, in whose characterization Coover exemplifies his most extraordinary demythification.

Indeed, if the Rosenbergs represent one extreme in this American morality play, what better figure could Coover have chosen to include in this Manichaean struggle than Richard Nixon? If Coover's focus is in fact epic, what better person than Nixon to characterize an era? Nixon is, after all, a man larger than life, a man who helped shape America's destiny. Indeed, what president in this century has had a longer stay on the national stage and a more sustained impact on national and international identity?

Before 1953 and in his Hiss and HUAC activities, Nixon was, many believed, a link back to the Salem witch trials. In the present time of the novel, he is involved with the Korean War, and, as he puts it, is the spirit behind the Rosenberg case. As the book ends, he is about to become president—the next scapegoat?—while at the time of the book's publication, he was to have survived both America's spreading of light to Vietnam and his own political demise at Watergate. Ironically, he was to be pardoned from the very courtroom in which he won his fame.

A man of extraordinary survival power, Nixon won the golden ring after repeated defeats, and even after Watergate he continued to engage a sympathetic public interest and, most striking, to be regarded by some as an elder statesman. Nixon is as much Coover's subject as the Rosenbergs, and his soliloquies occupy at least half the book.

He is also the novel's most interesting figure. What is most remarkable is that while most readers will approach him with some degree of distaste, it is difficult at the end not to feel sympathetic to him. This is, of course, Robert Coover's Richard Nixon, but that Coover accomplishes this may well illustrate his very point about the power of media and language to mold judgment and create history.

Watergate, finally, may be life's ironic comment on art. That is, when Coover was planning his novel, before Watergate, many readers would have been offended by his self-serving and megalomaniacal Nixon. On the other hand, Watergate vindicated Coover's portrait. Yet because Nixon's decency may go beyond the historical myth of his evil, and because his evil in the fifties and seventies may also conflict with the rewards he reaped, Nixon may be both more and less than history's record of him during the more than thirty years of his political reign.[7] Further, as one reads the novel today, not only with the laws of treason and capital punishment changed (in 1980 a self-confessed traitor was sentenced to seven years of jail), and when one considers how America's "image" has transformed since the fifties, he can't help but grant Coover his basic assumption regarding the arbitrariness of historical evaluations. *The Public Burning* is about the making and unmaking of heroes, villains, and scapegoats, whose classification is often interchangeable.

In his portrait of Nixon, Coover introduces such complex perspectives that the entire novel is set into a series of shifting planes. If Uncle Sam is the concrete manifestation of a fictionalized abstraction, Coover's Nixon is the fictionalized embodiment of a historical reality. If the Uncle Sam figure, like the Rosenbergs and the American people, are cardboard figures largely portrayed in external detail (the public "myths" of America), Nixon is, in great part, the complex core (the psyche) of America, and his varied responses to that external reality are detailed in emotional terms. If Uncle Sam is the objective world, Nixon is its subjective voice, its emotional system, as well as the measuring eye and judging mind. Yet, since he is a product of that world and very much an active participant in it, his lens is colored not only by his existential place within the scheme of things but also by his own conscious and unconscious needs in response to that world, as well as by the sum of his past experiences. Nixon is also, at times, the microcosm of Uncle Sam in his drive for power, sexuality, scapegoating, and order. His private burnings necessitate the authority of law and order, if not some regularized exorcism, whenever their eruption threatens.

Nixon's interaction with others, and his own changing ideas and responses, are the novel's most powerful evocation of the flux of personality and experience, and this is reflected in the variety of genres in which he is portrayed—a fitting way to characterize a man who, throughout, views himself as an actor. Because, for example, at a crucial point, he tries to intercede in the terrible execution, Coover moves him beyond what has been his sometimes epic role playing to that of the potentially tragic figure. In Nixon's final capitulation to tradition, however, he becomes the comic buffoon and an Every-man, the survivor of a multiplicity of roles and the pathetic partici-pant in a barbaric and Dionysian celebration of life. It is as though Coover were drawing, in his Nixon character's shift from genre to genre, the existential paradox of individual freedom within the context of inevitable constraint, concretizing the very metaphor most common to the existentialists, man as an actor in the universe.

Perhaps collage best describes this continuous shifting of perspec-tives. Coover sets up one view of an event, person, morality (or he uses a specific genre), which he then dissolves or replaces with shades or variations of other contiguous materials (or trappings from other genre forms). Despite the book's appearance as linear narrative (Coover's fidelity to time and place during these three days is virtually classical), its contours and moods, as well as characteriza-tions and significances, continually shift, and meaning lies in the tensions generated between the moving planes.

Nixon's voice, for example, though frequently alternating with Uncle Sam's, at times contradicts both itself and Uncle Sam's. Each also blends and then separates from the other in any number of different spatial relationships. Each voice refuses to synthesize, as it also utilizes a variety of dialects and moods with similarly fluid substrata of shifting classical and historical allusions. Thus, the lines between the "factual" and "created" narrators are in continuous motion, and as each grows more fantastic, it remains simultaneously probable. Lines evaporate between the real and fantastic, truth and fiction, "innocence" and "guilt." Finally, all the shifting planes are set against the only absolute in the book (and life)—the absolute fact of the Rosenbergs' death.

It is through Nixon's rich characterization that the novel's major issues emerge regarding history, morality, personality, and individ-

ual freedom. Coover's Nixon, first and foremost, is very open about
the sort of man he is. He reveals that like most people he is a
combination of often contradictory qualities. He is both compassionate and cruel, curious and narrow-minded, shrewd and corny,
fiercely aggressive, yet often inhibited and insecure, sentimental,
and cold-blooded. His actions are dictated by opportunism and
calculation, but he is also a victim of chance and unconscious motivation. His speech mixes media cliché, Hollywood gloss, tough-guy
bravado, and naïve sentimentality.

He knows perfectly well how the public views him—as a carnival
barker, used-car salesman, or "Tricky Dick." On the other hand, his
face is too serious and bookish, a sort of "Gloomy Gus." (He has, in
fact, to work "physically harder to smile," p. 142.) It's all apparently a
matter of his heavy cheeks and stern Quaker eyes which, he explains, give him his scowly and sinister look. His unvanquishable
beard peeves him in its injustice.

Nixon also perspires a great deal and fears his own halitosis; he
does push-ups to keep in shape, and for years he has suffered from
stomach troubles ("the Farting Quacker"); he eats a lot of cottage
cheese (with ketchup to make it palatable) and really enjoys a well-
done hamburger and pineapple malted.

A lonely man ("I wish I had a friend," p. 224), his only intimates
over the years appear to be George Smathers, Bill Rogers, and Bert
Andrews. He suffers humiliations from virtually everyone—from
his earliest teachers and girl friend (as the lead in the high school
Aeneid, he was called Anus) to his family and the entire political
community.

Often embarrassed by his own clumsiness (he frequently steps in
horse turds), he is the sort of person often caught with his pants
down (which literally occurs in two dramatic scenes, an ironic
literalization of what would figuratively occur during Watergate). In
typical self-pity bordering on self-mockery, he speaks of himself as
the unwanted child, boyfriend, husband, lawyer, and even vice-
president and president-to-be. But Nixon is not entirely without
humor; he enjoys, for example, playing lion tamer with the Republican senators in their cloakroom.

He is also living proof of the Horatio Alger myth—and proud of
it—not only the poor, small-town boy, who literally finished first, but
the loser who could come out on top. His recollections of a lonely
childhood in Yorba Linda (he was the first child born there, and the
sun eclipsed the next day) explain his strange combination of

ruthlessness and romantic dreaminess; he is a mixture of his mother's Quaker peacemaking instincts and his father's Black Irish temper.

Some of Nixon's most painful recollections are of the hard times he had with girls, who liked him only for his brains. (He loves word games.) An outsider even then, he learned the piano, and his nights were filled with lonesome train whistles; as we shall see, the train would develop into a major emblem in Nixon's life. Then as now, however, Nixon was sentimental and a dreamer. Though shy and inhibited, he might have been an actor, or writer, or even jazz pianist. Though one might accuse him of gross sentimentality, his concern for certain people was always genuine. Of his colleague, the ailing Bob Taft, he says: "I wanted to reach out and embrace him, . . . make him well again," and he adds, "make him President or something" (p. 46). Nixon always wanted the happy ending; his favorite movie was *The Best Years of Our Lives*. It is not surprising, then, that the Rosenberg's travails should deeply move him and that he should try to change what appeared to be their inevitable doom.

About Pat, his wife, he is similarly unrealistic. Though he recalls the pursuit of his "Tillie the Toiler" as one of utter romance ("If only I could win [her]," p. 54), he actually married because it was time to marry, and she was not the girl of his dreams. Now he has a passionless and bourgeois marriage with the prescribed two children and dog, and Pat is always cold and critical. Withall, he looks up to her as a standard of absolute goodness.

Nixon is, in fact, torn between priggish self-control and a deep yearning for passionate abandon. He admits his fear of intimacy, along with his susceptibility to passion, but his confession is another foreshadowing of what twice eventually occurs in the novel: "If you let your hair down," he explains, "you feel too naked. Yet, I longed for this nakedness" (p. 298).

Law was his solution, "a potent aphrodisiac"; furthermore, lawyers "ran the world" (p. 301). To be sure, Nixon has the legalistic sort of mind to entertain both sides of an issue, although he knows that this ability, if accompanied by too much imagination, can lead to paralysis. "Paradox was the one thing I hated," he repeats, but much of his trouble arises from his helpless immersion in dialectics. As though repeating Uncle Sam's words about manifest destiny, Nixon believes that his every act is a preparation for some "New Order that was my destiny."

Intelligent, foxy, and imaginative, Nixon is the "egghead of the

Republican Party." Though excluded from Ike's circle of friends, he is the real brain in the White House. Ambivalent about Ike's easy success, he asks: "Who else in all history had ever become the world's greatest living military hero without so much as firing a shot?" (p. 30). Yet it is Eisenhower's victory pose that Nixon adopts, and he frequently looks to Ike as a surrogate father and expresses admiration for him.

Nixon is extremely forthright about himself politically and admits to being a "shameless politician": "I'm a tough sonuvabitch to run against in an election. . . . I go for the jugular, no holds barred. . . . Even at its most trivial, politics flirted with murder and mayhem, theft and cannibalism" (p. 48). He understands how scapegoating the Rosenbergs is politically, socially, and pyschologically expedient "to keep things from just peterin' out" (p. 95).

Because Nixon is pragmatic about his career, he is concerned with ends, not means. Although essentially a man of moral conviction, he learned in his first law firm that he would have to scrape and struggle to get ahead. Moral convictions were well and good but utterly irrelevant to getting on in the world. His reports of Eisenhower and his cabinet well illustrate this.

Nixon loves a battle, a "straight-out power struggle, raw and pure," for its game quality. He would do anything to be president, even go bald, which seems to be the precedent. He is a compulsive worker, spends eighteen to twenty hours a day at his office: "The more I work the sharper and quicker my mental reactions" (p. 113). Well-organized and with an eye to the future, he writes notes to himself on index cards, a modern-day Hamlet.

He has always used everything to his advantage—e.g., the Secret Nixon Fund crisis, in which he immortalized Pat's cloth coat. (Actually, money means nothing to him; as he puts it, "If I were rich, the only thing I could possily want to buy would be the Presidency," p. 310.) He admits that his entire career has grown out of chasing Communists, and because of his success with Hiss and HUAC, he believes the Rosenberg case to be his "baby," though he apparently had little to do with their conviction. He also admits: "In a concentration camp, I not only would survive, I would probably even prosper" (p. 291). "Change trains for the Future" is his favorite motto, reminiscent of Uncle Sam's, and, as we shall see in one of the last, climactic scenes, Nixon literally does board a train to change America's future.

Nixon is also bright about life. He is aware of the impossibility of discerning "truth" in human events and of the relativity of all historical and moral pronouncements. History, he comments, "is never literal." If it were, "it would have no pattern at all, we'd all be lost" (p. 203). He knows that all accomplishments end in meaningless death ("I'd been scared all my life of dying and I was scared still," p. 346), yet he knows how people, including himself, must take refuge in a variety of structures. Law and marriage are part of his "unfolding pattern." This intelligence, and the conflict it provokes within him, isolate and elevate him above the masses around him. Thus, while he continuously speaks of the need for commitment and definition— "I'm no believer in dialectics. . . . It's either/or as far as I'm concerned" (p. 48)—he is torn by his awareness of the arbitrariness and transitoriness of individual accomplishment and human event. Reality might even be a dream, a verbal or imaginative construct: "What if . . . there were no spy ring at all? What if all these characters *believed* there was and acted out their parts on this assumption, a whole courtroom full of fantasists . . . [who] just dreamed it all up?" (p. 135).

But Nixon knows (much like Coover, who creates in the final execution the theatrical scene to match all others) that game playing and acting involve scripts or rules. He knows that it is too confusing to be all of one's conflicting selves and that one cannot communicate without the cohesive artifice of roles, which, in turn, facilitate morality and the social order.

What more sacred and uniquely American institution exists, moreover, from which to mold an identity than Hollywood with all its mythic heroes? Hollywood has, after all, provided the contemporary world a gospel of moral types and enough plots and happy endings to distract an entire population from the inscrutability of the real world. Throughout, Nixon describes himself as one of any number of Hollywood actors and roles. As a young man he was Douglas Fairbanks; today he may be Ronald Colman or Clark Gable. What troubles him about the Rosenbergs is their self-casting into "phony" roles which gives "the lie to their testimony" (p. 127).

Actually, all the novel's characters are described as actors, or they choose to perform as actors. Eisenhower's favorite movie is *High Noon*, and in one "Intermezzo," his words are set to the melody of the title song. (Throughout, *High Noon* and *The House of Wax* are used as analogues to the events of the time.) When a crowd gathers on the

White House lawn to await the verdict concerning Douglas's stay of execution (it is high noon), Ike outdoes even Gary Cooper in his towering role (p. 241).

The very trial is like a play and even a play within a play. Saypol *recites* a line from a play Nixon once acted; he has also "rehearsed" the witnesses and has been part of the prosecution's "backstage rigging." Kaufman is like the "director" of his own play, with his own "applause," "actors," and "script" (p. 119). Trials, Nixon implies, are merely presentations of competing versions of reality. Even "minor" characters are portrayed in self-conscious metadramatic terms although, as Nixon knows, regardless of one's number of lines, his role *to him* is always major. When, for example, a former Rosenberg friend is arrested, he reacts like Jimmy Cagney in *Angels with Dirty Faces*. The "fabulator" Gold, Nixon also observes, may have been "the real playwright here" (p. 126). The Rosenbergs quite reasonably fear some "irrevocable casting."

Nixon even connects morality—the Rosenbergs' death sentence —with their bad "style" and script. They were just too ordinary ("dowdiness *was* guilt," p. 122), as they capitulated to the human "zeal" for "story"; but they lacked sincerity, even in their letters, which were "hyperbolic . . . and full of political clichés." As a result, "the players had got bad reviews, the death sentence." Can one, Nixon asks, separate a person from his script ("Which was real . . . the paper or the people?" (p. 305).

In chapter 6, focusing upon the Rosenbergs in Sing Sing, Coover draws Ethel and Julius like characters in a play recalling other characters in a play, totally drawn into a metadramatic performance of life. The chapter begins: "The curtain rises upon the Warden's office," but the reader is unsure if this is Sing Sing or a play about it. "It *would* rain tonight" (p. 97), it continues, but, in fact, it did not rain even on Coover's warm and humid June 19.

As Ethel recalls her role in *The Valiant*, a play about a condemned prisoner, and the warden comments upon her role playing, it is difficult to get beneath the shifting planes to locate character and happening. One's attention is drawn to the metafictional quality of life, reflected in this fiction on fiction (metametafiction?). Reduced to cardboard figures, Ethel and Julius, like the characters in Ethel's play, are absorbed by metaphors. Ethel speculates that perhaps Ronald Colman played life better in *A Tale of Two Cities* (a film of a book about history) than Julius, whom she now compares to Colman (Nixon's "hero"). That the prisoners show signs of mellowing is, to the warden, perhaps "a ruse, the kind of trick Errol Flynn often uses." To Julie, however, everything *seems* more "unreal" than to Ethel, who has "taken the part on and made it her own." Lines also echo from *Hamlet, Romeo and Juliet*, and many other works.

The following chapter, in marked contrast, describes what is presumably the Rosenbergs' love for each other. Yet the narrative really indicates how each is locked in his and her own world. If the reader's sympathies are aroused, by virtue of their condemnation, Ethel's remarks put one off: she would like to see *The Crucible*, where audiences applaud the heroes' intent to "burn" rather than to be "stool pigeons"; again she recalls her role in *The Valiant*. Are the Rosenbergs innocent or guilty? Are they acting or not, and if they are, which scenario are they following? Even if they are innocent, are they to die with "pride" and "honor," *or* "as though in spite?" (p. 100). A rich summary of these ambiguities follows, and the reader can only sense the referential ambiguity of "farce" and "fascists": "The farce is exposed. . . . It is imperative to stand up to these fascists and nail them to their own lies!" (p. 101).

Nixon realizes that language lies behind and arbitrarily organizes all structures—all perceptions of experience, like drama, the media, or law. Regarding the impenetrable issue of the Rosenbergs' guilt or innocence, he describes any judgments as mere linguistic artifice, the pragmatic servant of an orderly society: "How could one . . . define the essential debate, keep it clean from diffuseness and mind-numbing paradox? . . . That was what language was for: to transcend the confusions, restore the spirit, recreate the society!" (p. 234).

Nixon is vocal throughout about language's function. That he speaks for Coover regarding the media, which have more generative, moral power than man, seems clear in two separate chapters presented from neither Uncle Sam's nor Nixon's perspective. In one, America's poet laureate is personified as *Time* magazine, and he proclaims himself as society's mythmaker (chap. 18). In a second, chapter 10, the *New York Times* reaffirms the press's similar mythogenerative function. In each, Coover deals with questions he has been raising throughout about the meaning of History (always capitalized): Is History mythic pattern that is replayed? Do men determine History, or does accident? Is History "process"? His conclusion, like Nixon's, would seem to be that history, like art in its many forms, is "arbitrariness as a principle, allowing us to laugh at the tragic" (p. 190).

Time openly admits his willing distortion of ("paralyzing") raw data and the need to subordinate "facts to the imagination" for meaning and "art." Successor to the *Saturday Evening Post*, and sibling of *Fortune* and *Life*, he is perfectly open about his bias—i.e., his belief in war—and he admits that his *style* creates not only social morality but the language with which men interact—with "rugged verbs" and a "ruthless emphasis on physical details" (p. 326). ("To name is to create.")

Like any God who offers comfort in the face of mystery, *Time* is committed to revelation. Yet with the self-righteous stupidity of Pope's bard of dullness, and illustrative of the kind of distortion that language and ideas fall into, he proclaims that "'TIME will reveal everything,' [as] Euripides prophesized" (p. 328); this is *his* "manifest destiny."

Less egomaniacal but ultimately as eccentric is the *New York Times*, which also provides a "struggle against entropy" with "randomness as design." Here Coover amplifies how language is an arbitrary pattern imposed upon reality. Newspapers provide a "tenacious faith in the residual magic of language," as they reconstruct "each fleeting day in the hope of discovering . . . some coherence, some meaningful dialogue with time" (p. 191).

The *New York Times* also creates an "orderly picture of life . . . no matter how crazy it is." It lies to the world about the commonplace; it places death into a perspective, and in so doing, it avoids "the sorcery, the terrible center, the edgeless edge" (p. 195); its statements like "Louis Applebaum will be buried today" are "sacred stuff . . . but ritualized."

Like religion, the media thus provide "a talisman against the terrible flux" (p. 188). To be sure, "men fear only surprises." Willing participants in the ancient ceremonies of food and drink, worshipers approach their newspapers by "breaking bread and sipping hot stimulants, muttering the traditional responses, snorting and farting, momentarily losing themselves, absorbing the positional metaphors that will preserve the earth's gravity one more day and stay their own panic."

But Richard Nixon knows all of this—and even more. He knows that a person is, finally, his linguistic function. One is his name. Thus, if one violates a man in the public record, one violates his identity and "mythology," as well as "History" itself. One's linguistic function, furthermore, is always defined within a priori structures so that linguistic function ("existence"), rather than substance or morality ("essence"), makes the man. Nixon calls Saypol's success an "accomplishment" more with "adjectives and style than with verbs and substance" (p. 122).

With this complex Nixon figure thus aware of such matters—of life as a linguistic function or predominantly a dramatic role—it is not surprising that he relates to people as an actor does to a role or an audience to a performance. Indeed, if identification is at the heart of all drama, Nixon identifies with the two main characters in this major contemporary drama, Ethel and Julius Rosenberg.

First, he cannot help but equate the Rosenbergs' dreams and inner lives with his own: he believes they share a similarly empty marriage; more importantly, he identifies them as Horatio Alger types. Their idealism, in fact, is most appealing. But Nixon also intuits real people beneath all the rhetoric and grandstanding. He feels a profound "There but for the grace of God go I" guilt toward them: "We all probably went to the same movies, sang the same songs. . . . We were the Generation of the Great Depression. Now I was the Vice President. . . . They were condemned to burn as traitors. What went wrong?"

Had Julius "come to Whittier" and Nixon himself gone to the 1936 International Seaman's Union Ball and met Ethel, their positions now might have been reversed. (Yet note the quality of Nixon's imagined success: "I might have become a Communist and changed the course of history," p. 138.) As ever, Nixon's mind is trapped in paradox. What would he do if his daughters married the Rosenberg boys? Nevertheless he and Julius were "like mirror images of each other." Each had similar childhoods: both had hardworking fathers who suffered hard times; both were religious and sickly children; Nixon cherishes the smallest detail: both boys loved candy bars. "I'd become Vice President," he repeats, "by a chain of circumstances not all that different" from the Rosenbergs'.

Nixon's identification with Ethel is completely romantic. Early in the novel, in a lyrical and innocent fantasy, he envisions her as a child within his own family. Later, after observing his cold, blonde, and naked Pat asleep, he has another vision. He begins to smell the sweat shops and fish stores on Delancey and Canal streets: Ethel and he were both children of hardworking but failed fathers and kitchen-bound mothers; both loved books, were honor students, were stage struck, shy, and lonely. Both were dreamers, and both married to give purpose to their lives.

He ponders Ethel's life as the possibility and/or illusion of choices.

Might she have found true stardom if her mother had encouraged her to sing? Indeed, was she ever free, or did she just trade one script for another? "Had she just said no to History," would she "have been home free?"

It is with this childlike romantic imagination that Nixon fantasizes a tryst with Ethel. He would be the knight rescuing innocence, Clark Gable saving Claudette Colbert, the victory of manly virtue over worldly violence and evil. His dream culminates with their childlike undressing of each other. As it turns out, Nixon is masturbating during this fantasy, and he is abruptly interrupted by Uncle Sam's sudden appearance: "You know, son," he says, "You'll go blind playing with yourself like that" (p. 318).

But the fancy compels, and Nixon is drawn to Sing Sing. This is, he believes, his chance to fulfill his destiny. He will get the Rosenberg confessions and thus release them from the death penalty. From this point on until shortly before the execution, Coover alternates Nixon's visit with the final preparations for the electrocution. As though a prelude to both of these, however, by way of tone, imagery, and meditations on life, art, the media, sanity, madness, and justice, is Coover's remarkable chapter 16.

A phantasmagoric descent into hell by an anonymous man (still wearing 3-D glasses from *The House of Wax*), this consists of a bombardment of concrete and surreal images within which reality and madness merge, along with countless evocations of fact and fiction, the Rosenbergs, Nixon, and a host of historical figures and Hollywood actors. Examples of art (and its destruction by fire), the media, trains, bombs, electrocutions, Einstein, and Armageddon — and an intensification of light and dark images — recur. The chapter, which accelerates like a frenzied strobe light, begins with a Rosenberg child watching television. News flashes on that his parents are to be executed, and the boy verbally evokes the "crazy" and "maniac" quality of the world. By the end of the chapter, the anonymous Forty-second Street man has been swept forward through the grotesque reality of New York and, no longer able to distinguish fact from fantasy, is incarcerated in the Walt Disney whale exhibit reserved for lunatics and criminals. (Recall Uncle Sam's earlier comment that kings and criminals create the world; Nixon will later take refuge here.)

Counterpointing this is the somewhat embarrassed Nixon traveling to Sing Sing, like a "beardy desperado arriving" for the "final showdown" (p. 359). To be sure, Nixon has literally changed trains for the future. Yet always a man of contradictions, he is shaky in making the trip. Ossining felt "like coming home," he says; nevertheless, he has found it necessary to disguise himself: he has literally pasted on a handlebar moustache and announced himself as Thomas Greenleaf ("like the poet"). In the following scene, Nixon at last appears to apply to himself what he has said about role playing, authenticity, and identity. It is as though he were going to follow that mysterious cabdriver's advice and free himself from "worn-out rituals." Nixon defines his crisis: "There were no scripts, no necessary patterns, no final scenes, there was just *action*. . . . [In fact] emptiness lay behind the so-called issues. . . . All men contain all views, right and left, theistic and atheistic, legalistic and anarchical, monadic and pluralistic; and only an artificial—call it political—commitment to consistency makes them hold steadfast to singular positions. Yet why be consistent if the universe wasn't [to which he farts]? . . . I had to step in and change the script" (pp. 362, 363).

Nixon's desire for authenticity is impressive but problematic. His statements, interestingly enough, bespeak the American ideal of freedom, political and personal; and their condemnation of role playing, in a sense, parallels an indictment of the philosophical notion of historical determinism. However, psychologically and practically, his "ideal" is impossible.

First, he fails to realize that despite the moral possibilities inherent in the individual act, whatever one's daily "plot," a "script" emerges with a scenario that contains the very grammar and referents one would reject. (That Nixon uses metadramatic language undercuts his very statement.) Furthermore, regardless of one's role and the difficulties of enacting it, his potential is always limited. The "conclusion" is always the same. Indeed, the flaw in Nixon's thinking reflects the contradiction of the absurd: one's freedom in a contingent universe is illusory.

Because Nixon makes this frantic leap from actor/victim to god-like author, what follows is as believable and unbelievable as his vision—a supremely melodramatic scenario that blends romantic idealism with sheer corn. One is reminded of Thomas Mann's ironic pose in *Death in Venice* and his use of a self-consciously effulgent prose to mirror Aschenbach's decadence. Just as one can view Aschenbach in paradoxical terms, as both destroying and saving himself in Venice, so too one can view Nixon's meeting and love scene with Ethel as the utmost in grotesque clumsiness *and* genuinely felt emotion. This is black humor in the extreme.

What is fascinating about Ethel and Nixon's love scene is that while it reads well, in isolating phrases or reading it aloud, it is often trite and excessive, like dime-store romance; yet one feels a genuine passion beneath Nixon's words. We are now dealing not just with experiential distortions inevitable in scripts or linguistic functions but also with the way vocabulary, phraseology, or genre defines. Perhaps the important point about spoken language is that words are meaningful only when they connect with real feelings, regardless of their complex, sophisticated, or original linguistic structures or vocabulary.

In this scene, and to himself, Nixon is at last the hero-rescuer, the great lover (like Henry in the *UBA*), and he fulfills the male child's most extravagant fantasy as conquerer and even savior of a nation. As he gets more and more into his fantasy (defined by both the Horatio Alger myth and Hollywood), distinctions between his inner and outer worlds blur. Both are, in fact, defined by the same clichés and myths.

As Nixon speaks to the reader, his words act out their own designs, as though they had a life of their own. At the end, in his ardent and heroic gestures, he is a buffoon and bumbler. That is, through the remarkable parody of the gap between passion (felt emotion) and language, Coover conveys the paradox of the hero-fool Nixon, a man both sympathetic and contemptible, a quixotic comic figure on the tragic stage set of the world.

As Nixon walks to Sing Sing, he announces his freedom: he will "step in and change the script"; he will make the entire nation "truly function again." His vision is grandiose and absurd: "I would make war and rebellion physically impossible, and world commerce would flourish." He would unite country and city, reinvigorate the myth of New America, and all of this, by the way, not just for the nation but also for Mom and Dad (p. 372). Nixon is euphoric, but as ridiculous as this sounds, how else does one express himself but in the often corny terms of his own experience?

Coover's prose changes radically as it captures the existential quality of life: "The sun was dipping low over the Hudson; not so hot now, and there was a breeze off the river. . . . The trees were full of birds" (p. 405). Nixon's zeal and obsession with the Rosenbergs gives way to the distractions of nature. Suffering does indeed take place, to paraphrase W. H. Auden, while the world goes on with its doggy life. Nixon strolls around the prison facilities, each thing in its own place; it is quiet and bucolic.

The warden describes to him the Rosenbergs' odd behavior. They are acting "like they're establishing historical models," like "they're on stage or something" (p. 408). When Nixon arrives at Ethel's cell, Coover plays riotously with the reader's responses. Potential tragedy becomes high melodrama, comedy, and finally, slapstick.

Nixon, for the first time free from the drive of power, is utterly compelled by the passion and romance of the moment. Ethel's first words (she even looks like Claudette Colbert) are: "I've been expecting you" (p. 429). The fairy-tale prince, he replies: "I've run away from the government. . . . I've come to save you" (p. 433). Thus relinquishing the frog for the prince (politics for passion), he continues: "I don't want your confession, Ethel! I don't care about the past, it's now I care about! . . . *You don't love him* [Julius] . . . *and you never have!*" (p. 435).

In his great and heroic moment he proclaims: "We've both been victims of the same lie, Ethel! There *is* no purpose, there *are* no causes, all that's just stuff we make up to hold the goddamn world together—all we've really got is what we have right here and now: being alive! *Don't throw it away, Ethel!*" At that point, "her lips parted. . . . I kissed her" (p. 436).

The reader is acutely distressed trying to discuss this, because despite the prose, this is really a moving scene. Not just an example of the disparity between felt experience and language, it is another example (perhaps ironic) of the ambiguous quality of human experience. That is, while in content Nixon's statement may be the moral core of the book ("All we've really got is what we have . . . being alive"), in reality, in the context of its utterance, it is ridiculous. As a proclamation, it is just as absolute as any other moral dictate. Yet the statement *must* be irrelevant to Ethel, who in the next few minutes is to be taken to her death and who, at least initially, seemed far more concerned with her "cause" than either death or passion. Ethel may, of course, be reacting to her own sexual neediness at this moment; she may also be using this occasion as a final political act, the consequences of which shall soon be evident. The fact is that when Nixon says "Ethel . . . let out a soft anguished cry . . . taken unawares. So was I. I had not planned this," one cannot begin to understand either one's motivation, and perhaps this is the point.

After a great deal of clutching, heavy breathing, "gasping," and "groaning," Nixon envisions the child he and his Beatrice would have. His comments are again moving but increasingly absurd: "I grasped Ethel's bottom and saw the face of a child . . . a poet, a

scientist, a great teacher. . . . He was America itself. . . . I saw all this
as my tongue roamed behind Ethel's incisors. I was weeping. . . . I
could hardly breathe . . . I was afraid I might have an attack of hay
fever" (p. 438). The fantasy almost real, he adds: "*I am making history
this evening . . . for all the ages!*"

Ethel's response is just what he wants: "You're so strong, so powerful!" to which he replies, once again using lines out of a play (and
what a play!): "*Gentlemen of the Jury*" (p. 439), to which she says: "Oh,
Richard! What's happening to us?" As they then speak of the acci-
dents of fate that afforded them their roles, Nixon admits, with
further self-consciousness, that he never wanted to be vice-
president: "I always wanted to be free," and he adds, "I wanted to be
a bum." Now the absurd hero, he utters: "I felt an incredible new
power, a new freedom. . . . I was outside guarded time! I was my own
man at last! I felt like shouting for joy!" (p. 442).

Ethel tells him her time is running out, and she must sexually have
him, immediately, on the prison floor. This is Nixon's finest hour as
bumbler: he cannot get his pants off, and he is caught in their tangle.
Ethel, whose purpose in getting Nixon's pants down will soon become obvious, tries to wipe clean his "filthy bottom." Her last remarks grant him his greatest wish: "You will . . . bring peace to
mankind [and] . . . they shall say of you: Richard Nixon was a great
lover!" (p. 446). She kisses him a last time and adds, "You need a
shave."

As they lead her out, Nixon, really a bad actor, says: "Ethel,
remember, the valiant die many—I mean, the valiant, uh, taste of
death—damn it, I've forgotten it!" (Recall Ethel's acting *The Valiant*.)
Always the moralist, he is now a ludicrous Christ or Sisyphus figure:
"A man who has never lost himself in a cause bigger than himself has
missed one of life's mountaintop experiences: only in losing himself
does he find himself" (p. 446). Ethel is off to die; Nixon is transformed.

The spectacle of the execution is an apocalyptic vision of the
burning of human flesh and spirit and a descent into hell that is
virtually unrivalled. Hundreds of American personalities of past
and present participate. The scene initially takes on the grotesque
elements of ritual sacrifice and early tragedy; with Nixon's
entrance—he is now a public buffoon—it becomes comic. Coover's
evocation of the primitive origins of all great art, the birth of tragedy
and comedy, stretches his canvas back to the beginnings of religious
ritual and the birth of civilization.

Coover has, of course, moved the execution from Sing Sing (a peculiarly inappropriate name for a prison) to Times Square, where "all top box-office draws since the days of the Roman circus" have played (p. 216). The Rosenbergs have become "no less then [*sic*] Valentino and Garbo . . . Rin Tin Tin and Trigger—true Stars . . . their fame assured for generations to come." Times Square is the "ritual center of the Western World," where all the great and mythic heroes once walked. One can still take communion with the modern-day gods ("break bread with Milton Berle . . . at Lindy's") and annually exorcise his sins in communal worship at "the world's largest New Year's Eve party," a "perennial charm against death and entropy" (p. 166). Yet one must always fear for his life here, where all the world's thieves, as well as its mystics, congregate. This is the "most paradoxical place in all America, and thus the holiest . . . the Heart and Cock of the Country" (p. 164), America's "luminous navel."

With all of America committed to the present ceremony, there will be no less than a full house. The Rosenbergs are scapegoats for an entire nation's violence and passion, as well as its secret sense of failure and inadequacy. Their dying light—literally in their electrocution—will concretely and symbolically defeat the forces of darkness and energize America's puritanical tradition. Their exorcism will promise a stay against entropy, death, and boredom. The dying gods shall herald to all a renewed sense of personal purpose and a "new excitement in the world."

The scene has all the trappings of Dionysian rite—sacrifice, carnival, and orgy. The mob has arrived frustrated and angry. (Traffic has been rerouted to cause maximum congestion and rage.)[8] An entertainment committee chaired by Cecil B. DeMille has organized a program to cater to everyone's needs. Preexecution festivities include all manner of entertainment, any of which can exceed the promised thrills of New York's popular theaters. In addition to Disney entertainment and exhibits (even the children are attended to) there is every sort of visual, verbal, aural, gastronomic—and finally, sexual—entertainment. The executions will take place amidst music, history, film, poetry, and dance, with a fifteen-round middle-weight championship boxing event immediately following. If, at any point, anything goes wrong or anyone is bored, there are backup movies.

Master of ceremonies at this "act of religious purgation" is naturally Uncle Sam, who says "Size me up and shudder, you scalawags!"

(p. 419), for "I am the Thunderer, Justice the Avenger." The event is a consecration, "a new charter of the moral and social order of the western world." It shall be of "Wagnerian scope," something befitting the grandest of all inaugurations, coronations, or religious investitures.

Countless bands perform: the Pentagon Patriots, for example, wearing Yankee Doodle uniforms like Nelson Eddy in *The Chocolate Soldier*, lead an old-fashioned sing along. As they march, they perform old American songs and "recall heroes and hangings, grief and grace, traitors and liars" (p. 398). The "real" Nelson Eddy is present, as are innumerable American box-office stars—folk heroes, magnates, and national sports champions—"winners" from every walk of life. Only Arthur Miller sits alone in a theater watching *The Crucible* and lamenting that art "is not as lethal as one might hope."

Among the celebrities present are Yehudi Menuhin, Dick Button, Gary Cooper, John Rockefeller, Bogart and Bacall, "Billy" Faulkner, Billy Graham, Busby Berkeley, and even America's answer to Michelangelo, James Montgomery Flagg. European bigwigs include Winston Churchill and Jean-Paul Sartre. Not only do film and cartoon characters "materialize," but every variety of filmgoer is also present, dressed in every sort of American costume. "Missionaries squeezed up with mafiosos, hepcats with hottentots, pollyannas with press agents and plumbers and panty raiders . . . an ingathering of monumental proportions" (p. 355).

There are hymns and prayers; Kate Smith sings "God Bless America"; minidramas reenact the major chapters of American history: actors wear papier-mâché heads modeled after official presidential portraits, but then the presidents are portrayed as their often derogatory public nicknames. (Do names or images now make the man?) These are then accompanied by iconic figures of the epics each president "represented." Coover sets up what might be called "metamedia upon metamedia," not unlike the "3-D man's" experiences of reality.

Contests follow—funny, terrifying, and sad—skits and readings of the Rosenberg letters by the nation's most talented comics. Hope, Crosby, and Lamour do a "Goin' My Way" routine on the electric chair; the prosecuting team actually reenacts the trial procedures. Celebrities mold whatever they can to their special talents: Boris Karloff and Elsa Lanchester, Martin and Lewis, Durante, Yogi Berra, the Marx Brothers, and, of course, Uncle Miltie. With all the "thrills, tears, and laughter," this is the greatest show of shows.

Throughout, everyone is aware of the main event; after all, Ethel and Julius are "the inner mechanism that sums it up and gives it meaning." They are, in fact, the libidinal force of the mechanism. As Nixon puts it, they have coupled with the Phantom and sought "nothing less than the ultimate impotency of Uncle Sam." Their union has generated a linguistic code—a script, identity, or even "new and appalling archetypes . . . to replace the comforting commonplaces of 'Stella Dallas' and 'Young Widder Brown.'" They even "hint at uncracked codes" (p. 352).

To be sure, the public associates the Rosenbergs' crime with excessive and perverse sexuality. Pornographic records discovered in their apartment were clearly "enough alone to hang them on." In Nixon's earlier scene with the cabdriver, he listened to a long, lurid description of a sexually promiscuous woman, whom he finally learned was Juliet Rosenblatt. (But Ethel's sexual immorality is assumed throughout.) Nonconformity is repeatedly translated into sexual deviation. When Justice Douglas grants the last stay, the narrator queries if perhaps he weren't touched by a "dose of venereal anarchy" which precipitated his own "satyr" role in "all those sex scandals" (p. 67).

To be sure, the Rosenbergs' punishment arouses the public sexually. Were a poll taken nationally, Nixon speculates, most everyone, including even Cardinal Spellman and Joe McCarthy, would admit awakening this morning "from the foment of strange gamey dreams with prodigious erections and enflamed crevices." Such an "unwonted appetite for risk and profligacy," which makes men—and women—nervous, must obviously be attended to. Lust, shame, guilt, repentance, and obedience: such will be the ritual.

Uncle Sam first fans the fires. He encourages close body contact, and he passes out free alcoholic libations and provides appropriate entertainment—e.g., Georgia Gibbs sings "Kiss of Fire." Though the government's executive, legislative, and judicial branches have now arrived, the sex and drinking accelerates. As Uncle Sam looks on, masses heave in copulative and masturbatory forms of every conceivable design. He comments: "Sex'll cause the flame to grow," and he adds, "You gotta plow up a field before you can grow something in it" (p. 358). The celebrants, not quite ready for the Rosenbergs, enjoy the prolonged patriotic and sexual brouhaha.

The action is incessant. The single clemency float is smashed, an old panhandler continues to reap unexpected wealth, and 435 members of the House, 96 senators (each introduced by Betty

Crocker)—and a host of other public figures—arrive. Supreme
Court justices slip in elephant dung and bump into each other "like
pigs." Everyone is equalized—the ordinary and the mighty—all
equally ridiculous and commonly vulgar. The Democrats' donkey,
with a "hard-on the size of Mickey Mantle's baseball bat," waits to
couple with the Republican elephant, which has just loosed its bowels upon several Supreme Court justices (p. 457). Significantly,
William O. Douglas, who issued the Rosenbergs' last stay of execution and to whom Coover dedicates the book, is exempt from this
unseemly baptism. One senses that Douglas is for Coover one of the
few uniquely admirable participants in this drama.

At the peak of this "frolic scene," with four minutes to go, Richard
Nixon enters, backing "bareass out onto the stage" (p. 469). "I AM A
SCAMP" is lipsticked on his butt. Confused and feeling as though he
were descending into a "black hole," Nixon faces the ultimate crisis
of his life and also his last chance to forge a new identity. *"I can't even
remember my name!"* he cries (p. 471). The helpless man is mocked by
everyone, his nakedness pelted by flying objects. Once again, he is
"front and center on the stage of human history."

It is important to remember that through most of the novel Nixon
has been a sympathetic, if not heroic, figure who, despite his opportunism and pomposity, has stood above the screaming and vindictive
mob. Though he may frequently have viewed others as extensions of
his own ego, he has truly cared for some, and he has also shown some
insight into himself and human experience.

What occurs now is complex. First, Nixon turns this humiliating
situation to his powerful advantage: "The only defense," he calmly
reasons, is "to talk my way around this humiliation" (p. 473). In an
extraordinary *tour de force* of legalese and psychologese, the drowning man does indeed save himself. He begs all Americans to bare
themselves for America in a new act of dedication. Everyone must
drop his "PANTS DOWN FOR GOD AND COUNTRY!" And
everyone submits—from Hopalong Cassidy and Walter Lippman to
Bess Truman, Captain Video, and Christine Jorgensen.

A jealous and wrathful Uncle Sam looks on. A potentially new
demogogue has interfered with his divine plan (his timetable) and
created his own spectacle. The favorite son has gone astray, Horatio
Alger stepping too far forward. (Perhaps Nixon has, as he earlier
wished, really caught Uncle Sam "from behind," p. 367.) In Uncle
Sam's capitulation, there is "a blinding flash of light and a simul-
taneous crack of ear-splitting thunder and then—BLACKOUT

[because no one can see the face of God?]!!" In the subsequent darkness are the final writhings of flesh, amidst pools and smells of semen and vomit.

Everyone is screaming for Uncle Sam and for rescue from his most detested fear—himself and "each other." This is a scene out of Dante, Brueghel, or Bosch, and all of American history is participating. Nixon, horrified, has been pushed into the audience and touched and jostled by everyone. He finally takes refuge in the Disney whale. As to exactly what happens to him at this point (like the conclusion of the *UBA*, where Coover dismisses Henry), there are few details.

The light returns, "like a mushroom," with the jackass and elephant still copulating, and Uncle Sam reminds everyone that thus is the Phantom's terrible power; but since a nation is *"larger than the scum of its parts"* (p. 496), redemption is possible. With everyone reacting as though he had just come out of a 3-D movie, Julius is brought out. (A straw poll had been taken to determine which spy should be burned first.)

The execution is, unfortunately, like a bad play. Julius appears like a "clown who has stumbled into the wrong room," and the crowd shrieks *"You have no moustache"* (p. 507). Levels of metadrama fold upon one another as most of the vicious and stupid mob screams, and Julius thinks about Ethel's letters, which also seem like distortions of their real life together. A documentary on the Rosenberg boys is on hand to reinforce audience "pity" and to retain the epic scope of the proceedings, now diminished by the ordinary size of the dying Julius.

Ethel, unlike Julius, remains more inscrutable. Her failure to react as the crowd would like is unnerving and infuriating. A martyr and actress to the end, she quotes Saint Joan and the Bible, but then "there is a sudden harsh metallic rattle . . . and Ethel leaps against the straps. . . . There's the odor of burning meat and smoke curling up from her scalp" (p. 515). She will not capitulate; her defiance is so strong, she demands another jolt. At last, her body "is whipped like a sail in a high wind, flapping out at the people like one of those trick images in a 3-D movie . . . sizzling and popping like firecrackers . . . haloed about by all the gleaming great of the nation" (p. 517).

In the epilogue Coover brings back Nixon and Uncle Sam to resolve unfinished matters—to unite his objective and subjective voices and the last scene's antagonist and protagonist. This is the only abrupt time-shift in the novel, noticeable because after his meticulous detailing of the last few days, Coover jumps ahead in time to protray Nixon at home. One is disoriented by the mystery of Nixon's behavior and by what appears to be his capitulation to the status quo—i.e., he is apologizing to Pat. Even more, one is disoriented by Nixon's alternation of verb tenses, as he tries to make sense of the events surrounding the electrocutions, as though he could now create some historical perspective. Ultimately, the reader's final assessment of Nixon is as inconclusive as his judgment about the Rosenbergs, despite the hundreds of pages during which he thought he "understood" the man. Not unlike Camus in *The Stranger*, Coover provokes his reader to judge characters who are ultimately unjudgable.

One may pose questions, nonetheless. When Nixon was on stage, transforming his humiliation into an act of political leadership, did he not perform a creative (existential) act of defiance (not unlike Henry's killing of Casey)? About this, Nixon says: "Christ, I'd leapt completely outside myself! [his Christ referent ambiguous]" (p. 524). Did he subsequently capitulate to a deeper, human fear of isolation, the fear of ultimately being forsaken by his God: "What was awful was the terrible *emptiness*—it had felt like there was nothing holding anything together anymore!" Although Nixon has understood the relativity of "truth" and the arbitrariness of all structures, has all his knowledge ultimately been worthless in the face of his own mortality?—"I'd felt like we were teetering on the brink of infinity. Scared the hell out of me." Did he really have a choice?— "The rest was simple reflex," he states (p. 524).

On the other hand, did he capitulate to "blind ambition"? Did he re-sign his pact with the devil? Or was he overpowered by guilt for his own private burnings recently acted out in his private orgy with Ethel? Did he react against his literal nakedness and punish himself for feeling passion for the first time in his life? (He felt singled out in "grace," he said about his sexuality.) Was this a necessary humiliation preparatory to the act of spiritual regeneration that would follow? Did Uncle Sam plan it all along?

Or did Nixon, like everyone else at the spectacle, project onto the Rosenbergs all his lusts and wanton fantasies? Did he see in them his own hostility to authority? Did they represent for him all those instincts considered anathema in American life? Did he realize the paradox of American political life, that while one is brought up to believe he can conquer the world, and one is raised on an ideology that verifies this as "moral," one's power is limited by larger social forces, and the true spirit of American life is not at all concerned with morality? Was it from this vantage point that he realized the larger paradox of human contingency? Whatever went through Nixon's mind during the darkness, he was, he now says, pushed through the crowd, and he became a part of every "grab-assing obscenity imaginable" in this "frantic all-community grope," which he continues to describe in genre terms: "like something out of *Fantasia* or *The Book of Revelation* (p. 526). It was in this state that he wandered into the Disney whale to become, like Jonah (like the man with 3-D glasses, perhaps not unlike Julius Rosenberg, whose Hebrew name, Coover mentions, is Jonah), the reluctant prophet.

But all of this is speculation. With the epilogue's abrupt time-shift, Nixon is brought out of the flux of events into the orderly present. Uncle Sam, the supreme deus ex machina, has returned to quickly finish the scenario, to win the war, to set Nixon back on the right track, and at least for the next several years, to reassure his kingdom on earth. As in old comedy, after the gods are portrayed in their greatness and meanness, they must be reintegrated into society.

"So jes' drap your drawers and bend over, boy—you been ee-LECK-ted!" (p. 530), Uncle Sam instructs Nixon, emphasizing the union of the political and puritanical ("ee-LECK-ted"). Ethel, he explains to unify plot, is now part of him "just as much as Poco-hontas"—a part of American history and American mythology. He has killed them to keep the family together. "It ain't easy holdin' a community together, order ain't what comes natural . . . and a lotta people gotta get killt tryin' to pretend it is, that's how the game is played" (p. 531).

What follows is, of course, the incarnation ritual Nixon has known about all along. Uncle Sam reminds him that if he really wants to be president, "You gotta love me like I really am: Sam Slick the Yankee Peddler, gun-totin' hustler and tooth-'n'-claw tamer of the heathen wilderness, lusty and in everything a screamin' meddler, novus ball-bustin' ordo seclorum" (p. 531). What he adds, however, licking his finger, is shocking. He confesses that the forces of darkness are his own creation and that the core of his power lies in his rapacious sexuality. He then instructs Nixon to accommodate himself to the Incarnation. The Horatio Alger hero must, after all, travel untrod paths for the extraordinary spoils of victory. The generation of power justifies any means. Coover's bitter humor is relentless: one must read the following in anatomical as well as political terms:

"They's a political axiom that wheresomever a vacuum exists, it will be filled by the nearest or strongest power! Well, you're lookin' at it, mister: an example and fit instrument, big as they come in this world and gittin' bigger by the minute! Towerin' genius disdains a beaten path—it seeks regions hitherto unexplored—so clutch aholt on somethin' and say your prayers, cuz I propose to move immeejitly upon your works!" (p. 532).

Nixon is consumed with paradox until the very end. After his rapid, painful ordination, a rape, he concludes: "Maybe the worst thing that can happen to you in this world is to get what you think you want [the presidency]." Yet, he continues, speaking of Uncle Sam, "Of course, he was an incorrigible huckster . . . [but] he was beautiful. . . . I was ready at last to do what I had never done before. . . . *I* . . . *I love you, Uncle Sam!*" he confesses (p. 534).

Nixon submits to his superior power in the way, in primitive forms of religion, men abase themselves before their gods. In "throbbing pain" and "bawling like a baby," he also speaks in joy, and his final thoughts, which echo Uncle Sam's parting message, reiterate every American cornball philosophy and platitude in the book, especially those of his predecessor, Ike, and the other popular entertainers of the day: "Vaya con Dios, my darklin', and remember: vote early and vote often, don't take any wooden nickels, and . . . always leave 'em laughin' as you say good-bye!" (p. 534). For the elected and the crucified, the saviors and the scapegoats, this is the final pain, elations, and loneliness, Coover's last paradox about the sadomasochism of powerful people.

Coover's manipulation of technique and form throughout is equal to his subject. He utilizes numerous forms of written and spoken language—from formal English to media hyperbole, from folk ballad to street slang. He moves in and out of a vast number of recognizable literary techniques and genres to stylistically portray the variety of published and historical responses to human event. Numerous sequences are self-consciously metafictional or metadramatic—an appropriate reflection of both a society that sees itself as part of a Hollywood scenario and an epistemology that considers the apprehension of reality as fictional. Some sequences portray fantasy against realistic backdrops—or vice versa, perhaps the most acute rendering of the contemporary milieu. And always to relocate the reader to the events of June 17–19, 1953, are the book's patriotic ribbons that decorate major chapter divisions and the highly structured table of contents, appropriate to any historical text.

The Public Burning is also filled with a variety of verbal interpolations of other art forms which also combine the "factual" and "fictional." An opera libretto is composed from the Rosenbergs' final appeal, and it is sung by the Sing Sing personnel. An "Intermezzo" is based on Eisenhower's speeches and set to the melody of "High Noon." News reports from *Time* magazine are restated in free verse.

Coover's brilliant parodies are worthy of special mention. In his Marx Brothers "entertainment," for example, he captures in remarkable fashion the comedians' humor, timing, and cadences in a routine that says more about the American sense of humor than the Marx Brothers. The comics, while playing on the government's "offer to commute" the death sentences "in exchange for information about the spy ring," take advantage of the media's insinuations about Ethel's sexual permissiveness. They play with "bomb," "bum," and "bottom" (so did Nixon in his Sing Sing rendezvous), which they connect to the frequent public statements that the Rosenbergs' crimes are worse than murder:

> CHICO: Oh, a Pinko, eh? We're gettin' to da bottomma dis!
> GROUCHO: You been there, too, hunh?
> CHICO: She'sa da one what's stole-a da bum', eh?
> GROUCHO: She didn't steal it, she was born with it!
> CHICO: And she gave it to da Russians?
> GROUCHO: She gave it to everybody!
> CHICO: Dat'sa terrible! Murder is dwarfed by comparitson!
> GROUCHO: Yeah, she gave it to dwarfs, too!
> CHICO: She's gonna get da hot seat for dis!
> GROUCHO: That's no good.
> CHICO: No good?
> GROUCHO: She's already got it. (P. 455)

Also of special interest because they reflect Coover's larger vision are the novel's endless epic lists, Coover's elaborate precedents for whatever event or response he is describing. He enumerates, for example, various public executions or last-minute acts of clemency; he tries to list all the women who, though incarcerated, avoided the death penalty. It is as though each and every event were archetypal and worthy of apostrophe, as though each were, to say the least, the "rule" in American society, the civil *and* natural law.

To list the last-minute acts of clemency, for example, raises interesting questions about history, law, and morality. Since one might be pardoned at one particular juncture in history and not at another, one is moved to ask: What forces determine the particulars, as well as the sweep of history—men, accident, or process? If history is indeterminate, is the same true of law and morality? One might accept the notion that laws serve changing social and political needs, but was someone like Joseph Conrad correct in maintaining that even morality is relative? Once man is taken out of a structured society, do concepts of "evil" and "benevolence" merge? Do society and its laws exist to protect the individual from his own heart of darkness?

Perhaps, Coover suggests, the only thing we know with certainty is that forces recur through time that are eternal, myriad, infinite, and variable, and the sameness of the world consists of its disorganization. Furthermore, only accident and point of view isolate for any given time this or that vector within these profound and eternal forces. Simply put, had the composition of the Supreme Court been different in 1953, the Rosenbergs might have been spared—and this, regardless of their innocence or guilt.

Interesting epistemological issues are also raised. While one might agree that all recorded determinations of history are arbitrary, these records always seem to fall into definite patterns. Whatever political or moral convictions predominate at a given time, there is always an emergent and opposing view. Historical, legal, and moral events always seem to generate their opposite. Marx and Hegel were thus perhaps wrong about a final resolution to historical process, for process, as they meant it, would seem to be a manmade matter, an interpretation. If anything, history, as the flux of events, like personality and morality, is an endless dialectic that never resolves.

Perhaps the only real patterns that exist are those of the endless tensions between life and death and between victim and victimizer. One can never know how and when he will be victim or victor. Like the Rosenbergs, every man's verdict may hinge on chance, the current interpretation of events, and the time in which he lives.

That perfection is process is, of course, the phenomenologists' posture; that people read process in "either/or" terms is the lesson of the structuralists like Lévi-Strauss. That Coover accepts this difficult paradox, which relates to the complexities of the existential, tragic, and comic visions, accounts for the intricate designs not only of these three novels but also of the shorter works, now to be discussed.

5

Pricksongs and Descants
An Introduction to the Short Fictions

Coover's novels focus on the human need for rituals in a world of time and flux. These "games," as one character calls them—of religion, art, history, and science—appear to organize and give meaning to life's intrinsic disorder. Coover sets up elaborate situations and vast canvasses on which to chart the survival or decline of those who construct and observe these rituals.

The short fictions, perhaps because they are short, differ in several ways. They take for granted the need for sustaining mythologies, but they focus on neither the deepest longings which motivate them nor the grammar of the creative mind that designs them. Most distinctively, they do not spell out the individual's creative/destructive involvement in his imaginative constructs. Instead, most of these short pieces, which include stories, plays, and filmscripts like the *Pricksongs* (1969), *Hair O' The Chine, After Lazarus, Charlie in the House of Rue, A Theological Position, and Spanking the Maid,* are self-reflexive, metafictional exercises. They often concentrate on archetypal roles or situations, or on generally familiar myths or Bible and folktales—those moral lessons generations have accepted as "exemplary." Coover takes the old designs and familiar stories and attenuates the ambiguities or metamorphic nature of their every detail. Whether dealing with a Bible story or Red Riding Hood, or a modern archetype like "the babysitter," he exposes the arbitrariness of every given. Serious, ethical implications that have until now been overlooked are suddenly illuminated, as are unsuspected dimensions of human character. At times, Coover focuses on a legend's "unimportant" characters; sometimes he rewrites a fable entirely; other times, he only partially restructures it. Implied

87

throughout is an indictment of our unthinking embrace of these mythic exampla and the foolish if not self-destructive lives we have modeled after them.

Although there is an enormous variety in the short pieces, Coover's "play" with familiar tales (especially fairy and Bible tale) is particularly interesting. To be sure, the reader's subsequent associations with, say, "Little Red Riding Hood," "Hansel and Gretel," or "The Three Little Pigs"—or even Shakespeare's *Tempest* or the New Testament's Lazarus or Hollywood's Charlie Chaplin—are never the same. Coover rejects Eliot's dictum that we live in the living moment of the past in the present (and vice versa), which suggests an ever-evolving historical/moral continuity. Although like Lévi-Strauss, he would seem to believe in persistent, omnipresent myths (e.g., all men in all societies create legends that define good versus evil), and although he would appear to believe that such structures may be useful at times, he is, in these pieces, artistically most concerned with the distorted representations of human nature in the classic Western myths and the ill effects of holding on to unworkable archetypes.

Closely examined, Coover's tales expose a variety of complex problems regarding so-called human virtue and moral truth. Implied is the notion that, like any other written documents (e.g., the chronicles of history), fairy tales or Bible stories distort the rich and often unfathomable, ambiguous nature of human experience. The Noah story, for example, carefully considered, contains less than salutary truths about human and divine justice—i.e., an inherent selfishness about the Noah who would abandon his brotherhood and a cruelty about the God who could author such a scheme. Coover's "The Brother" tells the story of Noah's gentle, generous, and appropriately nameless brother who, for many months, assists in building the ark. When the floods begin, however, he and his already pregnant wife are left to drown in the rains. The likely abandonment of such a couple compels the reader to question his preconceived mythology of God's so-called bounty and Noah's "elect" status as progenitor of a new race.

This type of realistic scrutiny of such familiar myths runs through Coover's work. In another sort of fable, he transforms the safe materials regarding ritual initiation into more disturbing revelations about human nature. He refurbishes the proverbial gingerbread house and restyles the crossings of any number of bridges; youth becomes involved in the complications of moral uncertainty and the intimate connections between life and death, beauty and the corrupt.

Again exposing the underside, variability, or ambiguity of human behavior implicit in popular myths, Coover focuses on minor characters—or at least those frequently ignored. "J's [Joseph's] Marriage" relegates Jesus to the background and is instead concerned with Mary's immaculate husband and his growing despair over her condition. Coover rearranges details and amplifies what suddenly appear to be crucial personal considerations—e.g., Mary's attitude toward marital sexuality and Joseph's loneliness.

Sometimes he retains only the most general or vaguely recalled details of a familiar story. His brilliant "The Magic Poker," an island tale with Prospero and Caliban figures, concentrates on the richly diverse yet similar textures of imagined and real experience. It also concretizes the existential confrontation with contingency.

Coover merges details from several sources. In "The Gingerbread House" and the later *Hair O' The Chine*, which incorporates much of this, are Jack and the Beanstalk, Little Red Riding Hood, the woodsman, Hansel and Gretel, Beauty and the Beast, Adam and Eve, and Mary and Joseph, among others. Some of the stories ("The Elevator," "The Babysitter," "The Train Station"), while not literary archetypes, reconstruct archetypal situations and portray the variety of fears and fantasies implicit in them.

Finally, among the most interesting works (although most could fit into this category) are the metafictions like "The Magic Poker," "The Elevator," "The Babysitter," "The Hat Act," "Quenby and Ola," *Hair O' The Chine*, *After Lazarus*, and the plays of *A Theological Position*. Many of these are written in a highly structured form, yet while they deny specific plot or characterization, like a cubist painting, film montage, or in many ways like symbolist poetry, they give rise to continuously metamorphic designs that reflect the nonfixed nature of both reality and human possibility. Their subject is process, and in each Coover captures an instant in time, or a specific landscape in space, or a single aspect of human nature. Then he suggests the infinitely rich possibilities that may grow out of, or cancel, one another in that specific time, space, or character. Once again, the transformational quality of the fictions mirrors the existential universe. Events lack final definition, and characters lack fixed motivation; meaning remains unshaped and unspecific. The author-narrator lacks final control over his medium. Coover's subject is process or structure rather than meaning.

These pieces evoke the reader's keen sense of the infinite possibilities of both the word and the world, and like the novels, they have an open-endedness in content, form, and meaning, also akin to much contemporary sculpture and collage. They propel an endless number of shifting surfaces into space—the infinite possibilities between felt, read, and then translated meaning, which the reader experiences. The act of imposing imagination upon the plenitude of experience is shared by Coover's persona and reader; the game of living is again reflected in the game of reading.

In many of these metafictions ("The Magic Poker," "Quenby and Ola," *Love Scene*), the author's voice is announced as subject ("I wander the island, inventing it"), and it expresses all the pleasures and complexities of writing a story. Here is a writer-magician, often pulling words, rabbits, or islands out of hats, self-consciously creating myth, wrestling with words and created landscapes—both God-creator of a verbal universe and victim of its emergent arrangements. Literature, rather than philosophy, religion, or politics, now structures the universe—tentatively.

The short fictions, then, share the vision of the novels regarding the flux of reality and the power and danger of frozen mythologies. Stylistically, their fusion of realism and surrealism within multiple levels of shifting imagery and a variety of prose styles bears the Coover signature. Again, he often utilizes a strong narrative line in order to counterpoint in fragmented juxtapositions of imagery the fluid and unfixed nature of human psychology, morality, and external phenomena. Finally, he creates an open-ended and infinitely evocative, almost metaphysical style in order to accommodate what seems to be his vision of the human striving for physical and spiritual harmony, to illustrate that the violations (or harmony) of the flesh are the violations (or harmony) of the spirit—to tie this world to the next and demonstrate the means by which one may connect his finitude with something more lasting. Once more, imagination is endowed with deity.

The title *Pricksongs and Descants* well expresses Coover's vision, as does the other apparatus appended to the stories—i.e., a prologue and dedication to Cervantes, two epigraphs, and, in the cloth edition, a dedication to the Virgin of the Post and a particularly interesting cover design. The two epigraphs are

> *He thrusts, she heaves.*
>   —JOHN CLELAND, FANNY HILL

> *They therefore set me this problem of the equality of appearance and numbers.*
>   —PAUL VALERY, "VARIATIONS ON THE ECLOGUES"

Cleland's "he" and "she," connected to Válery's "they," suggest the difficult though possible unity ("the problem") that exists between flesh, mind, and spirit. The cloth edition's tribute to the Virgin of the Post (on the dust jacket) similarly unites mystery and sexuality. Since it does not appear in the paper edition, it is quoted here in full:

> *Once, some time ago and in a distant land, I met a young maiden, known to her tribe as the Virgin of the Post, and she gave to me, amid prurient and mysterious ceremonies, a golden ring. Perhaps it was a local custom, a greeting of sorts. Perhaps a message, an invitation, a mission even. Some peculiar Moorish device of transport and return. Wand-scabbord. Open-sesame. Who can say? It bears on one edge an indecipherable legend, a single cleft rune, not unlike the maiden's own vanished birthmark, and I am inclined to believe that portentous inscrutability may in fact be the point of it all. Now, to that Virgin, I offer these apprentice calculations of my own, invented under the influence of her gifts, begging her to remember the Wisdom of the Beast: "If I carry the poison in my head, in my tail which I bite with rage lies the remedy."*

A "golden ring" and "mission," "transport and return," the "prurient and mysterious," distant lands, tribes, and wand-scabbords: "portentous inscrutability" is perhaps the object and lesson, as Coover says, "the point of it all." He has already set up the polarities and materials for descant—the maiden and beast, as well as the dualities of mind and matter. In addition, he announces his method, his use of narrative line from fairy tale or myth in order to explore the counterpointing mystery of experience. The wisdom of the beast would seem to be that there does indeed exist a bond between life and death, pain and recovery, gratitude and humility, mind and body, the organic and inorganic, sexuality and spirit.

The cover design of the cloth edition is interesting too, a detail from a Bosch painting of *The Seven Deadly Sins* united with an image of Christ and love—ironically two traditional and diametrically opposed mythic or moral views of human experience—which Coover perhaps utilizes as emblems of complimentarity. Finally, that he should reach back to older sources (Bosch and Válery) and that Válery should be writing "Variations" on an even older literary comment adds an additional and ironic breadth to his statement.

The sexual meanings and puns in the title are obvious. (In "The Door," Granny actually suggests that the "prick" sings only when the "cunt" dies; the concomitant pun on "dies" then undercuts the

violence and vulgarity otherwise implied.) Coover himself explains
his choice of words in terminology close to the *Oxford English Dictionary*:

> They are musical terms. In a way, the title is redundant
> because a pricksong is a descant. There is a shade of differ-
> ence, however. "Pricksong" derives from the physical man-
> ner in which the song was printed—the notes were literally
> pricked out; "descant" refers to the form of music in which
> there is a *cantus firmus*, a basic line, and variations that the
> older voices play against it. The early descants, being improv-
> isations, were unwritten; when they began writing them, the
> idea of counterpoint, of a full, beautiful harmony emerged.
>   Of course, there is also the obvious sexual suggestion. . . . I
> thought of the descants as feminine decor around the prick-
> ing of the basic line. Thus: the masculine thrust of narrative
> and the lyrical play around it.
>   The terms were useful to me because they were pre-
> Enlightenment, pre-Monteverdian, and so a part of the art
> forms that have been shunted aside by the developments of
> the last three hundred years. The choice of title had to do
> with my decision to focus on Cervantes as a turning point.[1]

Coover's remarks provide an interpretive handle, for one might
well consider his work in terms of melodies and counterpoints,
thrusts and counterthrusts—all the possible thematic textures and
tonal permutations in musical composition (not to mention sexual
dalliance).

That Coover is dealing with traditionally irreconcilable materials
and that he seeks to create new alliances, is clear in his dedication to
Cervantes, apostrophized for his transformation of the exhausted
romance into the novel form. Coover makes clear that, like Cervantes, he too is responding to a new world vision, one in which
mimetic, teleological fiction has become unworkable.

Since this dedicatory material, along with Coover's essay on Beckett, "The Last Quixote," could stand as Coover's *ars poetica*,[2] one
might examine it in some detail and observe even here Coover's wit
and stylistic virtuosity, as he imitates his master's style and diction;
he writes, in part, in Spanish.[3]

Coover's definition of the "exemplary" in Cervantes, in terms of
"game," well applies to his own work. Cervantes's intention, Coover

explains, was to provide a table of tricks, so to speak, so that everyone could entertain himself without pain or damage to soul or body (*"sin daño del alma ni del cuerpo"*). Such honorable and agreeable exercises, he continues, would improve the individual. Obviously speaking of imaginative rather than moral exercises, Coover echoes a variety of moderns from W. B. Yeats to Roland Barthes in identifying the fictional and life processes as creative games, where, as Yeats put it, "the body is not bruised to pleasure soul,/Nor beauty born out of its own despair." Furthermore, he continues, his comments again applicable to his own fictions, "Your stories . . . struggled against the unconscious mythic residue in human life and sought to synthesize the unsynthesizable." They "sallied forth [an appropriate verb for the author of the *Quixote*]" toward "new complexities" synthesizing "poetic analogy and literal history (not to mention reality and illusion, sanity and madness, the erotic and the ludicrous, the visionary and the scatological)." Cervantes (as would Coover) furnished better fictions—better stories, characters, plots, and dramatic situations so the reader could "re-form his notion of things."

Coover would recover the "optimism, the innocence, [and] the aura of possibility," which has today vanished in a universe slowly atrophying; he would reject the "closed" and "pessimistic" literature now popular (perhaps of the nihilistic, existential 1960s). The recovery of "Being," he continues, referring to the need for a positive view of man once again, remains a challenge to "the assumptions of a dying age."

In technique, one must return to "Design, to microcosmic images of the macrocosm, to the creation of Beauty within the confines of cosmic or human necessity, to the use of the fabulous to probe beyond the phenomenological, behind appearance, beyond randomly perceived events, beyond mere history." Coover's use of terms like "design" and "revelation," as discussed in chapter 1, must be qualified. Commenting on his *disbelief* in a transcending order and his ironic use of form he states: "The abstractions are empty. . . . Even so, they are useful." He further clarifies: "The reason is not that I have some notion of an underlying ideal order which fiction imitates," but "it is easier for me to express the ironies of our condition by the manipulation of Platonic forms than by imitation of the Aristotelian."[4] Coover thus dedicates himself to the honorable pursuit of literature with only the worn-out (literary) trappings available to the modern-day "knight": he will pursue his "adven-

tures of the Poetic Imagination" to the "New World" of "Being," and
"never mind," as he puts it, "that the nag's a pile of bones."[5]

The following remarks on each of the twenty-one fictions in
Pricksongs focus on what often appear to be most challenging to
Coover's readers: matters of linearity and point of view.

"The Door: *A Prologue of Sorts*"

"The Door" merges several fairy-tale and archetypal figures. Jack,
of "Beanstalk" fame, is also the vanquished Giant, Little Red Riding
Hood's lumberman-rescuer, her father, and her lover. Jack's
mother, herself once a Little Red Riding Hood now grown into the
grandmother, is both a siren and an innocent, wife of the beast
("Beauty and the Beast") that, in Coover's version, never transformed into a prince. She is a woman who, despite her own youthful
"myths" about love and sex, gave limitless passion and love to her
beast-husband.

Coover omits the evil wolf or any such scurrilous agent from his
storybook tale. Little Red's (or Jack's) initiation into experience is
through the necessary and wonderful knowledge of pain and pleasure experienced phenomenologically, imaginatively, and sexually.
Little Red, like the reader, is led through magical "doors" to shed the
ubiquitous red cloak and to then wander through ever new gardens
and paths toward mystery and wholeness. This is the first of two
prologues that introduces the reader to Coover's poetic landscapes.

Despite its metafictional or linguistic dimensions, this is one of
Coover's most tender pieces. Like the old woodsman and grandmother, Coover is gentle but realistic in his instruction: Come
with me, he says, to both ascend and descend the green stalk into the
world of toads, lizards, black flags, and wild dreams en route to the
knowledge of death and the harmony of "blood" and "essence"—to
the possible unity of sexuality and spirit, the word and the Word.
Come with me and embrace every possible role and experience; we
are all Jack and the Ogre, Little Red, Granny, and the witch (who
materializes in "The Gingerbread House").

What is especially remarkable in this six-page story is Coover's
psychological and sexual characterization of his family, particularly
the old couple. Ambivalent in their present, conservative point of
view (which includes their cynical and painful acknowledgment of

the ravages of age) and in their recollected youthful hunger for life, their separate comments—in distinctly different prose styles—serve as a counterpoint on vigor and death. The old woodsman would willingly die to save his girl, yet he understands her instinct to taste all of life.

He has sheltered her from "terror," pretending "there were no monsters, no wolves, or witches [or "itches"]," yet, he admits, "but yes, goddamn it, there were, there were" (p. 15). It becomes clear that the promises of life—e.g., the golden goose—did not materialize for him. He has had to pursue hard work, and although he has known pleasure from women, he has also shared with them the travails of growing old. Now he knows that once his Little Red takes her first step, he will never again occupy the same place in her life.

Similarly, the grandmother, who grew up when "virtue was its own so-called reward," knows better than to pass on the false old pieties (the "revelations of rebirthers," p. 16). Instead, she would lift the veils of those old fairy tales and admit the realistic nature of adult experience. Despite being "split with the pain and terrible haste of his thick quick cock and then still itchin and bleedin"—and besides enduring the ignominy of his infidelities—she grew to love "the damned Beast after all" (p. 17). Granny recognizes (and recalls) that the beast *in the girl* awaits, "lickin his hairy black chops" (p. 16).

Both Granny and the woodsman know that life consists of the eternal "birthing hopelessly sentient creatures into the inexplicable emptiness . . . [and finally of] then sinking away into addled uselessness" (p. 14). The girl must erase her "dippy smile" and enter the forest's different pathways and "doors." The story concludes with a powerful evocation of Little Red's anxiety, relief, and also exaltation as she enters the pulsating doors. Any encounter with truth, though momentary, is a miracle of birth. As Richard Eberhart puts it: One grows up into the "realm of complexity . . . Where nothing is possible but necessity/And the truth wailing there like a red babe." The girl loses her innocence and a new world of freedom and imagination awakens: "The air . . . full of spiders. . . . The lumberman's steady axe-stroke. The woods. . . . And so: she had known all along. . . . Though this was a comedy from which, once entered, you never returned, it nevertheless possessed its own astonishments and conjurings, its towers and closets . . . more gardens and more doors" (pp. 18–19).

"The Magic Poker"

"I wander the island, inventing it" (p. 20), announces Coover's writer-magician, inviting the reader, whom he also invents, into his island paradise—the blank page upon which his artistic shaping will materialize. This Xanadu of green snakes and dogwood trees and of love and isolation is, however, not only the product of his imagination; it also possesses an autonomy of its own: "I sometimes wonder if it was not . . . [one of my characters] who invented me" (p. 27). The island is also created by the reader.

"But anything can happen" (p. 20), the narrator explains, establishing the mood of his twenty-five-page chronicle. Two sisters, two men, a world of burgeoning and decaying objects, a poker (primarily the magical and generative pen, magic wand, and phallus) populate the island which, even within his fictionalization of it, is both real and fantasized, a fantasy within a fantasy. Everyone's imagined and real actions and thoughts weave in and out of everyone else's. Each is transformed and is the transformer, the artist and his object, both in control and helpless in the continuously generative linguistic universe.

One cannot begin to detail the endless metamorphoses here. It is as though Coover had combined Wallace Stevens's "resemblances" and Baudelaire's "correspondances" into his own open-ended and explosive medium, while redesigning their concomitant structural stays—i.e., their measured stanzas now in paragraph units. Coover fully accomplishes in this story the artistic goals set forth in the Cervantes prologue. He connects the sensual and the abstract, the concrete and the metaphysical—the disparates of experience.

On one of the most basic levels, he brings together details from other stories, which evoke specific associations in the reader, and then he transforms them: bright red doors, green and shiny snakes, black spiders with red hearts, clearings in deep and damp forests, protective and instructive grannies, and stiff black cloths. He establishes touch points in place and history ("My invented island is really taking its place in world geography . . . like the old Dahlberg place on Jackfish Island), and then he immediately explodes these within a timeless background or within the absurd, self-conscious admission of his metafictional role: "Yes, and perhaps tomorrow I will invent Chicago and Jesus Christ and the history of the moon" (p. 40).

Narrative elements from legend, folk and fairy tales, along with a plethora of archetypal characters, appear (e.g., the elegant and paternal lover versus the uncouth, bestial one; the sad, inhibited, and suffering sister and her more competent and extroverted counterpart), but again identity is unfixed. Although he invents as his major figures two sets of apparently contrasting men and women (and, of course, the narrator), all merge at points and then separate. Like words which the artist strives to use in fresh combinations, each character is both totally free from, and yet tied to, specific significances and contexts over which one has no control. The girl with the gold pants is the girl with the yellow dress which then becomes a rusty dress; her function to her surrogate self (sister) is like that of the rusty poker to the narrator-artist.

"Can the end be in the middle?" writes Coover, to which he quickly answers "Yes, yes it always is" (p. 33), an appropriate description of this continually evolving story. Near the conclusion, in fact, the narrator creates a number of statements that sound like introductions to a story we have already experienced, as though to remind us of our inability to finalize anything, even the flux thus far drawn. After a fantasized grandmother tells her children "I'll tell you the story of 'The Magic Poker,' " a series of disconnected historical and even contradictory statements follow—e.g., the island was founded by wealthy Minnesotans, by woodland creatures, and so on. The following typifies virtually any paragraph in that, while it may not move the story causally, it implies the broad panorama of private and public experience that the story treats; meaning goes beyond traditional logic: "Once upon a time, two sisters visited a desolate island. They walked its paths with their proclivities and scruples, dreaming their dreams and sorrowing their sorrows. They scared a snake and probably a bird or two. . . . They wrote their names above the stone fireplace in the hexagonal loggia and shat in the soundbox of an old green piano. One of them did anyway; the other one couldn't get her pants down" (p. 41).

Forms of meaning are here, although logic is askewed: "They walked . . . [the island's] paths with their proclivities and scruples"; they "scared a snake." Signs and words often float in referential ambiguity, sometimes attaching to corresponding lines of meaning or feeling, like tentative musical harmonies. Each character functions similarly and is thus "descanted" with contrasting and counterpointing details. Time sequences of past and present are also descanted. The nameless girl who can't remove her gold pants is a single detail that recaps the entire story, but major motifs repeat in isolated details in any given paragraph. Typically, this gold pants detail suggests male/female complementarity, an emblem of Coover's continual search for or evocation of the mind/body or material/spiritual union, the word in search of union with the Word. This girl becomes all women—the "beautiful young princess" in another tale recalled, the sister Karen, and the grandmother playing the piano to two children (one of whom is she). Similarly, the prince becomes all men, combining the innocent and the vulgar, the sensitive, sensuous, elegant, and paternal qualities that are separately and collectively attributed to the different males in the story—the Prospero and Caliban figures and the narrator himself, who is then ultimately identified with the poker.

The girl's sense of failure and exploitation and her heightened sense of violation and desolation are also repeated throughout—in the descriptions of the house and its furnishings and in the excesses or emptiness of nature. The sometimes erotic wilderness is also a projection of her neediness and wishfulness. The poker is her salvation, although she fears and yet caresses it. Indeed, there are half a dozen explanations in time and fantasy of the girl's activities with the poker—e.g., she kisses it and a suave, elegant man appears; she kisses it and nothing occurs. Everyone's fantasy, legend, reality, fear, and pleasure combine.

Yet the Coover-narrator is always prominent, the magician waving his wand before his audience, reminding it of his powers: "I have brought two sisters to this invented island, and shall, in time, send them home again." As though speaking of the built-in limitations of words—e.g., their dictionary definitions—he adds: "It might even be argued that I have invented their common parents. No, I have not. We have options that may, I admit, seem strangely limited to some" (p. 25).

At times, he clarifies wishful fantasy—e.g., that the girl would succumb to the beast as well as the prince. Or he (or his fictive selves) interrupts the narrative with speculations on meaning: "The tall man . . . has been deeply moved by the desolation of this island. And yet, it is only the desolation of artifact, is it not?" (p. 28). He even comments on the mechanics of fiction writing: "Wait a minute. . . . What happened to that poker? . . . I had something going there, archetypal and even maybe beautiful, a blend of eros and wisdom, sex and sensibility, music and myth" (p. 30).

This is a *tour de force* about the writer writing. One becomes spellbound by Coover's linguistic enchantments and is utterly incapable of touching the story's richness. Coover called this the anchor story of the volume.

"Morris in Chains"

Stylistically ingenious, this is "an epic of its kind" (p. 47) about a harmless and earthy, old shepherd who represents instinct, the Word, and raw experience. Outlawed and persecuted, he is finally captured by the inhibited and frigid urbanologists, the modern scientific and religious community. The story is fascinating, not only in its narrative elements but also in the way Coover's prose styles contrast with and "descant" each other. The shepherd is embodied in a first-person, informal stream of consciousness that incorporates humor, word coinages, and the conditional tense. He admits of himself: "I'm seekin . . . *yes* by damn! *women!* . . . why I've took on everthin short of newborns and old corses" (p. 51). The contrasting urbanologists are portrayed in the familiar polished, cold, and informational language of social science jargon.

Dr. Doris Peloris (Ph.D., M.D., and U.D.) heads Mission "Project Sheep Shape" to capture Morris and kill his sheep. Her ambivalence is apparent. At times she is attracted to the open, sensual, and instinctual life Morris represents and to his "own grit and cunning." At these moments her prose becomes more lyrical: "We might yet be thrilled . . . by the vision of bathing naiads' bared mammaries or of nutbrown torsos with furry thighs, by the one-note calls of hemlock pipes. . . . We are not yet freed from the sin of the simple" (p. 49).

Like the priest in *A Theological Position*, Peloris is dedicated to "an end to idylatry" (p. 48). She must rescue the "unredeemed" from "undeniable disorder" and "patternlessness." Our children, she explains "oblige us to grub up,once and for all, the contaminated seed of our unfortunate origins" (p. 49). A product of the sterile, new world, she is committed to ridding society of its instinctual life, "its old heroes, the old head."

Just as "style" fails to capture the essence of experience, all of Peloris's often very funny plans and rationalizations fail, along with her various acts of defiance. Morris's "excretions, emissions, irr [and] dreams" linger, as do his "loose shreds of shrill fluting [which] . . . reach . . . [her] ears." Morris entices Peloris and her group, like Kubla Khan's audience, to "approach [and] circle." How does one explain, they ask rhetorically, "simple song against our science?" (p. 47).

Near the end, after Morris refuses to take a job in the mutton factory and be domesticated, they put him in chains and examine him closely. They even study his semen. Still following the dictates of their morality machine, they explain: "It was merest Morris versus the infallibility of our computers." Yet at the end, like all raw experience and the instinctual life, Morris survives. Despite their belief that "even nonpattern eventually betrays a secret system," Morris "so far . . . is simply not apparent" (p. 49). His "story" may indeed "not be ended" (p. 59).

"The Gingerbread House": Fern Hill II

In "The Gingerbread House," Little Red Riding Hood transforms into Gretel, Eve, or even Mary, now deep in the dense and mysterious wood; her male counterpart, a Hansel type, is with her. Once again, a father figure leads or instructs his children on this journey into night, although his destination is uncertain. (It is possibly toward existential awareness: "The old man's gaze is straight ahead, but at what? Perhaps at nothing," p. 63.) A pied piper figure, he sings the old fictions, the nursery songs of wish fulfillment. Once more, like his counterpart in "The Door," his first impulse is to isolate youth from the knowledge of pain. Inevitably, however, his tuneful turnings also carry them out of innocence, albeit to the grace of earthy knowledge.

His female counterpart in the story, another instructor, is less the singer/artist than the active participant in experience, a seductress and formidable witch who demonstrates both violence and loveless sexuality. She is the witch of the original fairy tale now transformed into priestess. The children must also bear witness to her experiences.

Their destination, the gingerbread house or the candyland presumably promised all youth, punctuates the story; it is delicious and delectable, a sunny place with "mintdrop trees . . . candy cotton bushes . . . gumdrop pebbles . . . [and] lollypops . . . wild as daffodils" (p. 74). What the children, of course, come to understand is that the house can be entered only after the fall, through a jeweled door more appealing that the mintdrops and candy cotton: "The door is shaped like a heart and is as red as a cherry . . . red as a bloodstone, red as a rose" (p. 72). The door is actually a mirror of the witch's sexual bait—the heart of a dove, which she holds in her hands. She has acquired it by gratuitously assaulting the dove, a crucifixion analogue: "The burnished heart of the dove glistens like a ruby, a polished cherry, a brilliant, heart-shaped bloodstone" (p. 66). Only through youth's acceptance of violence and rapaciousness (as Goodman Brown *should* have acknowledged it)—their barefoot contact with the coiling and twisting shapes on the forest floor—can they finally open the door.

For a time, like the despairing and wan poet, the children maintain the old tunes. Like any conventional father, the old man would leave them in a house where, as Yeats put it, "all's accustomed,/ [and] ceremonious." Yet, despite the boy's efforts to follow the man in dropping crumbs (the conventional Hansel role), the crumbs are consumed by the dove. The old man's droppings, like his traditional songs, challenge the new world: Where "have all the good fairies gone?" (p. 70).

His children, like the girl in "The Door," intuitively know that reality consists of both good fairies and the witch's flapping black rags. What lies ahead, they already sense, is a house "where children come" but none may "leave" (p. 65). Their journey thus wavers between joy and fear as they eventually participate in the witch's gratuitous assault upon the dove. "She struggles with the boy for the bird. . . . Their legs entangle, their fists beat at each other" (pp. 66–67). As the witch maternally embraces her prey at her breast, the girl subsequently nestles it sexually between her legs. As Granny says in "The Door" (with shades of Baudelaire), human experience consists of the interpenetration of beauty and terror.

Then, as though witnessing a primal scene, the children, aging as the story develops, watch the witch couple with the old man (and there are corresponding role reversals and identifications with innocence and evil). The children embrace human time, passion, and human frailty; they also accept all moral possibilities.

As the door appears, they approach with arms entwined. Their eyes are wide open, and they stare ahead into the forest. The toads are forever akin to the dove; the old man's speech is the hooting of owls; strange shapes writhe.

This is a magical story filled with conditional words ("perhaps," "seems"), speckled colors, sweets and bitters, a rich and evocative prose poem. Typographically arranged in a series of numbered paragraphs, it evokes the merging of disharmonies, the physical and imaginative on vertical and horizontal planes. At the end, screeching bats and nonsense tunes sing of dappled horses and the slaying of dragons; lovers lie abed with the griefs of the ages in their arms. In Coover's universe, life's experiences *do* consist of beasts, doves, fairies, and witches: "Oh, what a thing is that door! Shining like a ruby, like hard cherry candy, and pulsing softly, radiantly. Yes, marvelous! delicious! insuperable! but beyond: what is that sound of black rags flapping?" (p. 75).

"Panel Game"

An unwilling spectator is called upon to sit on a television game show. The challenge is simple: the panel must locate the "meaning" of the game, analogous to the game of life: *"Why are you here . . .* if not to endeavor to disentangle this entanglement?" (p. 85). The answer, so everyone but the "Bad Sport" appears to know, is "Detail! Detail! [The] game's built on it" (p. 80). Answers, modulations of sound in the form of meaningful statement, are as follows: "So think. Stickleback. Freshwater fish. Freshwater fish: green seaman. Seaman: semen. Yes, but green: raw? spoiled? vigorous? Stickle: stubble. Or maybe scruple. Back: Bach: Bacchus: baccate: berry. Raw berry? Strawberry? Maybe. Sticky berry in the raw? In the raw: bare. Bare berry: beriberi. Also bearberry, the dog rose, dogberry. Dogberry: the constable, yes, right, the constable in . . . what? *Comedy of Errors!* Yes! No" (p. 80).

Juxtaposed to this brilliant wordplay, appealing in both sound and paralogical and associational meanings, are the panelists' physical responses, from casual grimacing to belly dancing. Although the contestant is tormented by the question "What does it mean?" and the moderator indicts him—"Muteness is mutinous and the mutable inscrutable!" (p. 84)—his silence communicates, at least to the reader (whom Coover identifies with the contestant early in the story), the inscrutability of the universe and the concomitant inability of language to reflect meaning.

The only comprehensible experience in life is that which may be approximated in the equally disparate and concrete elements of language. As Donald Barthelme illustrates in a somewhat similar story "Shower of Gold," one concretely experiences the absurd; one cannot explain in in language.

This is one of Coover's earliest stories, and everything is turned topsy-turvy to illustrate the concrete absurdity of ordinary experience. Stagelights and camera are "insecting" about; one of the panelists, Mr. America, is described as "fat as the continent and bald as an eagle" (p. 79). At the same time, the story functions like a series of chinese boxes, with each one set against a countepointing, controlling irony. The willing spectator never does get the moderator's point that life, in the most philosophical and existential terms, is "much ado about nothing" (p. 87) and is, in fact, the "Details!" Yet, in the process of losing the game, he is continuously, although unawaredly, participating in the fictionalized nature of his own experience. To both the contestant and reader Coover writes: "You squirm, viced by Lady . . . but your squirms are misread: . . . Audience howls happily" (p. 80). In a final irony, it is the television program, the contemporary transmitter of moral values, that becomes the mirror to the reader (if not to the Bad Sport) of life's absurdity.

"The Marker": La Belle Dame sans Merci

Although this could be read as an allegory of the deadening effects of (1) the traditional reading and writing of literature and (2) rigidly routinized life-styles—both with all their familiar "markers" —the breadth of Coover's detail and the variety of the story's moods and styles suggest even more.[6] The story treats, on the one hand, the realistic need for role play (markers) and yet the profound losses that occur when one pursues them too far. It dramatizes the horror of experiencing the dissociated sensibility—the rift between body and spirit, the self and the world, lover and beloved, the word/creation and referent, sign and signified—the loss of orgasmic fulfillment—when one takes advantage of "the givens" of human experience and fails to appreciate the uniqueness of every act. This is a comic, grotesque, and surreal tale about a man "deeply in love with his wife" who suddenly faces her rotting corpse and experiences the death of his pathway to ecstasy. He had marked her for pleasure perhaps once too often.

Coover literalizes this, as his Jason (mesmerized by his wife's golden fleece?) discovers that the body he has just made love to has become a stinking cadaver to which he is now genitally "hinged." Coover's treatment of what follows is as bizarre and grotesque in mood as his introductory material was traditional and banal. In mood, style, and event, the story touches upon both traditional and "kinky" extremes.

Until this evening, Jason and his wife would seem to have experienced each other both concretely and abstractly—both in motion and motionless, as Coover describes the harmony of language, art, and human experience in "The Elevator." On this last evening, she busies herself with concrete, ritualistic acts in motion—folding clothes and picking up objects. While illustrating the function of motion, however, Jason explains that "whatever meaning there might be in her motion exists within the motion itself" (p. 88). Like the woman playing to Wallace Stevens's Peter Quince, her motions strike a deep and passionate cord in him.

She views him similarly "with the same apparent delight in least motions." As they finish their separate evening preparations, he places a marker in his book, for tomorrow he shall return to his "place," hooks his pants on the armchair, turns out the lights, and then anticipates their sex: they shall now "swallow, for a moment, reason and its inadequacies, and . . . let passion . . . have its . . . way." Her "image [and his, presumably] fades," transformed "without definition," with "abstract Beauty" (pp. 89–90). Here may be the conquest of time, that union of the concrete in spirit that Keats captured on his urn, the transcendence of time and body through imagination.

Suddenly, the man is literally lost in the night. He cannot find the bed, and he fumbles toward her. Her laugh reassures him: she must be playing a game, but the furniture seems misplaced; perhaps the light is broken. Their sex, finally, is merely adequate; the room is still dark. Has she "pulled the plug?" he wonders (Coover not above punning: she is dead). As he tries to withdraw from her, he notices "a strange and disagreeable odor."

The police and four assistants enter, and the tone of the story, like Jason's reality, dramatically alters. This is concrete reality with talk of behavior, law, and even Jason's punishment. It reads like a Grade B movie about the setup for an exposure of infidelity. (Does Jason feel guilty for "marking" the evening's procedings? Is he reading his experience with her like an old story?) What follows takes on an even more surreal quality, again underscoring the terrible disjuncture between mind or spirit and body.

As the body is discovered ("without meaning") and the woman's hair, face, and breasts are described in their repulsive details, Jason struggles to extricate himself; he is glued to her. Finally wrenched free, the intruders pound his genitals to a pulp. (Only the punishment of hell is appropriate.)

Coover brings together, in this Kafkaesque room, archetypal and unconscious fears—misplaced objects, the dead wife, inextrication, castration—and conventional explanations (from the "lawmen"). When the connecting link in one's communion with the world, word, or woman dies—for whatever reason—the resulting pain, terror, and repulsion cannot be overstated. The love act is once again Coover's emblem of the means toward the harmony of disparates.

"The Brother"

The nameless farmer-narrator explains, in a sort of western lingo stream of consciousness, how he has always helped and even rescued his "buggy" brother, Noah, twenty years his senior. Now, for six months, he has ignored his farm and pregnant wife to help cut the pine trees for the odd boat that Noah, for some weird and probably crazy reason, is building. Like Noah's neighbors, the narrator cannot resist Noah's "weaseling" for help.

After completing the boat, the brother returns to Noah's house for a bit of wood to build a cradle for his expected child (note the ironic parallels), little Anna or Nathaniel. There, he discovers an ark already housing animal couples and a cold and uncommunicative Noah. Noah's wife, less a shrew than a victim of his cruelty, will presumably board later.

As the rains begin, the brother, now back home, and his wife celebrate: their crops will flourish, and they may finally spend some time indoors. As the rains continue, however, it becomes clear that the crops, the livestock, and they may drown. The brother runs to Noah to ask for temporary rescue in the ark. When the story ends, he is left out in the rains, weeping and begging for aid from the selfish and crazed (or is he divinely inspired?) Noah, who sails off, totally indifferent to the tragedy behind. Having observed his wife dead, the brother goes off to the top of a hill (a sardonic reference to Moses) to await his similar fate.

Coover bitterly challenges the selfishness and cruelty inherent in the original Bible story—the nature of a God who would design such a scheme and the "elect" (or mad?) Noah who works God's love (or is it wrath?). An additional and bitter irony operates through the story, as the brothers allude to God colloquially. Noah asks his brother-victim, for instance, if he will help him "for God's sake" (p. 92), and later the brother says: "by God the next day the rains" still come. In a final irony, Coover suggests that the only "divinity" one should revere (though Noah gains only reproach) is his brother: "GOD*damn* you" (p. 97), Noah is told, about to face his own death.

"In a Train Station"

As Alfred again awaits the 10:18 Express, which will never arrive, he spends his time with the stationmaster, a satanic instructor (master of Alfred's station in life?) performing a series of ritualized activities. These range from the most banal conversations on the "good" life, "good" wife, "good" weather, and "good" food to the murder of a drunk stranger. Afterward, the stationmaster resets the clock to 9:27, which is when the story began. Obviously, the events will be replayed.

One is tempted to discuss this as a surreal elaboration of the restrained though palpable violence and madness of Beckett's primary couple in *Waiting for Godot*. Alfred must also survive time, although as Beckett puts it elsewhere, "Waiting is to experience the action of ["accursed"] time," where "nothing real ever happens." But Coover interrupts the story early with: "Now, assuming both Alfred and the Express Train to be real" (p. 99), which introduces a metafictional dimension. Perhaps Coover wishes to underscore the artifice of fictional conventions within which grotesque and unnatural events are repeatedly drawn. Perhaps the story exemplifies the banal and horrific extremes of perception reflected through both the distorting lens of language and mood, as well as through the diachronic and synchronic functions of language. The victimized drunk man with eyes that focus on "no fixed thing" (p. 101) reminds one of Coover's sacrificial cat in *A Political Fable*, the personification of process and "perfection," also threatening to the lawmakers or (station) "masters." Here is pure experience and all the structures of language, each of which must be violated in the distorting translation of experience into communication. This is one of Coover's most enigmatic pieces, and as one struggles to discuss it, he is reminded of Donald Barthelme's story, "The Dolt"; also about writing, his story concludes: "Endings are elusive, middles are nowhere to be found, but worst of all is to begin, to begin, to begin."

"Klee Dead"

This story deals with the writer's (and world's) fascination, indifference, morbid curiosity, and fear toward the final mystery of death in what only *appears* to be a self-consciously well structured narrative. Like the experience of life or death, storytelling defies causal bonds. Just as someone's self-inflicted death shoud be (but is not) explainable, so too fiction, like life, lacks a structured beginning, middle, and end. Thus, the speaker's "assessment": his story about Wilbur Klee's death can only contain his own tangential and personal responses, as well as the ironic apology: "What is life, after all, but a caravan of lifelike forgeries?" (p. 111).

Once again in this metafiction, the writer is subject, although he tells us he is going to write about the unfortunate suicide of Klee, whom he neither knows nor, so he tells us, is interested in. What is fascinating is the pace of his report, with all its funny and odd digressions and with its alternating self-mocking and serious comments. The story reflects the speaker's response to death, and its inner structure of climax and denouement is the result of his emotional seesaw. All of this is set against Coover's evocation of the flux of everyday, experiential reality, which inevitably propels the narrator's several digressions. Everything is finally juxtaposed to the single, final denominator motivating the entire story—the present reality of death.

First, the speaker is angry as he observes that office bureaucrats coldly record Klee's suicide and that bystanders are actually titillated by it. But as he focuses on single responses, he free associates to the constancy of human needs. People may adapt to death and to time and loneliness, but they share a profound yearning for love, work, and family. The recluse Millicent Gee, for example, lives with an old ram, a stagnant aquarium of dead fish, and "interfiliated" cats. She has a boy, but he comes around only for "seasonal devotions." The narrator sounds like Miller in *Origin*, as he speculates on Millicent's life "impulsively driven to load up empty spaces, to plump some goddamn thing, any object, real, imagined, or otherwise, where now there might happily be nothing" (p. 105).

This is exactly what Coover is doing in the story, filling his spaces, as people do their houses or lives, with rituals or explanations to deal with the inexplicable. The note that may (or may not) have been found by Klee's side could never be adequate to explain his act, nor could a pregnant woman's unnecessarily feared venereal disease be just "reason" for her guilt-ridden husband's suicide. Yet the man, like Klee, killed himself. The only truth—about any of them—is "he . . . is . . . dead. . . . The proof . . . here in the pudding" (p. 106). Your "questions," he continues to the reader, "friend," are "foolish," a disease of the Western mind. On the other hand, "if you wish to assume a cause-and-effect relationship," then he is dead *"because* he jumped from a high place" (p. 106). What remains at the end for both the dead and those surviving, is the rubbish of metaphor, a few of Klee's personal effects, as well as "the farts" of the detached people who cleaned up after his mess. Finally, given this form of story and its low "entertainment" level, an apology seems appropriate: "I'm sorry," remarks the narrator. "What can I say? . . . Here, take these [circus] tickets" (p. 111).

The story is impressive in its range of tones. The first two paragraphs, for example, reveal not only the narrator's need for connection but also his essential and inevitable cosmic isolation. He would place himself and language between experience and the fact of death; he would attempt the impossible. "Klee, Wilbur Klee, dies. Is dead, rather. I know I know. . . . In some languages, it is possible to say: *to die oneself* . . . cunningly planting the idea that one's own hand was perhaps involved. . . . But unluckily I don't know any of these other languages. . . . And even if I did . . . it would be inconceivable I should know them well" (p. 104). Language reflects the limits of human comprehension, as it also reveals the human frustration in touching meaning.

"J's Marriage"

This is one of Coover's most remarkable stories for its wit, anger, and poignance. Coover takes the Virgin Mary story and elaborates its human dimensions, which are exactly what Christianity mythologizes. He concentrates on poor J. (Joseph), the forgotten man, who must have endured a variety of virtually unthinkable emotions, given his ill-matched marriage with the (presumably) eternal virgin, Mary.

The story begins with Mary (although she is never so named) before the marriage. Far from saintly, she is not unlike the young girl in "The Door" or even "The Gingerbread House"—fearful of sex and more taken with romance than flesh: Mary is wooed by J's words. Coover speculates on her inhibitedness: "What was it? a lifetime of misguided dehortations from ancient deformed grannies . . . [or] perhaps a dominant father?" (p. 113). Mary is, to be sure, no china doll. (She "spat" at J. "hatefully" and then "sought him out.") She knew she would always have the upper hand sexually with this adoring and patient husband-to-be, an older, well-educated, complex, cynical, yet patient, philosopher of the absurd. As it turned out, J. was unfortunately correct in his youthful belief that life would end in misery. He was also *incorrect* in his subsequent idealism that if Mary gave herself sexually to him, that final misery would be mitigated.

With great tenderness and psychological astuteness, Coover focuses upon J's changing responses to his inhibited wife, still virgin though not yet divinely impregnated—from his initial calm and delight in her "inexpressible beauty" (and his corresponding vitality in the natural world) to his frustrating progress in gaining a *sense* of intimacy with her. After his spells of weeping and loneliness, Mary finally appeared naked and announced: "I am expecting a baby." What follows, Coover writes, is "of course, a common kind of story" (p. 116). J. took ill and suffered a sort of breakdown, questioning God's "vulgarity in such an act," and although he survived the· experience, he reached that point of understated acceptance not uncommon among the terminally ill: "It was simply unimaginable . . . that any God would so involve himself in the tedious personal affairs of this or any other human animal" (p. 117).

Exploding the New Testament myth even further, Coover continues: "the boy [Jesus] played but a small part" (p. 118) in the rest of the story. (By comparison, Stoppard elevates Rosencrantz and Guildenstern to archetypal, heroic roles.) Then, he adds—although this is "perhaps too trivial"—it would appear that the couple did finally consummate their marriage. Indeed, the reader is so taken with J's human dimension, that he does find it trivial—whether the Virgin Mary was virgin.

At the end, in a remarkable last paragraph that reveals a warmth, irony, and yet distanced bitterness, Coover describes how J's life ended—without any comfort whatsoever in a child of his own or in any belief system. He even died in a "not especially appropriate" way (as though one could), just as everything else in this story has not been "especially appropriate." (What, in fact, *did* happen to Joseph, in the Bible?) More like Ivan Ilyich than Christ's titular father—and with a touch of senility and other normal problems, e.g., prostate—J. dies, mystified about life's absurdities and utter ordinariness. Once again, as in "The Brother," Coover asks the reader to reconsider the nature of a divinity who would ordain such a situation and the humanity of those who would happily comply.

"The Wayfarer"

Reminiscent of Morris and the man in "The Door" and "The Gingerbread House," this old man is drawn with numerous archetypal details: he is sitting on an "old milestone" and wearing coats that are "thick and many"; he is silent, unmoving, approving, and reproving. The "wayfarer" evokes any number of formidable figures—from the medieval wanderer and Chaucer's death figure in "The Pardoner's Tale" to the biblical patriarchs and prophets and Coover's own "Cat in the Hat" figure. A tabula rasa for both the reader and speaker (a law officer, a man of rules looking for meanings), he refuses the speaker's many proddings for verbal or physical response. In utter frustration, the speaker shoots him.

Raw experience—compelling, formidable, and irreducible to words—is violated by the speaker trying to fill his blank memo book. Close to death after his coats are stripped (all the structures imposed on him), he utters a random assemblage of fragmented speech "with neither [traditional] punctuation nor sentence structure": "Just a ceaseless eruption of obtuse language," (p. 123). With blood dripping from him (In "The Door" the lumberjack calls blood "essence"), he speaks "of constellations, bone structures, mythologies, and love . . . of belief and lymph nodes, of excavations, categories, and prophecies . . . Harmonics! Foliations! Etymology! Impulses! Suffering! . . . Immateriality patricide ideations heatstroke virtue predication" (p. 124).

Having assaulted the world of possibility, the speaker can now rejoin the death flow of ordinary society, like a linguistic part of speech that has performed its function. The story is about the inadequacy of capturing the richness of experience with language or any other structures.

"The Elevator"

Coover takes a number of fantasies that might be associated with riding an elevator and plays theme and variations on them in this oddly funny and frightening story. A generative story in the volume, it reminds one of "The Magic Poker," where Coover manipulates a number of literary forms to reflect the endless ways of describing reality, perhaps in itself fictional. More concretely, in the motifs that repeat in several variations, one is reminded of Picasso's *Girl in the*

Mirror in her multidimensional womb/tomb-sun/moon-drenched universe.

In each of fifteen sequences, appropriate for the fourteen floors and basement in the story's office building, Martin rides the elevator presumably to work. He experiences everything from boredom to wild sex, humiliation, and physical abuse, as well as deification for his "doodang [his "batterin ram"] . . . five feet long," (p. 135). He becomes a fertility figure and is even transformed into the Christian God pronouncing judgment upon all the fallen. An ordinary guy at the same time, he descends on this modern-day Charon to the silence and meaninglessness of hell.

In all of his various roles within and sometimes outside the elevator, Martin feels a variety of moods—passion, guilt, melancholy, fear, boredom, humiliation, impatience, and arrogance. "The Elevator" becomes any number of archetypal experiences relating to the sex act (with the opening and closing doors of its "tight cell" and the countless possibilities of each "ride" with the "shaft" and the "cavity") and to the artist and his encounter with the word. It represents the word in its fixed and moving possibilities and the individual in the universe. The elevator is emblematic of the universe. Finally, since each of the numbered paragraphs suggests a different genre from horror story to soap opera, Coover dramatizes the variety of fictional forms an individual's life may take. Life is, in a sense, a multiplicity of fictional possibilities and roles.

It is all here, as Martin himself comments, "space, time, cause, motion, magnitude, class," the individual "tyrannized" by the "arbitrary regimentation of time." Words, like life itself, remain "apparently motionless, yet moving," a wonderful condensation of the existential tension between personal belief and cosmic incoherence. Life is "Motion: perhaps that's all there is to it after all. Motion and the medium. Energy and weighted particles. Force and matter" (p. 129).

At the end, as Martin walks up the stairs (the work of art has taken on an autonomy of its own), he hears the crash below. He is both of and yet separate from his fictional creation. ("Inscrutable is the word he finally settles upon," p. 137.) Once again, the shape of this story, like "The Magic Poker" and "Quenby," is fascinating, for like a symbolist poem, the subject is infinitely suggestive within a very tight form. Yet, despite the story's specifics (the crash), Coover's endlessly mobile, fluid form stands firm against the specifics of violence, death, and joy, which are always his concrete subjects. Once again, the existential paradox of commitment and optimism in a world of contingency and inevitable demise is fictionally realized.

"Romance of the Thin Man and the Fat Lady"

Coover obviously enjoys the image of human society as a carnival or circus (*Origin*, *Political Fable*, *Public Burning*), where the bulk of humanity can gasp at, spit upon, or taunt the ludicrous or the unfortunate. The circus is the contemporary church of the unchurched, the place for ritual exorcism of one's deepest and ugliest drives. In this story, Coover focuses closely upon two of the more popular circus inmates. He discards any conventional or mythic rendering of the "comic . . . coupling" of the fat lady and thin man to instead tell a bitter tale of their romantic and literal coupling. His change in focus toward these normally acceptable, "beautiful" freaks and his intentional inability to smoothly resolve his story are a reflection of their unconventional and unsuccessful revolt against their ordinary and grotesque "functions." As he portrays them, the fat lady diets for love or fashion (it is unclear) and the thin man muscle builds for the same reason(s). Clearly, they defy their ordinary roles. Speaking of the couple, and writer as well, Coover asks: "Who can blame them if they see outside themselves symbols of their own?" (p. 140).

As one would expect, despite the sympathy they gain from the other circus anomalies, they are incapable of entertaining the ordinary public, which can only read them in conventional terms, and of earning adequate revenue for their godlike ringmaster, a wonderful label for the man who panders to the status quo. Each then tries to recover his original shape (function) but in so doing becomes the other's antagonist. After a great deal of turmoil, during which the fat lady is even sold to a rival circus and the ringmaster is disposed of, the narrator, reminding us that we are in the world of metafiction, admits that his metaphor "has become unhinged" (like Jason in "The Marker"). He then tries an absolutely ridiculous solution to glue the story together: the two suddenly and gratuitously return to their original forms, and when this fails to move the audience (or the reader), he makes them ride on a rocket. Even this fails. The "beautiful" has obviously transformed into the "ludicrous." At the end, the narrator might even make the rocket crash and thus destroy his fiction.

Once again, Coover's focus is less upon the specifics of his tale than its teller. Early, a narrator informs us that this circus legend has a broad significance and is "the ultimate image of all our common romances [a pun on love and traditional fiction]. . . . We are all Thin Men. You are all Fat Ladies" (p. 138). Possibly the man is the artist or the word and the Fat Lady is the world or the Word, a second metafiction within the larger one. Indeed, at the point the couple would seem to have their problems resolved (albeit through the narrator-author's absurd, well-made plot machinery), the story as story is *not* over. As the narrator puts it: "No easy label can be affixed." Speaking later as the ringmaster, he says: "Our precious metaphor . . . has lost some of its old charm." He would, if he could, work out a denouement, but as he admits: No, these two "are not the whole circus"; they can't be forced into an easy explanation. Nor "is life one [simple category, a one-ring circus]. There are three rings. . . . And then there are more. Who can grasp it all? And who, grasping, can hold it! . . . We can hang on to nothing [the loaded word again]. Least of all the simple. . . . *Look out!*" Coover's characters/plot/single words—his fictions—do indeed defy the "lawza gravity." All dance on a tentative tightrope and then actually take off into space.

"Quenby and Ola, Swede and Carl"

Here, in one of the most remarkable stories in the volume, Coover creates an impressionistic word-painting where, through a variety of conditional phrases and verb tenses and through his characters' continuously evolving fantasies, he captures both the existential and fictional qualities of life. Dreams, speculations, and imagery assume momentary reality, against the backdrop of a vast, indifferent, and infinitely mysterious universe.

Although the story deals, in large part, with a man's (Carl's) fantasied or recalled sexual passion with the young Ola (and possibly her mother, Quenby), it is the tentativeness of his fantasy or recollection that is the heart of the story. This is suggested in the open-ended or transformational quality of every detail, including Carl's relationship with Ola's parents, Quenby and Swede, and their relationship to each other and the girl, and so on.

That one's comprehension of an externally transforming reality is fictional is beautifully captured at the beginning where Coover evokes the mystery of the phenomenal world in its clear self-declaration in daytime and its magical disappearance at night. This Berkeleyan paradox of subjective versus objective reality unifies each seemingly disparate element of the story and each character and his or her fantasy, at once in its own light and dark. Through extraordinary word-painting and the use of subjunctive tenses, Coover evokes the precariousness of one's existential condition. The human comedy is implied in shimmering and fading textures, lights, and natural phenomena: "Night on the lake. A low cloud cover. The boat bobs silently . . . obscure humps of islands [with] . . . uncertain contours . . . more felt than seen. . . . The opposite end [of the boat] seems to melt into the blackness of the lake" (p. 150).

Coover invites the reader to join in the task of creating reality: "Imagine Quenby and Ola," he begins and then demurs, establishing and withdrawing his assertions of reality: "Their faces pale in the gathering dusk. . . . Can she even see either?" To Carl, who "wasn't sure" why he was here, or even of the islands in the background, Coover says "You know [them] . . . because you've seen them in the daylight." Yet despite his knowledge of birds (the "spruce grouse and whiskey jack"), he cannot fathom the moment: "You don't even know what makes that strange whistle that pierces the stillness now" (pp. 150, 151, 152). Perhaps tongue in cheek, Coover concretizes the famous Berkeleyan paradigm of subjective reality: "Forests have collapsed upon forests on these islands."

By the time one gets to Carl's sexual thoughts ("She is hot, wet, rich, softly spread"), fact and fantasy are inseparable. Indeed, the communication of experience, as Coover says at the end, consists of "telling stories" (p. 167). Each person's identity is then projected through his particular story, as Coover underscores the fictional quality of experience. As Carl sits in the boat, for example, he may or may not be speaking to Swede, who may also be a projected or remembered presence. Ola's story about her father's shooting her cat may or may not be true. *You*, the reader, is also Carl, who may only be projecting on to Swede's daughter his own taboo impulses toward his child. ("I have a daughter just your age," p. 164.) Ola's mother, Quenby, or even Swede, may have been part of his sexual fantasy. ("One or more may soon be dead . . . in revenge or lust or self-defense.") Carl may really be sitting in the boat with Swede, fearful that he is going to harm him; or he may be at the cabin enjoying an after-dinner drink with the others; he may even *be* Swede. (Both have bristly new beards which their wives dislike.)

As the shift from daytime to night is emblematic of the flux of

natural and human experience, Coover's highly structured paragraphs release counterpointing and infinitely expanding motifs that
touch on life/death; fear/passion; identity/anonymity. The writer-
narrator finally draws attention to his metafiction (though to a lesser
degree than in "The Magic Poker") and once again implores the
reader to undertake his role in the partnership of creating meaning.
By the end, the reader, like the fictional characters, is also involved
in the task of comprehension and articulation in a world of shadows
and continuously shifting surfaces.

"THE SENTIENT LENS"
"Scene for Winter," "The Milkmaid of Samaniego," and "The Leper's Helix"

Like "The Magic Poker," these three stories exemplify the transformational process of perceiving and then translating experience,
the relationship between the world, sense perception, thought, and
verbalization—the infinitely fertile nature of external and internal
"process." One is again reminded of Wallace Stevens's definition of
poetry in *The Necessary Angel* as "the creation of resemblances" which
bind together any combination of elements from reality and imagination. Poetry creates resemblances that do not claim to be experience; it is a magical tool that brings experience into the realm of
understanding.

Among Coover's most impressive metafictions, these stories are
lyrical and exquisite word-paintings. "Scene for Winter" is lovely in
its portrayal of the delicate yet self-sufficient birth of winter, its
falling snow a wonderful evocation of the lush, phenomenological
world unfolding in its silent innocence, fragility, uniqueness, and
sensuousness. The scene metamorphoses from silence and snow to
the appearance of a rabbit, a dog, and a man. It then moves back into
silence.

Coover also evokes the richness of anticipation and perception,
the world of the seer, as well as the seen. It begins: "No sound, it gets
going with utter silence, no sound except perhaps an inappreciable
crackle now and then, not unlike static, but our ear readily compen-
sates for it, hears not that sound but the absence of sound, stretches
itself, reaches out past any staticky imperfections there might be and
finds: only the silence." The moment's silence capitulates to perception and the pointillism of subjectivity. The fallen snow is at once
powdery, like infinitesimal flecks of light, and it is also a "mantel" for

mass, perhaps "ribbed beneath." But "we cannot know," writes Coover; "we can be sure only of the surface we see now, a gently bending surface that warps and cracks the black shadows . . . of complex patterns . . . yet tranquil" (pp. 168–69).

Perspectives are always structural pauses, arbitrary and precarious. Like camera shots, they are the records of attention paid to a sense or perception or perhaps the wide-angled view of a single, attenuated event in time: "A road passes . . . barely visible in the untrammeled snow" (p. 170). Coover writes, and suddenly we are transplanted onto that road which, given its own autonomy, makes everything else barely visible. The absolute silence becomes similarly charged with beautifully detailed sound effects.

Narrowing his focus (as one might interrupt a mobile's multiple definitions of space), Coover turns to a man (*perhaps* familiar) who is looking at an object that is "shrinking noiselessly into the horizon behind us." With the man looking behind our ken, Coover's camera angle can only capture his face, clothing, eyelashes ("strangely prominent"), and cigarette smoking (p. 172). The camera eye, while selective in its focus, remains limited by the givens and changes in the external landscape.

The scene contains, nevertheless, like the colors of the spectrum, the parameters of human response—humor, fear, beauty, decay, and of course, the ultimate mystery of response and causality. The man smiles, frowns, stands, or lies down; he urinates, and he plays. He is isolated, and then involved in his world, he is cheered and fearful. Like the other metafictions in the volume, this story once again conveys Coover's vision of the mystery and disorder that "descant" the structuring mind or ordering eye, the fluid counterpoint behind any narrative line. Despite Coover's several pauses throughout and the arbitrariness of each, reality continues in its disorganized, uninterrupted, unique, indefinable, and indefatigable way. The signs by which one pauses, and the particular paintings that evolve, remain entirely random.

"The Milkmaid of Samaniego"

This magical tale of metamorphosis recalls Coover's earlier trio of characters (the innocent girl, lad, and old man) now set in a pastoral world. It also looks forward to *Hair O' The Chine* in many of its details. Challenging traditional myth and symbolism, Coover reminds the reader, as he introduces the girl: "Its almost as though there has been some . . . precise structure of predetermined images . . . before our senses have located her in the present combination of shapes and colors," (p. 175). As he presents his now grotesque old man, he also spells out the traditional reader's expectations of him. Suddenly everything changes, and we have before us a lusty, self-sufficient girl, an aggressively sexual, male youth, and a rescuing and poetic, dirty old man.

As the girl walks alone toward the arched bridge, past "oaks and cypresses," her breasts appear fuller and "her hips broaden perceptibly"; her movements are gliding and assured. Indeed, "as she walks her skirt flutters and twists as though caught by some breeze, though there is none." Immediately after this, she encounters the old man. "No, no! the maid, *the maid!*" writes Coover whimsically (p. 176), as though one expected the man to harm her. Of course, nothing happens. The maid exposes a bemused smile, her vessel for carrying the milk, a pitcher on her head, undisturbed. Suddenly, it transforms into what it (or she) really is, a carrier of fertile eggs: "a kind of internal energy seems to take possession of the eggs" (and the girl). Chickens materialize, which become hens, which then become sows and all the animals of the traditional barnyard. Finally, a "tall lad, dark and fine-boned with flashing-brown eyes" appears and "gazes" at the girl "in wonderment" (p. 177). Yet, as Coover's reader might expect, he too breaks out of his mythic role, as he virtually accosts the girl. He grabs her and the pitcher falls; the animals disappear. At last, it is the dirty, old man who comes to her rescue. He, the poet, magician, and pied piper, then introduces her to the world of experience and "midnight suns."

Coover's pastoral, inverted even more than A. E. Housman's, choreographs Keats's "thou still unravished bride of silence and still time" both in motion and nonmotion (cf. "The Elevator"). The old man/poet introduces the mystery of experience and the wonder of imagination to the girl as his language and gestures stretch into wonderful new shapes. He reaches into his pocket for coins which transform into "nothing less than a whole private universe of midnight suns"; her pitcher has been violated and its milk scattered on the earth. Yet the story ends with an image of her urn breaking into a "thousand tiny fragments." With the milk soaking the earth, a new covenant is born. The pitcher (like the girl), Coover writes, "weaves, leans, then finally rolls over in a gently curving arc, bursting down its rust-colored veins into a thousand tiny fragments . . . not unlike the broken shells of white eggs. Many of these fragments remain in the grass at the foot of the bridge, while others tumble silently down the hill into the eddying stream below" (p. 179). Once again, the initiation ritual involves the bonding of the old and new, the embrace of black flags and ruby red cherry doors.

"The Leper's Helix"

The dancing leper provokes our every act, our every "progress" in life, and our relationship to him is like "describing a great circle on the desert surface, the leper's starting position as our compass point. . . . [We regulate] our own velocity as to schedule his arrival" (p. 180); we both control and are controlled by this raw force.

Our every response, mental and "hedonistic," is directed toward defying his power. "Puzzled by our behavior, he dances on." This powerful, disgusting, and yet seductive force will, nevertheless, finally be greeted by us and will finally surrender to us. We will embrace him despite his ultimate repulsiveness in the final dance, the final act of freedom. The leper, "tongue dangling—*god! nearly black!* . . . hurls himself into our arms, smothering us, pitching us to the red clay, his sticky cold flesh fastening to us, me, his black tongue licking my face. . . . Then, in the same instant, it is over. Purged of all revulsions, we free ourselves from him" (p. 182).

Beautiful and terrifying, the leper, with all the latent potential of both fiction and the universe, and with the energy and creative power of the sun, invites all into his totality. The speaker accepts and reaches a climax; he then prepares himself, like the leper, for the equally difficult task of seducing his reader, equally fearful and innocent of his true powers: "We wait, as he waited for us, for you. Desperate in need, yet with terror. What terrible game will *you* play with *us*? me." Surrendering his ideal of objective, cold art (the "perfect circle") for a more intimate expression that embraces brutality and death, the speaker is at last one with his subject. He must now occupy the same relationship to his reader.

This is a powerful, disturbing, and occasionally sardonic story that treats many subjects. A metafiction, it details the often grotesque nature of reality, both the subject and experience of life and fiction. More concretely, it treats in a contemporary, existential context Donne's famous "Death be not proud." One is reminded, particularly with all its sun images, of Camus's Meursault in his final welcome of that dreaded, final breeze similarly blowing toward him throughout his life. For the individual-creator, "me" is the ultimate measure of the universe.

"A Pedestrian Accident"

A funny, grotesque, bawdy, and sometimes surreal series of events are reported after the pedestrian Paul is gravely hit by a truck. Although he has lost his ability to speak, his perceptions provide the substance of the story. His neck may be broken, but, perhaps typically, he is concerned with whether or not the light was green or red when he crossed; he would know the source of his undoing. (The truck actually carries the advertisement "MAGIC KISS LIP-STICK.")

As he lies under the huge wheels, a crowd gathers. Initially solicitous, it soon grows bored. Fortunately, a series of performers entertain: a doctor illustrates his ineptitude in these matters of life and death; a policeman recites appropriate bureaucratic instructions ("Everybody back!"), although at points he seems genuinely moved by the suffering Paul; the truck driver is intent on proving his innocence and the fact that he's a good family man. Best of all is Mrs. Grundy, a latter-day Wife of Bath who, despite her mistaking Paul for another man, makes clear, at least to the reader, the nature of the luscious world the dying must leave. Like a Greek chorus, she chants a prayer that might well send any modern-day prince to his rest. Full of puns it ends "O mortality! O fatal mischief! Done in! A noble man lies stark and stiff! Delenda est Carthago! *Sic transit glans mundi!*" (p. 189).

Aware of his growing separation from the natural and social world, Paul seeks connection: "What *am* I without them? Could I even die?" (p. 188). Ultimate estrangement, the loss of the illusion of connection, is, of course, the final blow. At the end, Paul is literally left to the dogs, a potential hoard of Charons, and one rips a piece of his flesh. A satanic beggar who is mistaken for a priest waits for him, and the spit he hurls upon Paul becomes the rain of the universe. The real, ugly, lonely, and painful process of death is not yet over. Paul still awaits a comforter ("My God . . . why hast thou forsaken me?"): "For an instant, the earth upended again, and Paul found himself hung on the street. . . . There's nobody out there. . . . How much longer must this go on?" (p. 205).

The most compelling aspect of the story is its tone. Paul's mental and physical pain in his grotesque and imminent death is poignantly and ironically captured in his comments like the following, which reinforce both his profound isolation and the indifference of the world about him. The doctor says: "I know it's not easy to accept death . . . [but] death begets life"; Paul remarks: "The world was an ephemeral place, it could get away from you in a minute" (p. 184).

"The Babysitter"

Coover has played out a number of fantasies associated with "The Elevator" and with an island resort ("Quenby"). Here he objectifies an endless number of associations with "the babysitter" in terms of both her own fantasies and those of the people associated with her—e.g., her employer, Mr. Tucker, and two boys she knows. This is played out against the party the parents attend. In 107 paragraphs Coover develops at least 500 possibilities, and he even combines fantasies of several figures in single sequences. They range from the most sexually fanciful—the girl's rape by one, two, or three males, including Mr. Tucker—to the most boring, ludicrous, or frightening —the accidental or intentional deaths of the children, all set against a strict, logical timetable ("movement and non-movement" again).[7]

The ending is especially funny and grotesque. The mother, appropriately named "Dolly," who has been busy all night participating in a party game where she is stuffed back into her girdle, suddenly sees on the television news that her children have been murdered, her husband has disappeared, and a corpse has been found in her bathtub. Stoically, she turns to her reliable comforter: "Let's see what's on the late late movie" (p. 239).

In this, the ultimate pricksong, Coover descants upon the counterpointing realities and fictions of our lives and the violence, inanities, and sexuality that permeate the media which dictate our conscious and even unconscious behavior. He dramatizes how we are all creatures and products of fictions and how every act— imaginative or real—contains within itself an infinite number of narrative possibilities. Life contains no resolution apart from its own possibilities.

"The Hat Act"

Coover concludes the volume with a series of stage directions. His subject is the ultimate failure of the magic poker or the sentient

. lens—the artist-magician. What he implies is that after a series of truly fabulous tricks, the artist must capitulate to the jeers and hostility of his highly critical and demanding audience; he is also limited by the very materials he is working with. There is, indeed, a limit to his magic.

A disturbing rhythm builds. Initially, the man "dressed as a magician with black cape and black silk hat" gains warm applause and laughter as he busily pulls rabbits, himself, a half-naked woman, and hats out of still other hats, although it is always "a desperate struggle" (p. 241). These tricks beget newer and more unusual routines; he is able, for example, to decapitate bodies and then to put them together again. But as the performance goes on, his own demands, as well as those of his merciless audience, increase, as do their common hysteria and desperation. The work of art and the task of creating may well begin as an innocent trick, but it ends in mayhem or silence. The magician is destroyed by his own power.

Although the stories are very different, "The Hat Act" and Mann's "Mario and the Magician" are frightening portraits of the sexually energized artist whose initial powers over the simple and naïve turn to madness and violence. One hopes that Coover writes this and his last words tongue in cheek:

THIS ACT IS CONCLUDED
THE MANAGEMENT REGRETS THERE
WILL BE NO REFUND

6

A Theological Position
In the Beginning

Coover is unique among the younger postmoderns in publishing in virtually every genre—novel, short story, poetry, drama, and filmscript. His dramas—his "book of acts" (1972)—once more deal with the existential paradox, the difficult assertion of freedom and pleasure in a contingent and ultimately deterministic universe. Again, Coover focuses on the necessity, and yet danger, of imposing history and myth upon the reality of random event, the inevitable distortions of imposing structure upon felt experience. For the artist, these dangers are of special concern. Drama, for example, would seem to be the most distorting of forms, since in addition to its reliance upon the metaphor of language to convey experience, it relies upon an actor's reading of a director's interpretation—all of which must finally submit to an audience's final "reading."One might consider drama as both an emblem and metaphor of the problems of epistemology.

Especially innovative is Coover's technique. His drama resembles, in an unusual way, the morality play. It transforms the abstract characters of good and evil into anonymous figures representative of either the tabula rasa of felt experience or the flat and lifeless abstractions of legend, myth, and history. Nameless and often interchangeable, these "characters" are, in a sense, nonverbal vessels which, the moment the "action" begins, necessarily take on verbal identity. They are the word itself, instant projections of the individual-artist-creator-director-God—in the creative moment of feeling experience. Or, they are abstract, passionless, historical figures or archetypes. Their "development" involves their interaction with other verbal structures or with other mythic, historical, allegorical "significations." Defined by context, they may at times seem to take on an autonomy of their own, and they may reinterpret or enact variations, or defy a particular myth; or they may entirely lose or reject their linguistic or contextual place and function as awkward and nonsensical signs, like characters who have lost their identity.

Coover's dramatic characters are thus frequently metaphors of words on the page, which are metaphors of what is in the author's mind, or what is part of the written tradition (as in *Love Scene* and *The Kid*). At other times (*Rip Awake*, *A Theological Position*), they are legendary figures or philosophical or historical positions personified. The dynamic of the plays grows out of their consistent or inconsistent functioning within the structures in which they are defined. At times, the characters' efforts to be original—to create or illustrate fresh meaning (like asserting one's freedom in a limited universe)—is undercut (*The Kid*, *Love Scene*). At other times, they are entirely successful, brilliantly creative, and infinitely suggestive (*Rip*, *A Theological Position*).

Most fascinating are the different, concrete forms each of the four plays takes, the first (*The Kid*, produced in New York and London), a wild-west scenario with countless and nameless cowboys and belles; the second (*Love Scene*, produced in New York and Paris), a "voice" trying to direct actors in passionate sex; the third, *Rip Awake*, an encounter with a disoriented and angry Rip Van Winkle victimized both within and outside his legend; and the last (*A Theological Position*), a sexual intercourse performed between a priest and pregnant virgin, the Word and word made flesh.

The Kid

At one point in *The Kid*, dozens of western belles and cowpokes both listen to and perform (with microphones and sound effects) an old cowboy/cavalry/Injun saga. The Indians have alarmed the white man. Suddenly, dynamite pours upon the Indians, and so do curses (about plagues, right out of the book of Exodus); a deus ex machina in the form of a freedom train stampedes through the western terrain and destroys the charging buffalo, and everyone sings "The Battle Hymn of the Republic." All of this occurs among numerous other evocations of American and biblical history. It is the good versus the bad guys again. This is a sequence within Coover's main story, just one of many tangents that synthesize time and history and evoke the subject of brutal power over individual freedom—the unpopular story of American history and politics.

Like *Rip Awake* and *A Political Fable*, *The Kid* begins as a reworking of an American folktale, "Billy the Kid." As it develops (also like *The Public Burning*), it exposes America's need for national identity as the force of light (the good guys) invariably victorious over the force of darkness (the outlaws). Power is the name of the American game.

The main plot has the same anonymous and interchangeable cowpokes and belles as the subplot. Everyone sits in a saloon awaiting the arrival of the virile hero "the Kid," in reality a murderer and thief. Coover's stage directions insist upon stereotypes: "The BELLE and COWPOKE lines . . . should be passed out randomly enough to make it difficult to distinguish the character of one BELLE or COWPOKE from another" (p. 14). The sheriff, like everyone else, sounds like a composite of all the hayseed characters ever filmed in Hollywood. But while his language is properly provincial, his corny sentiment is not. He is so grateful to these folks for electing him that he is going to prove his mettle by killing the Kid: "I was mighty proud the day yuh all seen fit tuh make me yore Sheriff. . . . It's the greatest goldurn thing ever happened tuh me" (p. 21).

In the sheriff's promise to make his political platform good (to fulfill his role), he fails to understand that the folks not only respect but also desperately need, the Kid in their lives; the force of light can only exist in relationship to the force of evil; to be blunt, these people worship the Kid's power, and as Coover thoroughly investigates this in *The Public Burning*, "he" is a projection of their aggression and power lust. Nevertheless, given the conflict between the sheriff's and the Kid's "roles," perhaps (so the audience speculates and the townsfolk must think) the sheriff will demonstrate his even greater power. Is not politics, like American history, a tale about the orderly transfer of power?

As the Kid is about to appear—this incarnation of Billy the Kid, another Horatio Alger sort—they all celebrate in a combination of Greek chorus, "dance-hall routine, and country gospel singing: a hillbilly mix of sex, sentiment, and self-righteousness" (p. 17). They sing the glories of his towering criminal status. He is also a sexual wiz, so the ladies believe, although the men talk of his famed impotence. He is remarkably handsome, "a real impressive piece of magical meanness" (p. 24).

The Kid says nothing but "Coma ti yi youpy youpy yea," but his behavior is absurdly predictable. He shoots up shot classes, whiskey bottles, the eyes of the jacks in playing cards, and the marshall. He even shoots words ("jist say the word 'Injun' ")—all for no apparent reason except that he is programmed in his role to do so. His silent power and manifest violence stir their religious fervor (They chant "Youpy yeas"), but they also enjoy exploiting his violent displays: "Hey, Kid! Behind the bar! More Injuns!" (p. 34). They wind him up and play out their violence.

The sheriff, who should really polish their idols rather than destroy them, remains true to his role: he's going to keep the peace. When he spots the Kid, he announces: "I've come tuh take yuh in" (p. 39) and almost accidentally shoots him (an entirely playful version of Camus's Meursault on the beach).

Though the people are briefly astonished, disappointed, and even disgusted, they almost immediately give praise to their new hero, along with a new title. The sheriff is now *"the fastest gun in the West"*: he's "done made *histry*, boys." But he repeats the same old platform: "Crime . . . don't pay," to which they all chant the only prayer they know: ". . . YOUPY YOUPY YEA" (p. 44).

The sheriff would actually bury the Kid, in good classical fashion, and say a proper prayer for him, but the only words they know are of the "YOUPY" sort. At the word "prayer," the deputy recalls the "law's" earlier victory over the Injuns (cited above) in which "prayer" was the magical word that brought victory (the freedom train). Actually, what his lengthy story reveals is the arbitrariness of morality, the *"good* guys" and the "law." The white men who now rule the west (the forces of light) were the plunderers who ravaged the prairie innocents (just like the outlaw "Kid"). They might just as well have been shooting at the word "Injun." The sequence is full of anachronisms and unusually interpretive stage directions: "The DEPUTY's performance should suggest priestly rituals, the magic gestures with validity of their own. . . . [Words] can well be lost. . . . BELLES and COWPOKES may form shifting choral groups that respond antiphonally to the turns of the story" (p. 47). In addition to being a self-conscious metadrama, a drama about drama, this story within the story is an allegory of the human, and especially the American, scapegoating mechanism; its details range over the history of the blacks, Indians and Hebrews.

At this point, everyone passes on to the sheriff the Kid's gun and clothes. (The ladies pass on to him the Kid's sexual charisma, although the men again balk.) Like the Cat in the *Political Fable*, he would strip the population of its last illusions: "They ain't no such thing as the fastest gun in the West. . . . Me and the Kid there, see, it jist happened like. It don't mean a thing" (p. 69). And introducing them to the reality of accident and arbitrariness, he proceeds to his revelations: "The fastest gun, well, we jist make all that up. . . . Yuh gotta face up to it! I don't wanna hurt yuh, but I love this town, and sometimes, why, sometimes love hurts" (pp. 69, 70). While they could apparently accept his slaying of their Kid, they cannot accept his wholesale murder of their belief system. As the deputy tries to remove the Kid's magical guns, they "blast off" and kill him. Evidence at last of the survival of their power lust and violence, they chant "THE KID'S COME BACK!" (Violence is always generative.) Then, in the hands of the sheriff who would throw them away, the guns blast off again.

The sheriff talks too much, and he would still convert them. Like the people in the *Political Fable* and *Public Burning*, however, they cannot do without their mythos that there *is* an external force of evil. They would rather destroy the truth than face it. The sheriff will simply not play *their* role for them; he is still trying to reason with them. Thus, they sacrifice him (another "Kid," like all the messiahs) and conclude with the ritual of a new song—*to celebrate his mythic status*. What is fascinating is how they take his goodness, honesty, and integrity, those qualities for which they kill him, and transform them into their own values. The sheriff is celebrated for his power, sexuality, and beauty. He has become the law: "He was mean, he was magic, he was real!/Sweet Jesus, he was somethin tuh see!" (p. 74). From the beginning of the song until the end, they write a history in which they create another "Kid." Note the change in the refrain, as "The West was a place of grace and glory/ Till the day that they strung up the Kid" becomes "Since the day . . . " (Earlier in the play, the first "Kid's" sexual inadequacy was transformed through one woman's song, and he became the "biggest" and "blackest" gun in the west.) Once again, fictions, including songs and myths, create reality. The final irony, regarding Coover's title, is that the Western world, and this goes beyond the American west, may have been freer and filled with far greater possibility *before* it embraced any of its "Kids"—i.e., Christianity.

Love Scene

Coover sets on stage two undefined and silent people—projections, in a sense, of a third "character," a voice that "can come from anywhere" (p. 79). A director, author, God, Everyman, the voice is the subject of the play. He instructs the two in acting out passion and sex, and as he does (in every clichéd historical and literary example), he grows increasingly frustrated and angry. "Come on, this is . . . the whole goddamn saga of the western world. . . . Now, move it!" (p. 87).

Mostly, he fails to arouse the two as he wishes. Although at one point they kiss and at another they move toward foreplay, their timing is different from his or they are negligent of ceremony. At the end, the voice achieves either an ecstatic or partial and masturbatory release. Then, having finished with his couple, he calls upon his last character, a "deus ex machina," to verbally shoot them dead.

Especially playful, the opening dialogue might even be regarded as a satire of method acting or of the tenuous connection between sex (or love) and passion, or the sign and the signified; it may also be an ironic parody of the mechanics of the human and literary drama (the artist and his medium, man and the universe). Finally, it may be about the nature of pleasure.

The conclusion is fascinating and open-ended. The line "I-MAGINATION RULES . . . SHITHEAD" may indeed be Coover's thesis, but it may also be a final irony, depending upon how one responds to the deus ex machina's "bang bang" (p. 98). Coover may be erasing the words "IMAGINATION RULES," as well as the rest of the play (and punning on "bang," his final consummation) to indicate the more likely release his speaker has had. In this case, the words have outlived their usefulness. On the other hand, he may be expressing his frustration over the limitations of language. Masturbatory pleasure is not enough; one must write something else. The closing lines are similarly ambiguous: "Yeah. That's great . . . just beautiful." Coover's sexual metaphor—with the bad timing and orgasmic "shooting"—may finally be his metaphor for any kind of transcendence, any personal, *unshared* pleasure. (Perhaps one should extend Roland Barthes's discussion about the eroticism of literature to all heightened human experiences.)

Drama is at the level of language. The director announces his subject in general terms: "There's something happening here. . . . It's what makes the world go round." But communication depends upon explanation and hence metaphor; his language becomes trite: "It's . . . light from heaven . . . the sacred flame." He can't help but interpret his own comment, so now criticism, psychology, and philosophy intrude: "So much gets said about pattern" (p. 80).

He returns to directing the couple in sexual passion, now using romantic terms: They should illustrate "the sound of trumpets."

Perhaps he could fire their fantasy with another story (a story within this story) or some pictures; perhaps he could evoke recollections of childhood wishes. Torn between his awareness of all these metaphors and the uniqueness he seeks, he says: "I'd hoped we could make something brand new here." He returns to analogies and myths, but the couple look hopeless, as though they're "taking a morning constitutional" to keep their "bowels regular" (p. 85).

The drama, as drama, turns here. The voice has become more stimulated than his actors. "Stay with me," he implores. Meaningful on a linguistic as well as sexual level, he pleads "that space there between you has got to come alive . . . charged with necessity" (p. 86). They finally perform a (dull) kiss. He is furious; they have proceeded without him: "You left out the whole goddamn courtship sequence," which he explains, again in frustration and rhetoric: "What is it, am I using the wrong words? . . . Get it up now!" Again the tension grows; excited by the prospect of their arousal he cries: "Lemme *see* it! Lemme *feel* it." He continues: "I want tension! . . . mysticism and melodrama! . . . It's not crazy enough. . . . appetite and cruelty . . . GO!" Again as they kiss, he interrupts: "HOLD IT. . . . We're rushing it," and he explains, connecting the rhythm, spirit, and passion of sex with tragedy and all great art forms: "We invented tragedy . . . let's not mock it. . . . Not just attraction . . . but resistance, too." The sexual, artistic, human, existential, and tragic plight are one: "push, pull, push, pull. . . . You're excited and you're scared . . . sensations sweet . . . but the stink of death" (pp. 88, 89, 90).

The author cannot perform. In bitter humor now, he emits an exhausting catalogue of metaphoric and allegorical abstractions. The final consummation is every fantasy: "the princess and the blackamoor. . . . That thing he's got'll split you wide open, honey! . . . yin and yang! . . . *the beginning and the end*! SYNTHESIZE!" (pp. 91, 92). Virtually depleted of the old metaphors, he says: "Put your life into it! . . . The backwards look toward the primitive terror. . . . Eat her up! Suck him dry! I want action! Shock! Deception! Rape! Transfiguration! Come on! Make it weird!" (pp. 93, 94).

While they kiss, the voice, far more aroused than they, cries: "My God, are you still *kissing*? . . . JUMP HER! . . . Oh hurry! Come on boy, stick it in her deep!" However he tries, he cannot bring his creation (still literally and figuratively clothed) to his pitch of eroticism and strip them to his essential feeling; he cannot share his orgasm: "Go! Rip! . . . Faster! . . . Sorry! Ah! Please—*Aaahhhh*" (pp. 94, 95).

Having himself finished, he relaxes and tells them to "knock it off," and to round things off neatly, he calls for an eraser, the "deus ex machina" (an "Indian . . . Mafia . . . whatever") to destroy the entire tradition in which he has sought to verbalize his experience, "the whole western world . . . history . . . *A* to *Z*" (pp. 96, 97). He concludes: "That's just beautiful . . . all used up"—exhausted, depleted, desperate, bitter, indifferent, or fulfilled?

Rip Awake

The appeal of Washington Irving's *Rip Van Winkle* to Coover is easy to understand. Irving tells of a good-natured man, helpful to all his neighbors, who is plagued by a nagging wife. Rip doesn't care much for the Horatio Alger work ethic. In fact, he despises "profitable" work; he is an artist.

One day he and his dog, Wolf, "unconsciously" climb a mountain. Rip gazes at the magnificent Hudson River below and its surrounding calm and wilderness; suddenly a stranger dressed in the old Dutch fashion appears and calls his name. The man gains Rip's assistance in carrying liquor up the mountaintop where, in an amphitheater, Rip discovers a group of similarly dressed and odd-looking men playing at ninepins. The entire group "reminded Rip of the figures in an Old Flemish painting." They maintained a "mysterious" and uninterrupted silence: only the noise of the balls "echoed along the mountains like rumbling peals of thunder." As Rip approached them, the "figures" stopped "their play and stared with such a fixed statuelike gaze," Rip's "heart turned within him." He drank their magical draught and fell asleep for twenty years, the knight in Keats's "La Belle Dame sans Merci," the poet in "Kubla Khan," drunk on the milk of paradise.

In Irving's part 2, the awakened Rip slowly discovers the time elapsed, his rusted gun, Wolf's disappearance, and his own weakened body. Alarmed by what has happened and always fearful of his wife's scolding, he looks for an explanation and the amphitheater but can find nothing.

Once back in the foreign-looking and much-grown village, Rip realizes that the people are not only dressed in a new style but they are also changed in "character," unfriendly and suspicious; even a familiar dog, possibly his Wolf, has forgotten him. A placard of King George has been replaced by one of George Washington. Indeed, a revolution has passed him by, and many of his friends have died.

In the last section, everything ends happily. Rip recovers his daughter and son, his identity is confirmed, and the local historian, Peter Vanderdonk, verifies his story about Henry Hudson's legendary reappearance on the mountaintop. He also learns, to his great relief, that his wife has died. He retires to his daughter's house, rediscovers some old friends who inform him about the Revolution and becomes a teller of his tale.

Even in Irving's version, Rip's identity is created by *his* working out a mythology of his own life. A man apart from the everyday, practical world, then as now, "changes of states and empires made but little impression on him." Rip is the creative, romantic figure, and like the Ancient Mariner after his return, he tells his story "to every stranger." At first, "he would vary some points," but finally it settled into a fixed story, known to all. Though some people, Irving concludes, "pretended to doubt the reality" of it and insisted that Rip was mad, the old Dutch inhabitants believed him, and it became "a common wish of all henpecked husbands . . . [to] have a quieting drink from Rip Van Winkle's flagon."

Irving's story is perhaps an allegory of America's change from the old-world communal society to democracy, with an implied attack on the new citizenry—efficient and acquisitive but cold and mocking, if not suspicious and cruel to the suffering in their midst. (Rip's wife is the epitome of the new capitalist ethos.) It also contains the descent into hell motif, and most dramatically, the poet's surrender to ecstatic vision. Perhaps of greatest interest to Coover, it is an allegory of the storyteller who connects the new and old worlds (the author of history), and it is also a metafiction with numerous interlocking stories.

Washington Irving, or to be more accurate, his persona, the late Diedrich Knickerbocker (whose history of the Dutch settlers was a mixture of fact and fiction), tells a story which is actually a reworking of a German folk legend. His is, he vows, a "precise" rendering of Rip's story, told originally by Rip in several versions but now finalized and even committed to memory by everyone in his neighborhood.

Though Knickerbocker (let us call him Irving) tells of the twenty-year nap and awakening, the events prior to this are mysterious in detail. Was this, as Hawthorne might ask, a fact or a dream? Was it an enactment of an older Henry Hudson myth? All that Rip knows is that after an "unconscious" ascent, he gazed at the river which, as in a dream, precipitated Hudson's appearance, which was then followed by his Dutch mates, described like a painting. Was Rip's long sleep his consummation with creative fancy, or a surrender to the extremes of natural beauty? Might it have been a new or remembered response to his parson's Flemish painting? Was it a descent into the unconscious? Whatever the mystery of Rip's experience, his subsequent fiction romanticized his life for future generations, and whatever else he represented, he was an inspiration—an escape— for henpecked husbands. (Note: One of the boxes within other boxes here is that Rip was better understood by the old Dutch inhabitants than by most of his henpecked audience which ironically, had it drunk of his draught, might have been moved to vision.)

Coover exposes Rip as an angry victim of Irving's myth, resentful that Irving ignored his mental and physical pain. Yet, as Coover sees him, Rip is unaware of the positive significance of that "journey," his communion with imagination (creative passion), which then became a part of him. Coover, that is to say, first focuses on Rip's profound loneliness and physical debilitation, on Rip's wish to clarify for the modern-day audience the anguish, rather than historical immortality (whitewashing), he endured. But then, Coover expands the original story (or his reading of it) and not only betrays Rip's obliviousness to the imaginative visitation that was part of Irving's character but goes so far as to portray how such acute visionary powers culminated in Rip's awareness of the intensely concrete and mortal dimensions of human experience. In the end, Rip sadly understands and sorely experiences man's fragility. Thus, as Coover repeats many of Irving's details and invents many of his own, he ironically rewrites the Rip legend for his own audience (or technically, for Rip's, since this is a monodrama). Coover's Rip then also becomes a victim of Coover's reading of Irving's myth, a "text" offered to an audience, to be read and mythified in each person's own terms. Coover capitalizes on the transformational qualities of legend—as history—in all their variegated dimensions.

If, in a sense, Irving's story revolves around the enchantment of imagination (and its powerful intoxication, as Keats described it), Coover's revolves, in part, around the pathos of one's indifference to it. The saddest thing about Rip is his failure to appreciate his "dream." All he can do in the present time of the play is try to separate himself from Irving's (or what he calls Peter Vanderdonk's) history, while at the same time he is in many ways tied to it. Multiple ironies resound in Rip's "Maybe I've been living with my stories so long I've got senile and started believing them": he is speaking of (1) Irving's, (2) Coover's, and (3) his own distortions about his life.

As the play begins, Rip steps before the audience and implores it to see him outside of any scripts. What one sees, however, is a reluctant Sisyphus frightened to return to the rock, while at the same time intent upon confronting those forces that have instigated his fate. Well-intentioned though naïve, he is a character out of E. A. Robinson's Tilbury Town. Coover's first stage direction removes Rip from Irving's mold: "[He is] more ancient than ever, toiling up a mountainside" (p. 101). He carries his own wine jug now, a replacement for that taste of magical draught of many years ago.

Rip understands his "story" in his own terms. It will be different now, he says, because this time he has willed his journey. He will go "all the way" for his "con-su-mation" with "those little buggers" who "messed up" his life. Poor Rip has slept through both his own and society's Revolution. "Maybe if I hadn't," he speculates," I wouldn't be needing one now" (p. 102).

Melancholic, he reflects on the past, on how those "weird little dwarfs" involved him in drink. They were, at least as he now sees them, a "depressing outfit," like humorless gods, unfeeling and gloomy; he drank "so as not to feel like shooting" himself (p. 105). But his ordinary vision failed, and he couldn't distinguish one thing from another. He may even have shot Wolf by mistake.

Unaware of what happened to him, he asks why he was singled out for this experience. He then tries to rationalize why he was victimized. Punning on "thunder," the mock tragic hero defying nature, he admits that he did "steal" the "little fellas'" thunder, in a sense, to become the main character in their legend (to rewrite it). Perhaps like the classical deities, they are jealous of his (questionable) fame and want to be like him, the "guy" who had "it done to" him. On the other hand, perhaps they are totally indifferent to him.

Why then is he returning? Rip turns to the audience, angry and abused by the role he's been dealt, about to create a more authentic identity. Think about it in concrete terms, he says; his life was robbed of twenty years; into posterity he will always have been just an old man. To be immortalized through legend is "damn well" not worth it. History and legend distort.

That he was a great and happy storyteller, for example, is untrue. Everyone ignored the substantial part of his tale, his dream material, and then became bored. The truth is that after he awoke, he was miserable and decrepit—with twenty years' moss on his teeth and a variety of physical ailments, let alone long and enormous, ingrown toenails. The "worst" thing—and this is one of Coover's most ingenious interpolations—was that he could never really feel completely awake while, at the same time, he was understandably afraid of falling asleep.

Actually, he could never tell if he was asleep or awake: "I just couldn't get my head clear," he explains, and in his rich and evocative exposition, the audience realizes that Rip's greatest loss, now as then, was his inability to appreciate the keen imaginative power born on that mountain, that ability to function between dream and fact, the void and the concrete. There is a sad irony about his statement, a naïvety belied by rich and lyrical language: "I kept trying to wake up even when sometimes I probably *was* awake! You know how when you're sleeping and the cock starts crowing, . . . or the bells are ringing, . . . but there's something inside you, way down inside you, . . . and its smarter than you, . . . so . . . it turns the bells into a bobsled and you go off for a holiday" (p. 109).

The reluctant poet carrying the old-world (pre-Revolution) dreams did everything to shake off his condition (like jogging and dieting), but for a time, nothing worked. His enchantment to a dream was his constant reality with everything in a state of flux and transformation: friends appeared to him to say they had died in ways different than Irving had reported; he was even informed that there never was a Revolution. The terrors of his vision were most debilitating: his worst dream was that his daughter, not his wife, had died.

At this point, Rip awoke (as in the title) with a "pounding heart" and, as Keats experienced it, a mouth "dry as a bone," his epiphany marked by a sense of the "itness" or the particles (or "specks") of human experience. With all of physical reality speaking to him of transience and death—cracks in his walls and "webs on the windowpane"—he said: "I saw it, I felt it all" (p. 113), an unwelcome insight and dour modification of Wordsworth's visionary experience. With such a vivid vision of the concrete and final extremities of experience, rather than its infinite transformational possibilities, he could never sleep again.

What Rip yearns for, in the present time of the play, is to regain his first vision; thus, he would ascend the mountain as he did in youth. Transformations of dreams, he explains, are infinitely preferable to those of reality. (One has the salvation of metaphor and endless possibilities.) "There ain't *no* relief for having to watch things turning into themselves," he explains. Indeed, fictions alone keep one together and "them goddamn specks from blowing apart" (p. 116).

What *would* Rip do to the figures on the hill? He would "whup" their "fat little arses" for imposing on him his role, his fate, his old age. Clearly not the nineteenth century's lovable and local innocent (whose portrait, he says, was the raving of a madman), he is *not* the fictionalized "Rip" but, rather, the essential man, naked of fixed identity, "alone." He has moved from one extreme to the other—from imaginative vision, from youth, to "knowledge," an awareness of time and the void. Now he affirms the need for balance. Life consists of trying to keep "them goddamn specks from blowing apart," he says, ironically the purpose, though not always the accomplishment, of religion and history, as well as of art, and of course, storytelling.

What Rip wants is some harmony between these two sides of himself, the imaginative and logical faculties. He would be Sisyphus. "By damn," he says, "we have to balance things out. . . . I'm too old to keep on living a stranger to myself and kin" (p. 117). An additional irony, of course, is that to accomplish this, he must return to the Dutchmen, to his roots, his "kin," the mythic frameword that "invented" him; the word and the Word are again one—imagination and the concrete.

In Coover's typically ambiguous and open-ended conclusion, Rip may be foolish or admirable. One cannot, he says, "just stand around . . . and get killt for nothing" (p. 118). (That is, of course, the *only* "reason" one gets "killt.") Furthermore, he continues, extending his message to the "living theater," if the audience should see old Peter Vanderdonk, his historian-author, tell him, he urges, Rip "aint sleeping through no more Revolutions," that his "old national heritage was last seen proceeding back up the mountain to rassel with the spooks in his life!" (p. 119). Though Rip longs for the transformational faculty once again, what he cannot understand is that one may not be able to acquire it on demand and that he may be projecting onto the dwarfs what alone is within him. There may be a final irony in his last words which imply that the conscious choice for authorship is automatically redemptive. Perhaps neither conviction nor old age allows one to regain the farm forever fled from the childless land. But then again, a tangible amphitheater remains before him.

A Theological Position

A Theological Position is one of Coover's most provocative and irreverent works. A priest performs sex with a woman—a demure, smiling, silent virgin who is six months pregnant—all in the course of duty to clear her of potential heresy charges. Though he is physically and imaginatively aroused, he finds it easier to ejaculate words than seed. She, on the other hand, in her nonverbal responses, exacerbates his growing impotence and drives him to stab her. He is then assaulted by her surviving "cunt's" diatribe against him and the inhibiting law he represents. As the play ends, the priest finally kills her, and his and her husband's "pricks" comment on the scene.

The "theological position" is this: sexuality derives from Eve, that part of Adam, the devil's tail, from which woman was created. Mary's later and redemptive conception was nonsexual and virginal, the incarnation of a mystical and transcendent Consciousness. The purpose of Christianity and of the Word is "preventative"—to lead mankind away from its primitive itches to "regeneration" and "freedom from nature" (p. 128). This can be accomplished either through reason or faith, but these can never "intersect."

If one is looking for symbolic meaning in this ultrachic mystery play, the man and woman can represent anything from a middle-class couple with domestic problems to the mythic Joseph and Mary. But since the man and woman also alternate with each other as symbolic words and "witnesses," each, in addition, can represent the writer and his audience and/or the dialectical flux of experience, the diachronic and synchronic functions of language, history (or any structure) and time, God and his Son (or Daughter).

With the priest's major involvement in the plot—as its "complication"—functions continue to shift and interlace. The priest is the male chauvinist, the catechist reexperiencing his catechumenate, the writer, the critic, the "word," or language's different functions, Sartre's *soi* and *pour soi*—one of any number of roles seeking fulfillment. Any combination among the three characters is possible. Most compelling are their playful interchange within (1) the holy trinity; (2) their linguistic functions as the concretized "In the beginning was the Word"; and (3) their comic/serious sex roles.

This manipulation of roles and allegory is reflected in Coover's subtle wordplay. A change in spelling in a repeated phrase thoroughly transforms meaning. For example, the change of "fetal" to "fatal" in the statement that one must be liberated from his fetal/fatal "attachments" condenses Coover's attack on the seductive appeal of death to the church fathers (pp. 129, 169). Puns also abound. "Let's not beat about the bush" evokes not only idiomatic meaning but also sexual and religious signification (the "burning" bush common to both). Words are used, at key points, as signs that point in entirely different directions—e.g., "fantasy" signifying both traditional, blind ("peasant") worship and inhibited sexuality. Indeed, Coover's collection is partially dedicated to Gail "Goodwin," while this particular play is addressed to Gail "Godwin"—a typographical error, or a private communication?

The plot is this: a man and woman seek council from a priest, since the woman is presumably bearing an immaculate conception. There is no problem, the priest happily reports, since the woman can *now* be "penetrated" to satisfy church law. If her husband is too inhibited, he will accommodate—a worthy shepherd well servicing his flock. What he discovers, however, after a wildly funny climb atop the table and aboard her (and subsequent plungings into her) is that the lady is no virgin. Although he could stop now, and probably should, since he has served his "function," he nevertheless whacks away. (Why has the man tricked him? Does he know that once aroused, the priest will not be able to stop? Is he the teacher, the priest his "recalcitrant pupil?")

It becomes increasingly clear that the woman's pregnancy may indeed be immaculate, in a manner of speaking—not because she hasn't had sex, but because the priest, like the man, is incapable of climaxing within her. If this is so (the audience realizes), then the priest's problems will just begin, since she will be repeating an experience sanctioned only in revelation which cannot be a part of ordinary experience. Indeed, the latter possibility is considered "repugnant," "infantile," and "depraved" to the priest. To be sure, he has argued from the beginning that there can be no connection between the incarnation and real experience, or "reason" and "revelation": one should seek out the Consciousness that "fathered" the Mary myth, rather than continue "idolatrizing the extravagant sow, the immaculate whore" (p. 129). That is a dirty story.

From this point on, however, the priest forgets these distinctions, and as he plows away, he reaches a sort of linguistic ecstasy. He also appears close to a coronary, since he cannot seem to "finish." The woman, on the other hand, responds physically. While he is like a machine upon her, also spouting words to turn himself on, her body is like a mouth sucking him in. Initially furious at his own limited "condition," he deteriorates into monosyllables and then harsh threats, which stimulate even more vigorous thrustings. At this point, her vaginal mouth bites him. Mortified, he extricates himself, ejaculates on his robes, and stabs her. Though she warns, like the narrator in *A Political Fable*, that her power remains (her belly is like the Cat's "hat"), her manifest form as a pregnant woman "collapses," and her more "essential" nature is "resurrected." A sort of spirit materialized, she is now a talking "cunt," the source of life, the primal origin of sensual pleasure—the true "word" and mouth, whose experience can only be retold by metaphor. The word incarnate, the cunt then delivers a diatribe on the male's abuse of the female; it attacks the moralities that respond to the infinitely rich and erotic world of experience through inhibiting laws.

This difficult play becomes more lucid when one pays close attention to the priest. In fact, the play's dramatic tension consists of his exposure to the merging of fact and Revelation and the way concrete experience and belief systems (his myths) are one. The priest is allowed to bear witness to both the spirituality of the sensual and the sensual base of the spiritual. Indeed, he demonstrates that both mind and body gravitate to the concrete. Whether or not he changes at the end, however, is questionable. Coover's audience, at the least, observes that sensuality alone is transcendent, as Coover once again illustrates that the dancer and dance are inseparable.

The priest has associated the "arbitrary" interpretation of the "spirit" and law with the devil (cf. the phantom cab driver in *The Public Burning*), maintaining that they are "utterly transparent" (p. 130). For Coover, the reading and rereading of myth, like any act of imagination, is divine. Like sexuality, it demonstrates one's creativity and (illusory) transcendence over flux (and time). The woman is actually an example of both transcendence and flux, of the original Christ myth and the arbitrariness of its sign in time. She is the embodiment of the magical in the real, the magnificent pregnant reality that carries the word or the child—the reservoir of infinite possibilities, whose "delivery" (a curious word in both religious and medical circles) is accepted purely on faith.

Through the interaction of these two figures, Coover parodies the priest's view: "There has never been such a conception, and there never will be another" (p. 129). One comes to realize the limitless varieties of "conception." Coover not only ironically verifies the original fiction (its "essence" on a diachronic level) but in his depic-

tion of contemporary inhibition and denial also reaffirms its synchronic "existence" in time. Possibilities regarding Christ's actual
"conception" (another curious word) increase with geometric pro-
gression, as do Coover's additional assertions regarding value and
freedom in a contingent world.

The priest's emergent sexuality is passionless. Sex to him is like his
belief in the church: it lacks love and surrender. Although he un-
dresses the woman, for example, his response is abstract: "I've
forgotten some of the words," he begins: "Yes, I think we speak of
marble" (p. 141). He delights in her "plump . . . [breasts]"; he cannot
bring himself to say the word. Only after familiar words and rituals,
like crossing himself, can he continue. It is both funny and grotesque
(p. 143):

> MAN: Maybe you'd rather I left you . . .
> PRIEST: No . . . there should be witnesses!

Coover naturally mocks Christianity for blindly substituting
communal identity for the more frightening alternative of individual choice and personal responsibility. He also plays with Sartre's
l'autre as a necessary confirmation of one's existence (with Sartre's
metaphor of "gazing" literally exaggerated throughout). Indeed,
the paradox of survival, on many levels, involves witnesses (e.g., the
dramatist and his audience, the lover and his partner), yet one's
ultimate condition is that of solitude.

The priest, then, while falling prey to passion, holds firm to his
puritanical morality, as well as to his ego. He would really want the
woman to be a virgin enjoying sex for the first time with him. (What
if, he asks, "it were really" her first time?) His (linguistic) ecstasy is
more than he ever "imagined": he used to concretize the sexual in
order to apprehend the mystical: "It [the Spirit] was always 'she'"
Now, since he is actually experiencing, and not just contemplating,
the flesh as word, he can make "'she' a 'her,'" and unify "substantive
and verb," "matter and spirit." He continues: "Oh my God," and
speaks one of Coover's best lines: "I've got the sweet taste of trinities
in my mouth!" (p. 145). He is, of course, his own worst enemy, the
self-conscious lover, like the writer-critic. His subsequent "tran-
substantiation" is totally bizarre. As the priest traditionally transforms the wafer into the body (at least four levels of metaphor are
involved), he now performs another metamorphosis—the transformation of passion into grammatical units.

He obviously knows she has been penetrated. ("Maidenheads," he explains, "I have had converse with," p. 146). Also, although he has shown no personal interest in her, her body has contracted and, "like another mouth," has truly spoken to him as felt experience qua experience. He "wriggles" gratuitously (p. 147).

He is aroused although, once again, he could, or should, withdraw. "Strange we should speak of marble," he says, weakening. "[There are] too many statues." But the fear of engaging in his own sexuality frightens him. There is, he rationalizes, "truth in marble. . . . It lasts." He wavers again, distracted by passion: "Imagine. The soft letter of the soft law" (p. 148). Especially in his last mataphor, he seems redeemable.

Nevertheless threatened by the wordless embrace of the woman's body, the priest "irreverently" begins to work faster. (In counterpoint, the man watches, eating the apple, a witness and vicarious participant.) As her passion grows, so does his guilt: "It was better when . . . it might be . . . 'she.' " His words, rather than his seed, spill: "Yes, I like words . . . Velutinous! . . . Oleaginous! . . . Heavenly! Diabolical! . . . Oh, it's good!" (pp. 150, 151).

The woman remains, fecund and functioning, despite her partner. She seems perfectly content to thrive on her own terms. He becomes increasingly enraged, his system all the more threatened. Still incapable of ejaculating, his fancy words become monosyllables. Once again, although he should withdraw (the cock crowing the magical thrice), he continues. In a sense raping her, his hostile language excites him further. Close to orgasm, he collapses.

While earlier her body was sucking him, now it is biting. He finally pulls out and discharges all over his frock. (It will wash out, he knows; have his thoughts about the original myth so stimulated him before?) As he insists he will still get to the "bottom" of this and its devilish origins, her "bottom" speaks: *A rich husky cascade of laughter issues forth from beneath the* WOMAN's *skirts. Her* CUNT *speaks*: 'The bottom of it indeed!' " She takes his remark "I beg your pardon" both literally and figuratively, adding that he couldn't recognize the "Devil's unguentiferous oleoginous ass" from "God's tit if we provided . . . survey maps" (p. 161).

He is astounded at the possbility of a talking "cunt," but she explains: "I use your language, having failed with my own." (She has already tried sucking and biting him.) What follows is extravagant metaphysical comedy. He bends to examine her anatomy—lips and perhaps even tongue—and cries: "My word"; she insists: "And the word is flux" (p. 162).

Christianity, like male chauvinism, she explains, loses the forest for the trees: "You boys get misled by the rigidity . . . of your own organs": You care so much for your own safety and pleasure, you lose the mystery of life. Continuing to attack male-dominated thought, she goes on: "You work up a hard-on [like "a rock" and "as cold"] and like it so much you call it a system, but you're afraid of orgasm and call it death" (p. 162). Fulfilling the life instinct involves surrender to "process" and *all* the pure experience behind the "dirty language."

With the priest now chanting (*"vagina qui verba facit"*), she recalls the moment he might have accepted a new fiction: "Now, the soft letter of the soft law . . . you nearly broke through there." The theological position, however, is "murder": "You've got [no] . . . chance of fucking the world alive with that." To be sure, "only man could hang himself with glossaries. . . . If you ask [man] . . . what genesis is . . . it's a book on jurisprudence" (pp. 162, 163, 164).

One needs a new fiction, an affirmation of Eve and sexuality—no more "assaults . . . by the old sausage gods [written by men]." Indeed, the cunt enjoys "foaming floods of boiling seed." Although she knows she is going too far, she pursues: "We have to stir the senses, grab you where it hurts! Any penetration, however slight, is a bloody business" (p. 166). Both the husband and priest are unwilling to accept this, for neither has been penetrated or shed blood. The husband cries out for her subordination: "I work hard. . . . We all have our place, and she has hers!"

Her response, a nonverbal but very clear communication, offends all—"*a loud wet fart*," after which she chants to the priest: *"Te oro, pater!"* She is the "wild bear" he referred to earlier: sensuality, rather than sin, is one's true birthright.

Though the priest now tries plugging her up, she finally bites him and explains that real salvation is in living. One has "to suffer" the cycle of surrender/gain/and ultimate loss. His only alternative, with echoes of the *Political Fable* and *The Public Burning*, is to destroy her. He must fulfill, as she puts it, his "covenant with holy inertia," his need to "kill and codify" (p. 168).

"Stop," she finally pleads; stop telling little boys to be liberated from flesh and death. Stop teaching that "Adam had a tail and that's what God made Eve of." The priest grabs the ritual knife for the last concrete/symbolic communion act. He shall kill her. "Think of her," he says to her husband, "as a host" to be "liberated" from the "demon," another political crucifixion from which another (rationalizing) fiction will undoubtedly be created. Ironically, he is about to act out the final details of the Christ story: after the denial of flesh (the Incarnation), the "father's" sacrifice of it.

Punning on "come" and insisting that life need not consist of good versus evil—again, the forces of light and dark—she pleads that nothing is profane, and certainly not the body: "Why do you fear a Second Coming when you haven't yet heard the announcement for the First?" (p. 170). "Do you think," she concludes, "you can stay the moving spirit in an alphabet?" (p. 171).

At this point, "IN GOD'S NAME," he plunges the knife into her belly. Her voice trails off, and she collapses, "cradled" by the man. "It is done," the priest concludes his ritual. At this moment, another "transmutation" (and climax) occurs: both the priest's and man's "pricks" speak (p. 172):

> PRIEST'S PRICK: It's all emptying out . . .
> MAN'S PRICK: Why is it we always become the thing we struggle
> against?
> PRIEST'S PRICK: Because of love . . .
> *Pause.*
> After all, there's something to be said for talking cunts . . .

Perhaps now, or tomorrow, they will fashion another myth, to borrow Yeats's words, to vex to nightmare another twenty centuries of stony sleep.

7

More Innovations: Old and New

A Political Fable[1]

Coover borrows Dr. Seuss's Cat in the Hat for his 1980 fable of the rise and fall of a U.S. presidential candidate. This mischievous and magical creature can pull anything out of his hat and transform any activity or object into whatever he wishes. He makes people laugh and "lift" their chin" and feel that they "will win" (p. 1). Since he is a cat, however, he lacks common speech. Thus, his story is told by the minority party's national chairman, Mr. Brown (nicknamed "Sooth-[sayer]"), and his political position is articulated by his own Mr. Clark, another magical figure out of Dr. Seuss's *One Fish, Two Fish, Red Fish, Blue Fish*.

Brown's major capability is predicting elections. He himself could never aspire to the top job because of his fat lips, empirically un-popular and obviously unelectable. Brown understands the "kin-etics," rather than the nonissues, of politics. Terms like "liberal" or "conservative," he explains, are "mere fictions" of the press "which politicians sooner or later . . . adapt." Actually, politics is "a complex pattern of vectors, some fixed . . . some random . . . even cosmic"; a politician's job is merely "to know them and ride them," (p. 7). Once again, politics is just a way of organizing life's flux.

This is, nevertheless, an election year, and Brown's party has conceded that the opponent, the incumbent, is a shoo-in. But to keep the political game rolling, it will push two losers (a Boston, Irish Protestant named Riley; and a tall, western descendant of Daniel Boone); this may blaze their trail toward victory four years hence. To be sure, the incumbent has everything; he is a man of all the people: "a member of everything from SANE and the NAACP to the Ameri-can Legion, Southern Baptists, and the National Association of

Manufacturers" (p. 5). Coover compiles a list of characteristics that covers all possibilities.

Despite this well-oiled strategy, the Cat suddenly appears for the minority party's nomination. Brown is upset for obvious reasons. Though Dr. Seuss's Cat entertains the children by instigating and then undoing their devilment, it is hard to imagine this political cat orchestrating an adult divine comedy. "I CAN LEAD IT ALL BY MYSELF," nevertheless, is the Cat's motto. A couple of maverick midwesterners, in the meantime, are busy engineering madcap preparations for his convention appearance with the usual political hoopla and slogans like "Let's Make the White House a Cat House" and "What This Nation Needs Is More Pussy!" Before long, everyone is wearing the Cat's red-and-white-striped floppy hat or singing Cat songs and enjoying tantalizing fun and games—i.e., "a hundred gorgeous milk-fed Midwestern co-eds [real pussycats]" leaping "in and out of laps" and licking faces (p. 16).

The Cat flaunts all the rules. He appears on the convention floor before his nomination, interrupts the opponent's rallies with magic tricks, and, most appealing, he concretizes and thus exposes the meaninglessness of his competitor's political jargon and strategies. The nationally televised convention is transformed into a grotesque spectacle. Coonskin hats, for example, which Boone distributes as his trademark, are turned into live raccoons that scamper madly about. Cat hats beneath the "Boone-skins" begin "raising a din of happy Cat-Calls." Most of the coons then start "humping each other" (pp. 20, 21). Mr. Brown faints.

The Cat becomes an instant national sensation. Mortified Mr. Brown tries everything he can to return things back to normal. After a long talk with Clark, the Cat's political visionary, he at last comes to understand the Cat's charisma and vision of "a vast reconstruction of human life." That Boone hat, for example, is really less a "ridiculous" than a "failed" metaphor (p. 29). Leaders need symbols that can emotionally mobilize people. Everyone has had enough of the Daniel Boone vision.

The Cat understands the modern age. A revolutionary, he can free people from their dependence on history and all the other structures and illusions that have inhibited and depressed them. "The Cat is funny," Clark explains, and "dramatic." The modern world has "a terrible need for the extraordinary . . . [and is] weary of the misery under our supposed prosperity, . . . of dullness and routine, . . . of all the masks we wear." The Cat "cuts through all this.

We laugh. For a moment, we are free. [To paraphrase Merleau-Ponty, it is only the ordinary that is extraordinary]."

The Cat will cure the Great Western Disease of History; he will free men from tradition, from their isolation from the here and now; he will bring them to the "actual and the possible," thus performing "a kind of racial historectomy"; one will be free at last of his "irrational terror of reality," which the "mystification of history" has produced (p. 31).

The Cat is the "agent of the absurd," his most potent gift his "ambiguity," his breaking "the rules of the house"—any rules, of any house. As Dr. Seuss's Cat frees the children, Coover's Cat also has a liberating function—to perform whatever each person needs, a custom-made deus ex machina. His "Voom" can thus mean anything —whatever one reads into it: the bomb, freedom, reason, being and nonbeing. His promise remains "Something new!" (p. 44).

So much for theory. The Cat, who easily receives the nomination, must now gain the public trust; he must convince a nation of its own creative and magical powers. This he does when, arriving on roller skates and with a cake on a rake, he performs incredible tricks and suddenly allows a fish tank to overturn. The hall is transformed into an ocean. With everyone swallowed in a whale's body, there is a great deal of physical, mental, and even spiritual excitement. At last, the imprisoned population contrives its release—through the utterance of the magical "Voom." (Would such an explosive syllable generate enough gas to force the opening of one of the whale's orifices?)

Their minds now free for new metaphors, the population is both exhilarated and threatened by this "soul-finding" experience. As Clark explains: "The structures we build to protect us from reality are insane ... [but] comforting. ... Their loss is momentarily frightening." Yet, if humanity can experience reality concretely, "without mystification . . . [and] unencumbered by pseudo-systems" (p. 47), perhaps elections will no longer be necessary. Because all myths are defenses against loneliness, one might learn to face the absurd, to tolerate direct experience and feeling. One could become the Cat in the Hat.

As the campaign continues, the Cat performs increasingly unpredictable, magical, embarrassing, humiliating, sensational, outrageous, and unmanageable things to his opposition. He turns a five-hundred-dollar-a-plate political dinner into a "stable full of braying polka-dotted donkeys wearing Cat Hats." He causes the clothing to fall off a speaker at an American Legion convention, leaving the speaker "diapered in Old Glory, noticeably soiled" (p. 53). He continually forces his opposition to represent concretely what he says he is, and he gets increasingly more vulgar and extravagant, performing "exorcisms" that release a nation's "long-repressed belly-laughs," (p. 56). By now, the opportunist Brown is utterly swept up with the minority party's certain victory.

Finally, on the national television debate, the Cat performs his most "devastating" act, which forces his opponent, the man of all the people, into literal madness. The Cat metamorphoses his small-town fedora into a bowler, biretta, golfer's straw, miner's helmet, beret, ten-gallon hat, mortarboard, earmuffs, crown, feather, and flower. As the poor man rattles on, with each phrase tailored to each constituency (concretized in the hats), all his words run "together in one mad gibberish of sound. . . . He seemed to swallow his tongue," reduced to a final "ME-YOU," which not only ended the campaign but sent him into some "idiotic" state and political retirement (pp. 59, 60, 61).

Brown has come a long way in his support for the Cat (his candidates surrendered long ago), and he agrees with Clark and Sam about human psychology: "[People] have been programmed the wrong way from birth, all of them stuck to the earth with hungers and sex grabs, scared to die or even get hurt," (p. 67). But he also maintains—and, as things work out, is ultimately right—that people cannot be completely transformed, that the psyche is not formless and empty.

Brown's opportunism, nonetheless, is always his most striking characteristic. Even if the Cat is victorious, this is of less importance to him than the Cat's "function" four years hence: "It scares the hell out of me to think of no elections," he admits. The implications of the Cat's victory are in fact too frightening to everyone, who needs "the reassurance of . . . the familiar." Though the Cat opened a "shutdown world" and involved a nation in the "process" of living, freedom has become intolerable.

If the political machine seems to have taken on its own life, the Cat has similarly transcended political categories. He has exposed the illusions that sustain an entire nation. He has taken to bouncing out of television sets to confront the comfortable citizenry with everything from "spies" and "sob-sisters" to "elephants out of Indian documentaries" and "unwed mothers."

Everyone begins turning against him; an army coup is planned to assure victory for the incompetent, insane opponent; all traditional political and military options are considered. Things get so bad that the multitude of bigoted groups throughout the country are assembled to finally deal with the menace. The Cat is skinned alive and crucified. Sam, his vice-presidential candidate, the most decent politician of all, is shot. Like the spectacle of *The Public Burning*, a mass orgy of brutality, sex, and drunkenness takes over, "the Great American Dream in oily actuality" (p. 82). The scapegoat Cat is finally torn apart, each celebrant eating of his body and then "tripping" on it—with visions of American history and all its "massacres" and "motherings" (p. 83).

The ritual over, ordinary life is at last restored. Riley is elected president; Clark is put under house arrest. (He may still have the Cat's hat, although one was turned over to a Princeton Museum and Library, and many others, perhaps, still survive); the speaker, Brown, has become attorney general, and a holiday is declared during which to commemorate the Cat (October 31, considered by many now to be "Halloween"). *A Political Fable* is one of Coover's most bitter and funny works. Though on an entirely different scale from *The Public Burning* and *The Kid*, it again treats the birth of an American civic religion.

Whatever Happened to Gloomy Gus of the Chicago Bears?

People are wonderful. . . . They can get used to everything in this world. (P. 94)

Another political/religious satire, *Gloomy Gus* (1975) tells the bitter tale of the ultimate plastic man who, programmed to respond to the roles of lover and football player, runs the gamut from Horatio Alger hero to sacrificed political/religious martyr. By virtue of compulsive and ritual practice, Gus trains himself to be a great football star and fabulous seducer of women. Had he a soul, one could call him a Faustian figure bedevilled by success, but lack of "a center" (p. 51) is precisely Gus's shortcoming: "Gus not only lacked political awareness, he lacked awareness of any kind. He had no core at all. . . . It was this nothingness that we all settled on as the essential Gloomy Gus" (pp. 50, 51). In a sense, Gus represents human possibility—an "empty vessel," in all its dangerous potential. As such, he is as responsible for the destruction of the innocents at Guernica—the backdrop of the story—as for the decimation of the enemy quarterback on the football field.

Numerous details from Nixon's portrayal in *The Public Burning* are also used to characterize Gloomy Gus in this story. Devoted to cottage cheese and ketchup and "paranoid" about his bad breath (p. 73), Gus (whose real name is Dick) is the "Fighting Quaker," the "Iron Butt" (p. 42)—a graduate of Whittier, a scholar, politician, organist, pianist, braker, gas station attendant, debater, entrepreneur, journalist, and so on-now become "National Hero." He is, Coover warns, "a kind of walking cautionary tale on the subject of fame and ambition" (p. 43). To be sure, Gus has worked his way up the ladder and become every boy's dream hero. An American cult figure, he has gathered all the chits one associates with the rags to riches legend.

The story has numerous comic sequences. Since Gus is too constricted to comprehend the nature of football, he must be programmed to blindly react on the field to a single stimulus—the number "29." When his lover, Golda, tells him she is twenty-nine years old, he charges her like an end rushing the quarterback, blackening her eyes, and knocking out her front tooth. Golda, mesmerized by Gus's impeccable, unvarying seduction techniques, is enthralled, despite the fact that he barely knows her name. Elsewhere, when Gus overhears a conversation about the year the stock market crashed, he lunges through a stove as if it were a goal line. Finally, at the close of his record-breaking season, when the opposing players realize that he plays entirely by rote, they give him stimuli for seduction responses and completely destoy his game. As one might anticipate, a human engine like Gus might well serve any political organization; indeed, at the end, he is wound up to lead a union demonstration and, along with ten others, is killed.

Coover's details—i.e., setting the story in the thirties against the backdrop of violent labor and management disputes, Guernica, and other Nazi depredations—transform vaudeville routine into serious political allegory. If the Cat in the Hat is an emblem of spontaneity and immediacy and if he struggles to have the nation accept freedom, Gus serves the opposite function. Although living in the present, Gus operates entirely by programmed roles and blind rules— the American dream gone wrong, freedom without conscience and responsibility.

Gus is also frighteningly resilient. Driven insane by the role confusion on the football field and failing to recover through all conventional therapies, he is rehabilitated only through more role playing—by becoming an actor. Gus is so "free" that he can even become programmed to his final and most dangerous role. Always in motion, he never reflects; he lacks the balance that his own game, football, presumably represents, that balance of reflection and action which the narrator says is also essential to art, history, and civilization—which Coover elsewhere calls the perfection of process. Gus's problem, as the narrator sees it, is not that the game of football is inherently brutal, imperialistic, and capitalistic. Rather, it is that like many of his coplayers, Gus does not think enough to really understand the meaning of his game.

Because of the many allusions that tie Gus to the Richard Nixon of *The Public Burning* (where he is even called a "Gloomy Gus"), the story may be read as a portrait of what might have happened to Nixon if he had indeed associated with the Socialists, as he fantasizes in *The Public Burning*: "I might have been there myself" (p. 138). More generally, it treats the dangers of any political or social power that neglects purpose and morality for action and blind commitment, the dangers of role playing without constant vigilance over the metaphors that control one's life.

Coover gives a sympathetic portrait of the young leftist idealists through his narrator-artist, a "lyrical socialist" (p. 37). A friend of Gus's, he seems to speak for Coover in his fascination with the flux and ambiguity of history and experience. ("History is . . . [a] minute-by-minute invention," p. 40.) He also understands the need for balance between what Coover repeatedly calls "reflection" and "action" (p. 71). At the same time, he—or at least his friends—exploit Gus's blankness. They observe his copulation with Golda as though he were a Pavlovian dog; they rationalize his death by calling him a "police informer" (p. 47). These Socialists manipulate Gus as much as his football coach, and eventually they trigger his stimulus-response system so that he leads their union demonstration and is killed. Possibly like Nixon at Watergate, the great star, Gloomy Gus, is finally destroyed because the signals change and his responses no longer bring victory.

The Water Pourer

My rod and my staff, it comforts thee. (P. 13)

In the preface to this "unpublished chapter [one of several] from *The Origin of the Brunists*," Coover defines art as a polarizing lens upon the explosive texture of human experience: "The infinite is all we have. All narratives, like the universe, are explosive. Man's weak vision is not suited for these infinite explosions. To avoid going blind, he attempts to focus on this or that vector, spark, trajectory.

But there is too much in the corner of his eye. The eye is jittery, distractable. There is more and more to see on all sides. Into the center, out to the edgeless edge. But if he relaxes his eye altogether, he sees nothing at all. Art is a polarizing lens. . . . I can make an attractive and curious shape and drive the narrative through it, absorbing part of your peripheral vision."

The artist, while modulating adjacent materials, thereby manipulates one's attention; there remains, of course, a world of tangential, *excluded* material within the artist's peripheral vision. *The Water Pourer* (1972) is about one such exclusion from the fictional world of *Origin*, a twenty-two-page chapter omitted from that book and published separately. It portrays the vision and character of Charlie Patterson, a man who is the antithesis of *Origin*'s opportunistic, indulgent Justin Miller. If Miller is, as his nickname Tiger suggests, "experience," Patterson is the slaughtered lamb, the sexually innocent and professionally dedicated man, the water pourer, the end of the Age of Aquarius, the rendered Christ. That his story is omitted and that "no one else in . . . [*Origin*] noticed he was there" is a gloss on the fallen world of West Condon both before and after its new religion.

Timid and self-conscious, the high school history teacher Patterson is a middle-aged bachelor nearing the far side of his forties. In style and language, he is a leftover from the late 1950s (his favorite phrases include "What the *h*" and "superhistorical"); he likes to talk and has a corny sense of humor. But he is profoundly lonely, and with this important birthday around the corner, he is in need of renewal—perhaps even a sexual dalliance. As he puts it, this is the time when "out goes the old goat . . . and in comes the grim water-pourer," (p. 3). In his particular case, the grim reaper is associated with bladder trouble. *The Water Pourer* portrays the poignant passing of sexual potential.

Pat's connection to the people in *Origin* is minimal: he lives in West Condon, and like most people there, is superstitious to some degree (interested in the zodiac). He writes voluntarily for the local paper and therefore knows its staff—Miller, characterized here in flattering terms, "a prince of fellows"; his assistant, Jones; and naturally, Miller's secretary, Annie Pompa, the object of his last romantic dream. There is no mention of the mine disaster, although the dates coincide to some extent. Patterson's birthday is one week after Washington's Birthday, the explosion sometime earlier.

Minor details also connect with the novel, such as Patterson's awareness of West Condon's many failed marriages and the sexual promiscuity of the high school students. A different world of experience is heightened here, one that emphasizes the loneliness and helpless desperation of a man tied to lost values and time. Pat is both attracted to, and victimized by, the past. (It is thus of some interest that Coover virtually repeats one passage in both works.)[2]

Coover's style is once again impressive as it wavers between articulating the self-conscious Prufrockian man and his less frequently tapped, sexually imaginative, funny and self-mocking, dapper-Dan self. When slightly inebriated, Pat is a regular roué. There is, at moments, a touch of Leopold Bloom about him, although if one wishes to compare him with Joyce's people, Pat more often resembles the sober shades of *Dubliners*, like "Maria" and Little Chandler (from "A Little Cloud").

The plot is this: with his birthday less than a week away, Pat accepts an invitation for "raviolis" and birthday cake from his office chum, the fat, nonsexual Annie Pompa, descriptively nicknamed "the Girl Fried Egg [Friday]." Nervous about the evening, he stops for a few drinks and enjoys a savory fantasy:

> Ply plump/plow plumb plunk and pluck the old efficacious. Little hot and cozy raviolis and then a little: hmmm. Something to think about, Charlie. Candlelight scene. Alone. Ittabitsy kneeknocking under the table-o. Scusa me, signorina. Heh heh heh. Those knockers! hoo boy! those magic moun tains! Does she do it? Don't they all, Charlie? And alack! poor Annie! In her thirties. Impossibly obese. Obese: still got the old words, head is full of them. Never miss a trick. Old and obese. So: it's all up for her, isn't it? And no girl wants to tumble into the tomb without having at least tasted the prod of thy little old staff, does she? No, Charlie! A thousand times, no! My rod and my staff, it comforts thee! A thousand times! (P. 13)

By the time he gets to Annie's house, his bladder is sorely stimulated, and although he has to urinate throughout the dinner, he is too shy to excuse himself from the table. In the witty juxtaposition of his abdominal discomfort and Annie's relatives' nervous conversation and eager efforts to make a match, Coover creates a powerful concretization of the grim reaper/carpe diem theme, which has occupied so much of his work, as it now focuses on Patterson's ailing organs. Finally, in what is really a very funny sequence, Pat urinates

"wolf"), as though one could ignore this in Coover. To help us distinguish language's different functions, he illustrates his point about wolf/wolf: the man grunts and as he rises to enter her, the piggy says "Not by the hair . . . " On the other hand, lest Coover lose his reader in excessively strenuous and esoteric mental gymnastics (and to parody his own style), he shifts to the most conventional use of imagery as he describes the girl's violation and/or ecstasy—always a matter of perspective. She responds with "one small white hand balled into a fist, soft whimpering noises. The fist slowly opens, revealing: crushed flowers, a small trickle of blood" (p. 9). The subsequent vigorous and mutually pleasurable sex will be described as the man's plowing of the field and her breaking of a water jar on the ground. But this sort of self-consciously unsophisticated imagery (Coover both mocks and imitates a variety of interpretive and literary styles), while reinforcing the reader's hard work, accounts for only a small portion of a very difficult text.

Coover's real *tour de force* is (1) his juxtaposition of the Voice's commentary with the couple's activities, and this runs the gamut from formal and esoteric to kitsch and gibberish, (2) the Man's identification with the Voice, and then (3) the Man's and Maid's identification with, and then (4) their deviation from, the fairy-tale figures. The Voice first retells the plot behind the tableau, which parallels the Man/Maid. For example, when the Man first captures the Maid, the Voice says: "The wolf requests entry"; but then it also interprets. With the Man and Maid chasing around the farmyard, the example, we learn that the duel between the pig and wolf involves the conflict between chaos/order; mind/matter; the sun/moon; life/death; dialecticism/synthesis; unconscious/mystical illumination; the priest/his flock, and, as he so well puts it, "(op. cit.) all that shit" (p. 20).

Among his concerns with color symbolism, numerology, and etymology, the Voice asks some amusing, if curious, questions: Why *did* the wolf wait each time until the houses were finished? Coover achieves some extraordinary effects setting the sober, sometimes sophisticated, jaded, naïve, or silly academic voice against the lively sexual activity.

Despite the chic, kinky, and ultrasophisticated qualities of this filmscript, it is, in addition, one of Coover's most interesting psychological pieces and is actually quite moving in its portrayal of one's initiation into sexual pleasure—at least up until the last third. For all his comedy, Coover dresses his couple in very human garb. In their (magical) three sexual scenes paralleling the intricate, tripartite structuring of the fairy tale (are they, as Barthelme's characters say in *The Dead Father* the three notes in the sexual aria—stimulation, climax, and release?), the girl is portrayed as increasingly more aroused, participatory, and playful; indeed, at the last, she is a bravura coloratura. The Man, also sexual and playful, grows increasingly inhibited and self-conscious. If she begins with panic and he with confidence, their positions reverse at the end. Indeed, he capitulates to the old rules, as though an innate guilt or fear were dissipating his vital energy.

Psychological details appear in poetic images. The first scene, with its smiles, panic, grunts, and sobs, is well captured in the passage partially quoted above: "The Maid's sobs now partly covered by his own heavy breathing. . . . Snap and crash of twigs . . . [a] small white hand balled into a fist . . . slowly opens" (pp. 8, 9). This is followed by a transitional period of playfulness, anger, embarrassment, flirtation, and withdrawal—in images of blood, broken windows, and wet mortar. The ax digs deeper in the tree, and the surrounding stumps grow fewer. The Man, while aroused, builds a brick house—rebuilding the temple to her radical innocence, or perhaps the house to which, as bridegroom, he shall lead her. (Perhaps this is where *he* will finally take refuge.) Each detail conveys a complex interplay of law, innocence, and sexuality.

The Voice, in the meantime, expresses the wolf's strategies to get the pigs, in terms of "encounter," "temptation," and "epilogue" (p. 12). Amid much farmyard activity and more crying and teasing, the Man and Maid are ready for their first truly sensual experience. The Maid moves with "elegance and graceful self-confidence," a "steady" water jug on her head; he "steadily" ploughs the field with a hand plough (p. 21). The sun is bright and hot. Though the tableau and epigraph flash on, she breaks the water jug on his plow; the field, sun, and plow echo in "forceful music." From each one's orgasm and ejaculation ("Water drips off the plow onto the soil"), they paint their faces and body (p. 24).

Up until this moment, the reader has subordinated his interest in the couple to the Voice's interpretations. Now this reverses. The "moral" Voice becomes the comic foil to Coover's sensual action (with metacomedy a commentary on metacriticism?). At one point, for example, the Voice, reminiscent of the impotent priest in *A Theological Position*, makes some wildly funny speculations, the silliness of which even he recognizes: the wolf, he says, miming the

theologians who query everything as man's search for transcendence, represents man's wish to eat God. The hair of the pig's chin, he
then explains, is, after all, part of a beard—an attribute of God.

What follows between the Man and Maid connects all of this (the
diachronic, synchronic, concrete, metaphoric—indeed, the ridiculous). The Maid, herself now on all fours, acts out what the Voice has
just said about deity—by painting on herself a handlebar moustache
(from their ejaculate) and by getting astride the prostrate man. After
more "little popping sounds, like the bursting of little waterjars
against miniature plows" (p. 26), they roll about the muddy, plowed
field and raise their hands to the sky in prayer. Rain falls upon their
seed which is echoed and propagated in nature. Corn grows, as
though magically; she reaps it, shows it to the camera, and fearless of
punishment, sings "Who's Afraid of the Big Bad Wolf?" (p. 27). She
not only plucks the corn, but greedily blows, teases, and bites it.

With such female liberation—midpoint in the script—the Voice
reverts to a more rigid reading of the fairy-tale tableau: the death of
the first two pigs (punning on "death," perhaps her first surrender?)
established the "voracity and true destructive power of the wolf."
The Voice would reestablish the glum mood of "conflict, violence,
[and] death" (p. 28).

The Maid, free and mischievous, like the Cat in the Hat, is totally
involved in the corn. She even sucks it and swallows its juice. (The
cob has a single kernel on top.) Then she eats it up—cob and all. The
Voice goes through a hilarious, etymological history of "straw" and
"twigs" and though everything is viewed in the cold light of semantic
analysis, "meanings" are now all sexual. Straw, for example, derives
from the Anglo-Saxon "streowian" and Sanskrit "str" meaning "to
spread"; stick means "to pierce or thrust in" (pp. 29, 30). The Voice
is noticeably upset, and as she plucks an apple (which she smears all
over herself, also smiling at the camera), he asks for a "brick."

The identification of the Voice and Man, the girl and audience, is
growing. (The Man is now both actor and witness of his own behavior). Of the Maid's eating the corn, Coover writes: "She seems to
include us in her greed," and similarly with the apple, "She is
holding us in her gaze." She winks, giggles, and winks again (p. 29).
The Voice is overwhelmed by the sudden crunch of her apple, and
"off camera" says ("as though clamoring for action"): "Please! Let us
hurry on!" (p. 33). (Is the Voice sexually aroused, like the director in
Love Scene, and is the entire script his vicarious experience?)

At this point, the Voice struggles to get back to his exegetical study of the three pigs' temptation scene (as he now puts it, Christ founded his church on a brick) and a variety of other esoteric interpretations. She remains eating, winking, and drooling, about to mount the butter churn, which, earlier, the Voice associated with labor in exile (the apple with the temptation, and the corn with Eden).

The Voice, though recapitulating the climax of the fairy tale, is clearly commenting on the Man and Maid. As he also gives the etymology of corn and grain, his terms are even more sexual: "Corn is a 'grain' . . . a provincial word for 'groin'; [the] . . . spike of corn is an age-old sign for . . . " (p. 36); he cannot even say the word.

He shouts "Cut," but the Maid continues stimulating the butter churn. Naked, she runs out, chased by the Man, also naked and whooping. Dismayed to see the camera, the Man would cut the scene. She pulls him away nevertheless, and he worries about how his behavior "looks." (He is, after all, before a camera.) A tableau returns, and the Man, now the Voice, explains that what follows—in traditional terms, the temptation scene at noon—will be the grand climax, and the "whole world" will stand as "witness." But he returns to his text, rather than to the girl. "What happens," he explains, is disturbing: "The pig buys a churn," which he defines as "the love act"; but the pig then turns it *against* the wolf!" (p. 38).

Trying to achieve some control and to assert herself, it would appear, she upsets the applecart. ("The wolf didn't know what hit him," p. 38.) Indeed, as the Man describes her ravenous sexuality—in which he gleefully participates—he mostly assumes the attitude of self-conscious prude, the aloof intellectual; as we hear the "rhythmical beat of the churnstaff being agitated," for example, he cites Professor Smoots's theories of male sexuality. As she stimulates the butter churn between her legs and licks the butter from her fingers, he grips "the churn staff like a rifle," his back now turned to the camera. In a wonderful line, tying together all the levels of action beginning with the fairy tale, Coover writes: " "Let me in," says our wolf—' says the Man" (p. 42)—and we might add, "says the Maid."

Indeed, although he has been crying "Stop it," the Man goes off with her into the woods. When he returns, he again avoids the camera. He resumes his lecture, now commenting on both the synchronic and diachronic levels of meaning, a witty exposition of the meaning of chine, cleft, split, and hair, with the Maid enacting the earlier scenario (her indulgence in the corn, apple, and butter). He "pays no attention to her" (p. 47).

We then move back to the tableau detail with the Man now the academician/technologist. (Coover has captured their sexuality during the three cycles of civilization—the hunting, agricultural, and now the technological age.) Since he now understands the significance of history, he can comment on meaning and morality, as well as on how they "erred." What follows is very funny, as the Man/Voice responds to her inexhaustible overtures *in words alone* and offers as his final reply: "YOU HAVE THE DUTY NOT TO BE THE CAUSE OF MY RUIN!" (p. 48). Because of his intellectual expertise on male/female relationships, she swoons and begins taking notes, even taping his history of events. As one can well understand, he would devise new structures for these "more formless and public times" (p. 49). He is the modern hero, the academician, the scientist, the writer adored by women, and the Maid now begins literally eating everything up, including the paper and tapes. But as she also hears about male submission and female domination and about how the woman ensnares the man into marriage and still hoards her wares, she begins, in a sense, eating him up once again. If she earlier consumed his corn, she now consumes his tales and, parallel to her smearing him with mud and butter, she now binds him up in his own words. She perhaps has her own tale to tell; or perhaps she realizes that behind all his research, he is like his colleague who investigates virginity for his linguistic researches but who really just wants to look up women's skirts. She reduces him to the ridiculous.

At best, if one is looking for a serious overview, Coover again suggests that the flux of experience frequently assumes the shape of conflicting forces, but the significance of these forces is entirely arbitrary. They may be interpreted however one wishes—good versus evil, male versus female. The eternal truth of the world is its randomness. Human understanding is like Hegel's dialectic without synthesis, a shifting from one set of opposing vectors to another. But such serious considerations are, one feels certain, less Coover's intention than that his reader enjoy the play of his ingenious game.

After Lazarus

I myself am Resurrection and Life. He who believes in me will live on, even if he dies, and no one who is alive and believes in me will ever die. Do you believe that? (John 11:25–27)

As Jesus tells Martha, Lazarus's sister, about man's personal resurrection through faith and then illustrates his powers in resurrecting Lazarus, in verses fifty to fifty-three, Caiaphas, the

Pharisee high priest who fears Roman domination, explains that Jesus's sacrificial death will unite and save a "whole nation [from] being destroyed." In the biblical text, Jesus is thus viewed as both individual and group savior.

Coover, bypassing both aspects of Christ's powers, creates in his Lazarus figure, as well as in those who reject him, a parable of the artist as Everyman and of the word and the Word. This elaborate metafiction (1980) treats the eternal striving for personal and linguistic authenticity. Though revealing endless new energies in the search for originality, the individual, like the word, is limited by inexorable a priori patterns.

Coover utilizes the filmscript again with the camera eye capturing random and undifferentiated experience. He begins by moving across a shadowless, empty, white world (like the blank page of the mind), which gradually takes on the shapes and sounds of a poor, small village with a prominent cathedral. The Lazarus ceremony is scheduled. Before long, like an Ionescoesque series of proliferations, a single mourner transforms into other mourners and pallbearers of both sexes; all have the same face, gestures, and dress; all are described in similar language and are identical to the awakened Lazarus. The pallbearer, rejecting what Lazarus "represents"—his role in the Christian myth—hurls the arisen figure back into his coffin, races through the empty town, and in an effort toward originality, undergoes a series of metamorphoses. At the same time, he retains his original form, the diachronic and synchronic merging. As he puts on a woman's dress, for example, he instantly transforms into a woman *and* faces himself: "He pulls on the [woman's] clothes, stoops, peers up at: at the pallbearer, now grinning." He gets the black dress on the chair, puts it on and stares "at the pallbearer standing before her" (p. 18).

At the end, failing to discover his own freedom and yet structurally fulfilling his function in the ritual, he returns to the coffin and provides the necessary corpse to complete the Christian ceremony. He is now both the priest and the deceased performing traditional and prescribed roles; he is witness to his own functioning, the Word (authority, law, and tradition) and its manifestation in time, the word (motion and nonmotion—cf., "The Elevator").

The variety of one's associations with this filmscript will depend, as ever, upon his literary and psychological history. One might compare it with *The Kid*, for example, in its focus on a blind, homogenous society that centers around empty and incessant ritual.

Every detail reinforces Coover's parody of popular birth and death ceremonies (e.g., the mourners bite their lips uncertain whether to laugh or cry). However, the appeal of the work is clearly more emotional than rational, like the surrealism of de Chirico or even Ingmar Bergman. Although Coover's images are unique, there is an eerie familiarity about them. He has created a poetic transcription of archetypal dream landscapes, the recesses of the mind in its lights and shadows—preconscious thought patterns and felt experiences associated with emptiness and death.

This is a landscape with endless mourners, all projections of the single consciousness; as in dreams, images take on meaning only through the imposition of logic and structure. As Lazarus cannot rise without Christ, the word cannot be meaningful without a context and referent points. Like the legend of Christ, this is a vision about death and the illusion of victory; it is also about the mind's deepest division between belief and negation. Coover evokes the fear of surrender, the ambivalence toward sacrifice, the universal resistance to structure and one's inevitable capitulation, in the end, to the pattern of tragedy.

The pallbearer tries to free himself of structures, like the Cat in *A Political Fable*, performing unique feats (with flowers, flowerpots, shawls, tattered white cloth, and even sexuality), all of which reach toward new connections but finally fail to signify. His hands even fly to the camera, as though to break the very images that define him. In the end, the old mythologies (like Andy Warhol's Marilyn Monroes) remain and proliferate. Coover's vivid images arouse no small amount of terror, especially when the dead body rises and exchanges /connects its identity with the pallbearer/reader.

Charlie in the House of Rue: An Anatomy of Comedy

In Pinter's world, sexual inadequacy, symptomatic of human vulnerability, is often expressed in weak tea or poor eyesight. In Beckett, the same vulnerability is concretized in urinary problems, ill-fitting boots, and broken bicycles. In much of Coover (*Theological Position, Political Fable, Origin, Public Burning*), dropped pants and naked behinds function similarly. In *Charlie in the House of Rue* (1980) the wild antics of the ordinary-become-bizarre people one associates with Chaplin culminate in the comedian's dropped pants and exposed behind. Charlie fails to rescue the beautiful, rich lady from her grotesque hanging: "He clings to her, pants adroop, . . . gazing out into the encircling gloom with a look of anguish and bewilderment," (p. 44). This is not the Charlie Chaplin we have known.

Chaplin's Hollywood slapstick reminds one of the commedia dell'arte and its later offspring, theater of the absurd. This is a form that concretizes dream sequences, and one can watch the acting out of his deepest, aggressive drives toward authority figures like the police, for example, or toward the powerful, exploitive upper classes. As in farce and dreams, the clown-hero is allowed the outrage and hostile expression of his deepest thoughts (his unconscious) without punishment or retaliation from society. Both innocent and destructive, he can act out the interplay of the conscious and unconscious mind.

Coover's novella is fascinating as it re-creates Chaplin's style and yet removes a legendary figure from his legend—i.e., the Hollywood scenario where everything works out for him. Initially, Charlie "blinks, his eyelids flicking shut and open like camera shutters. . . . His little patch of scruffy black moustache twitches with anticipation in the middle of his pale face" (p. 9). Charlie appears in a familiar setting—with a policeman who has a helmet for a hat and a six-pointed star, and a beautiful but cold lady and her oversexed maid. There is the usual Chaplin slapstick—pie throwing, a policeman slipping on a bar of soap, races of eating overflowing bowls of soup. But everything moves toward the grotesque in a series of dreamlike metamorphoses: chandelier globes look like bowls of soup, a douche bag transforms into rabbits; a man becomes a woman with a man's eyes about to fall from their sockets; Charlie grabs the loose eyeball which turns into the maid's behind. There is blood, soup, pies, tears, and urine.

Most frightening is Coover's pursuit of what is not even suggested in the Hollywood films—the sadness ("rue"), gratuitous suffering, and hostility that truly define the bourgeois world of cardboard types. Despite Charlie's efforts to interact with these people, he actually has no power whatsoever to affect their lives. As they are gratuitously injured into their various metamorphoses, so is he victimized by their indifference. It would seem to be their initial coldness to him, in the first half, and their subsequent and bizarre transformations which occur independent of him, in the second half, that result in his final frustration and despair. This is dream or nightmare experience where nothing works out.

Coover creates an unusual background against which to chart

human experience, his measurement no longer, as in Beckett or Pinter, the disparity between conscious and unconscious thought and behavior. Instead, his landscape reflects the amoral texture of the unconscious—a mosaic of cruelty, dread, instinct, and emptiness. These he sets against a universe of gratuitous event. Beckett's and Pinter's counterpoint of conscious and unconscious behavior gives way to a portrait that consists entirely of the irrational and the contingent.

Finally, one might comment on the metafictional dimension of the piece by looking at Chaplin's last lines (quoted above), spoken with his pants down: "He clings to her . . ." Charlie, in the end, is the impotent, speechless observer of human experience. Those he has sought to entertain, and thereby rescue, have a life of their own and, despite his efforts, know a despair that ends only in death. As the comic artist who would but cannot change the world, Chaplin is helpless.

On the other hand, in a final Coover irony, despite Chaplin's unrelieved pain, he remains the subject of an audience's laughter—the people on the opposite side of the stage—as it identifies with him and laughs at its own helplessness. Charlie's absurd performances, like those of the Cat in the Hat, in the midst of the ordinary and grotesque, may ultimately change nothing, but they still provide humor and comfort. Charlie looks both within and without the proscenium, at the stereotypes before him and at the reader, as he says: "Who took the light away? And why is everybody laughing?" (p. 44).

Spanking the Maid

Traditional, as well as structuralist and deconstructionist critics, can have a heyday in the complex and highly whimsical *Spanking the Maid* (1981), a tale "of callipygomancy" (p. 52), with its series of repeated rituals and repeated phrases. A maid, with "all her paraphernalia," enters her employer's bedroom; he awakens out of a dream with an erection; she tidies about nervously but efficiently and then commits "a fundamental blunder" (or, is, in effect, "blundered to") in an odd and funny, somewhat Ionescoesque way. A well-made bed, for example, becomes undone. Finally, the master performs his "obligation" to "administer the proper correction" (p. 28)—and he spanks the maid.

That this is repeated in a series of subtle variations gives the story a metafictional dimension which suggests both the difficulties of re-porting the simplest activities (e.g., the woman's passive "serving" and her male "superior's" active judgments) and the complex struc-tures within which fiction and language function. If in traditional literature, words and plot represent human activity and are there-fore metaphoric, here human activity once again represents the functions of language and the problems of writing. In addition, Coover's serial design, which repeats through time and space, is counterpointed by basic, natural functions both within and outside the narrative pattern—the sun rising, birds singing, bees humming, the man urinating, the fact of death.

The man's act of punishment and the woman's happy submission are the reader's focal point. She is, in fact, more eager to receive his strokes than he is to impose them, and the story expands to sym-bolize matters of teaching and learning, confession and contrition. ("Oh, teach me," she repeats, in a whimsical parody of the Ash Wednesday refrain: cf., T. S. Eliot's version.) Coover stretches his paradigm of human experience to play with the central abstraction that suffering (even if blood is drawn with a leather belt, for exam-ple) purifies the soul, and that hard work builds character. In the maid's ritualistic cleaning of the toilet or in her proper handling of sheets (for bed or book? as emblems of the mind or psyche? as a shroud?), she comes to "understand that the tasks, truly common, are only peripheral details in some larger scheme of things which includes her punishment—indeed perhaps depends upon it" (p. 33). Punishment or "chastisement," after all, Coover adds, more seriously clarifying the universal condition of living, prevents "natu-ral confusion and disorder."

In the man's high-sounding pronouncement and what may be his death at the end, Coover may be expanding his allegorical resources to encompass the man as God the Father, as well as priest, teacher, writer, lover, or any social or economic force. The man, however, may also be the pupil or any subordinate, for the roles of confessor and victimizer, on any level, may reverse and attach to the woman. ("He knows that it is he, not she, who is forever in need of . . . explanations," p. 11.) This may be a tale about the act of creating on any level: "Her soul . . . is his invention" (p. 35); "When . . . did all this really begin? . . . Long ago? Not yet?" (p. 10). It may be about the different functions of language; it may even choreograph the sexual act. In each case, nevertheless, as the man explains, each spanking is due to "some kind of failure of communication" (p. 34).

Whatever one's specific reading, Coover once again parodies the need for (and rationalizations about) structure and ritual, and he is very funny. "A maid's oppressive routine," the man says, seems like the "sudden invention of love" (p. 11). "Drudgery," he adds, must seem like "divine service." "True service," after all, is "perfect freedom" (p. 7). In his wonderful pun on the woman's "hired end" (her hired derrière) and the man's "hold on it," Coover parodies traditional religion's efficacy through its dependence (or *hold*) upon a belief in life's higher purpose or *end*. Her behind is "destined by Mother Nature for the arduous invention of souls" (p. 45). Unfortunately, for the man, this gospel doesn't always comfort: "Sometimes . . . watching the weals emerge from the blank page of her soul's ingress like secret writing, he finds himself searching it for something, he doesn't know what exactly, a message of sorts, the revelation of a mystery" (p. 46).

Interested neither in moral absolutes and the laws they give rise to nor in the traditional paradoxes accepted through faith, Coover stylistically verifies that concrete and imaginative harmonies are possible within the disparates of life. In the larger sense, one remains both in servitude to and master of his fate, but specifically, in apprehending the totality of (so to speak) the chapters, characters, and meaning of his life, one cannot separate role, word, act, or value from anything else that touches it even peripherally. The dancer and the dance are again one, the word and Word. Indeed, the whole story reads like a dance, with pattern, implied sexuality, and verbally choreographed thrusts that connect evocations of flesh, spirit, time, and space. Coover's vision and what he has tried to recreate verbally and visually—with a series of bird, womb, and snake transformations in the text from the most formal designs to the fetal and sexual shapes within them, and vice versa—is the "riddle of Genesis": "a condition *has* no beginning. Only *change* can begin or end" (p. 10). Once again, "process" within the human condition, even one's subjugation to time, chance, and passionate transport, is perfection.

One of Coover's remarks in a 1981 review of an Ernesto Sábato novel is appropriate to this, and all of Coover's, work: "Events in the outer world mirror events in the inner world. Telepathy is possible. Everything is portentous and—not because this is fiction but because, contrarily, this is the way the universe works—everything is symbolic."[3] Thus, the reverberations throughout, of language, gesture, color and mood, as well as Rikki's pictorial decorations which illustrate not only the metamorphic relatedness of all experience but also the relationship of art and life. There is a connectedness between all experience and all knowledge, from life to death. At the same time, every act, perception, signification—and person—exists in utter isolation.

Language once again thus functions throughout on many levels and is simultaneously concrete and metaphoric. Evoking the sexual/spiritual unity defined in *Pricksongs*, "the room seems almost to explode with the blast of light" (p. 6) and the man's erection is "the day . . . hard upon him" (p. 19). With repeated phrases and loaded words throughout ("gravely," "crosses," "flooding," "radiant"), puns expand philosophically, and traditional word meanings are fragmented or expanded: the man, in his dreams mostly, connects humanity/homonymity; utility/futility; lectures/lechers; holes/souls; humility/hymnody; and even humor/tumor. One lives in the Edenic world with "dew . . . still on every plant in the garden," also the world of "time lost" (p. 4).

Both in the most serious and comic of terms, the act of "tidying" is the life of every person as artist, the supplicant in search of belief. Coover's "maid" "enjoys this part of her work: flushing out the stale darkness of the dead night with such grand (yet circumspect) gestures—it's almost an act of magic!" (p. 7). Actually, the act of making the bed is the existential act of encountering fear and dread, but it is also the moment when one's imagination may redeem and transform: "Today . . . when she tosses the covers back, she finds, coiled like a dark snake near the foot, a bloodstained leather belt" (p. 9). At the end, the maid (and we) learn that "change and condition are coeval and everlasting: a truth as hollow as the absence of birdsong (but they are singing!)" (p. 51).

Notes

Selected Bibliography

Index

Notes

1 The Universal Fictionmaking Process
An Introduction to Robert Coover and the Avant-Garde

1. Regardless of debates about nomenclature and membership, excellent introductions to the avant-garde include Jerome Klinkowitz's *Literary Disruptions: The Making of a Post-Contemporary Fiction* (Urbana: University of Illinois Press, 1976); Raymond Federman's *Surfiction* (Chicago: Swallow Press, 1975); and Robert Scholes's *Fabulation and Metafiction* (Urbana: University of Illinois Press, 1979).

2. "The Literature of Exhaustion," *Atlantic* 220 (August 1967): 29–34.

3. C. W. E. Bigsby, "Interview with Robert Coover," in *The Racial Imagination and the Liberal Tradition*(London: Junction Books, 1982), p. 82. (Coover and Barth have subsequently met.)

4. Ibid., pp. 81–82. See also Frank Gado, *First Person: Conversations on Writers and Writing* (Schenectady: Union College Press, 1973), pp. 142–59; Leo J. Hertzel, "An Interview with Robert Coover," *Critique* 2, no. 3 (1969): 25–29; and Alma Kadragic, "Robert Coover," *Shantih* 2 (Summer 1972): 57–60. See also Federman; Donald Barthelme, *Shenandoah* 27 (Winter 1976): 3–31; and William H. Gass, *Fiction and the Figures of Life* (New York: Knopf, 1970).

5. Bigsby, p. 87.

6. Gado, p. 143.

7. See Robert Towers, "Nixon's Seventh Crisis," *New York Review of Books*, 29 September 1977, pp. 8–10, or Celia Betsky, "*The Public Burning*," *Commonweal* 28 (October 1977): 693–96.

8. Hertzel, p. 28.

9. Gado, p. 152.

10. Ibid., pp. 149–50.

11. Bigsby, p. 87.

12. Gado, p. 144.

13. I am especially indebted to Theodore and Jane Beardsley for information regarding Coover's school years. See also Larry McCaffery, "Robert Coover," in *Dictionary of Literary Biography*, vol. 2, ed. J. Helterman and R. Layman (Detroit: Bruccoli Clark/Gale, 1978), p. 107.

14. *New American Review*, no. 11, ed. T. Solotoroff (New York: Simon and Schuster, 1971), pp. 132–43.

15. Ibid., p. 137.
16. Gado, p. 153.
17. Ibid., pp. 153–54.
18. P. 156.
19. McCaffery, p. 108.
20. Gado, p. 146.
21. Kadragic, p. 60
22. "Dedicatoria Prólogo a don Miguel de Cervantes Saavedra," pp. 76–79.
23. "The Last Quixote," p. 132.
24. P. 138.
25. Gado, p. 148.
26. Kadragic, p. 59.
27. "The Master's Voice," in *American Review* no. 26 (November 1977), 361–88, is an excellent introduction to Gabriel García-Márquez. In addition, Coover not only translates Spanish literature into English but also translates his own work into Spanish. See Selected Bibliography.
28. Gado, p. 144.
29. Geoffrey Woolf, "An American Epic," 19 August 1977, p. 56.
30. Ibid.
31. In a meeting with this author on 8 July 1981.
32. In a meeting with this author on 9 July 1981.
33. Seaver's remark.
34. Woolf, p. 56.
35. Bigsby, pp. 83, 87, 88.
36. Kadragic, pp. 59, 60.
37. Gado, p. 156.
38. Hertzel, pp. 26–27, 29.

2 *The Origin of the Brunists*: The Origins of a Vision

1. (Bloomfield Hills, Mich. and Columbia, S. C.: Bruccoli Clark, 1972), discussed in chap. 7.
2. Coover defines an entire society in both psychological and socioeconomic details. Those who run the town include the better educated and better heeled Ted Cavanaugh, the banker; Whimple, the mayor; Fisher, the hotel entrepreneur; Himebaugh, the lawyer; and Castle, the storeowner. Clemens, Minicucci, Moroni, Collins, and Strelchuk are among the working class who die in the mine; surviving them are their families (e.g., Clemens's sister, Dinah, the book's Mary Magdelene figure) and also Bonali and Bruno. The religious community includes the Catholics (Father Battalione and Bonali) and the Protestants, like Cavanaugh and Edwards; those who join the Brunists (the Brunos, Nortons, Collins) and their evangelical opposition (the Baxters). The media people include Lou Jones, Annie Pompas, and Justin Miller.
3. Compare, for example, Marcella and Happy, two women with whom Miller is romantically involved: Marcella (p. 108) begins, "He arrives"; Happy (p. 238), "It was widely."

4. These include several memorable lost souls like the orphaned student, really in search of a parent, and Ben Wosznik, whom the widows pursue and who becomes the group's balladeer.

3 *The Universal Baseball Association*: The Props of Meaning

1. Historians of the sport consider Ruth to have been the savior of baseball following the "Black Sox" scandal of 1919.
2. See the interesting "Robert Coover's Playing Fields," by Brenda Wineapple, *Iowa Review* 10 (1979): 66-74. See also Régis Durand, "The Exemplary Fictions of Robert Coover," *Les Américainistes*, ed. I. and C. Johnson (Port Washington: Kennikat Press, 1978), pp. 130-37; Neil Schmitz "Robert Coover and the Hazards of Metafiction," *Novel* 7 (1974): 210-19; and Robert Scholes, *Fabulation and Metafiction* (Urbana: University of Illinois Press, 1979), p. 208.
3. R. E. Johnson, Jr., "Structuralism and the Reading of Contemporary Fiction," *Soundings* 58 (Fall 1975): 281-306.
4. Margaret Heckard, "Coover, Metafiction, and Freedom," *Twentieth Century Literature* 22 (1976): 210-27.
5. Henry's final surrender to fantasy is marked by his abandonment of simile and metaphor for a kind of hallucinatory equivalence of real and fantasized people and things. Early in the novel, for example, as he walks in the rain, he says: "Hunched-up cars pushed through the streets like angry defeated ballplayers" (p. 46).
6. After their sex, a "consecratory romp," they perform their "ablutions and purifications"; foreplay for Hettie includes a ritual with her knees. (One of Henry's players always precedes playing by squeezing "his bat for luck.") Hettie also communicates her sexual pleasure in terms of language. She "used to let a man know he was in with her, getting the true and untarnished word" (p. 22). The use of baseball jargon for sex continues in today's youth culture. "Paradise by the Dashboard Light," by Jim Steinam (recorded by Meatloaf) tells of a young couple's "scoring" through Phil Rizzuto's baseball commentary.
7. Rooney, for example, would take the day off and get organized; for him, the "game" (life) must go on. But Rooney also throws up; Shadwell wants to protect his own son from baseball and aging. Jaybird Wall makes practical jokes, and Fenn McCaffree, the chancellor, observing all through a T.V. (another fictionalized godhead, created by Henry), relates everything to his own political position.
8. As each of Stephen Dedalus's epiphanies is associated with a "communion" meal, so is each of Henry's—from his first pastrami sandwich to the duck now, and pizza later.
9. One could, of course, read the entire book as an allegory of the God who creates an utterly orderly universe (and "a Book") and then abandons it or is irresponsible to his creation or is a victim of his own creative machinery or acts according to personal whim or irrationality. The book is thus a parody of the Old and New Testaments and of various contemporary religious debates. Such a reading, while fascinating, ignores the particulars of the book—e.g., Henry's emotional drama. Recent psychoanalytic theory has, interestingly, emphasized an unconscious wish for omnipotence as a central force in the human psyche. Cf., Hans Kohut's *Analysis*

of the Self (New York: International Universities Press, 1971), considered by some to contain the most significant theory since Freud's revolutionary ideas.

10. Mallarmé's "Un Coup de Dis" is divided into three sections: "JAMAIS"/ "N'ABOLIRA"/"LE HASARD."

11. Coover remarks: "The Henry book came into being for me when I found a simple structural key to the metaphor of a man throwing dice for a baseball game he has made up. It suddenly occurred to me to use Genesis I.i to II.3 — seven chapters corresponding to the seven days of creation — and this in turn naturally implied an eighth, the apocalyptic day. Having decided on this basic plan, I read a lot of exegetical works on that part of the Bible in order to find out as much as I could which would reinforce and lend meaning to the division into parts." See Gado, p. 149.

12. Regarding Damon's death (Daemon, Demon, Diamond, Nomad):

(1) For Henry, in his middle-age slump, Damon represents pure, unrestrained freedom, a mental/physical state Henry is long past. In a bitter concretization of the God/Son relationship, *He*-nry is the creator who kills his son out of envy, then disappears from the world and leaves it to its own ignorance to play out a difficult and predetermined drama. The father is in eternal competition with his son. Reversing the traditional association of father (the inscrutable one) and son (human love), Coover writes of Brock and Damon: Brock was a "public phenomenon," Damon, a "self-enclosed yet participating mystery. His own man, yet at home in the world, part of it, involved" (p. 9).

(2) Henry punishes Damon for wanting to "top" his father's record; about this Henry "laughed irreverently" (p. 10). The novel is filled with fathers and sons and the rivalry between them: e.g., Lou asks if Damon is Henry's "bastard" son; Henry and Brock are the same age — also the same age as the Association — Damon their mutual son; other fathers include "Pappy" Rooney and even Zefferblatt, whom Henry calls "Dad"; the latter says "Don't kid me baby."

(3) Henry is the father who vies with his son for youth and power and envies that his son is better loved, that he has greater potential. He kills Damon in order to save himself. This is survival of the fittest.

(4) In the tradition of literary figures who slay their sons (Cuchulain, Rustum), Henry commits an unforgivable sin, which may account for why he is cast aside from the last chapter, where his personal vision transforms into myth.

(5) Henry kills Damon in order to save himself morally and spiritually. Damon's death permits Henry his own descent and rebirth; it gives him the opportunity to find himself so he can later choose to kill Casey. It is the vehicle for his learning that perfection is process, the place of death in life.

(6) A part of Henry wants to die: "Why was he murdering himself?" (p. 129). Although Henry would kill the entire Association, "process" outside of him, continues. The work of art gains its own autonomy.

(7) Damon's death appeases Henry's guilt for having pitched him too soon after the perfect game. Aware of his increasing hubris, Henry must have Damon die in order to restore (Swanee) Law (whom Damon defeated in the no-hit game).

(8) Damon's death teaches Henry another lesson about pride: Even in fantasy one cannot fix perfection. "Without law, power lost its shape" (p. 157); one must create within forms. Damon's death humbles Henry creatively and personally.

(9) Pursuing a romantic impulse, Henry wishes to keep perfection alive. Since he knows Damon must eventually age and die, he preserves him (contrary to no. 8) in perfect youth. He dies on (Good) Friday, in the bottom of the ninth inning, is the ninth batter, in the forty-ninth game, with Henry's ninth chart.

(10) Pursuing a metadramatic device and the pattern of all myth, the artist must satisfy his audience, which has borne witness to Damon's perfection and which must also see him die. The essential paradox at the heart of all religious ritual, this is the "story" Henry invents as author of the universal baseball association.

There are also a multitude of possibilities regarding Casey's death:

(1) Henry cannot tolerate having projected death, Damon's fate, into his game, so he kills Damon's "murderer," an eye for an eye, to restore balance.

(2) It keeps the league going and permits Henry's "resurrection," the vehicle for understanding once again that perfection is process, that death (Damon's) gives life its value. Henry gains humility and stoicism.

(3) In his own way perfect like Damon ("He played the game, heart and soul, like nobody ever," p. 201), Casey, another child of Henry's imagination, is killed for all the above reasons discussed regarding Damon. For example, as artist-criminal and tragic hero (with even overtones of Moses), Henry must suffer and celebrate the autonomy of his greatest enterprise. Casey's death, again in its J(ock) (esus) C function, allows him to finish and separate from his creation.

4 *The Public Burning*: The Making of The President

1. "Uncle Sam and the Phantom," *Saturday Review*, 17 September 1977, pp. 27-28, 34; "Coover's Revisionist Fantasy," *Commentary*, 9 October 1977, pp. 67-69. More reasonable reviews include Donald Hall, "Three Million Toothpicks," *National Review*, 30 September 1977, pp. 118-20; Celia Betsky, "The Public Burning," *Commonweal*, 28 October 1977, pp. 693-96; and Thomas R. Edwards, "Real People, Mythic History," *New York Times Book Review*, 14 August 1977, pp. 9, 26.

2. See Hall, Bell, and Benjamin DeMott, "Culture Watch," *Atlantic* 240 (November 1977), 98-101; Thomas LeClair, "The Public Burning," *The New Republic*, 17 September 1977, pp. 37-38; Walter Clemens, "Shock Treatment," *Newsweek*, 8 August 1977, pp. 75-76.

3. Among the other accounts of the Rosenberg trial, see E. L. Doctorow's *The Book of Daniel* (New York: Random House, 1971); Louis Nizer's *The Implosion Conspiracy* (New York: Doubleday, 1973); Walter and Miriam Schneir's *Invitation to an Inquest* (New York: Delta, 1968); Robert and Michael Meeropol's *We Are Your Sons* (Boston: Houghton Mifflin, 1975); and sections of William O. Douglas's *The Court Years: The Autobiography of William O. Douglas, 1939-1975* (New York: Random House, 1980).

4. See chap. 15.

5. Baseball fulfills this same religious function in the *UBA*.

6. For a fascinating discussion of these matters, see William O. Douglas.

7. "History" continues to reevaluate the moral status of former presidents, especially in regard to their private lives—e.g., their financial difficulties after leaving the White House. Jefferson's lavish style in Mt. Vernon was so indulgent and financially ruinous he was forced to sell his library, which established the Library of Congress.

Madison exhausted all his cash in paying his son's debts. Monroe was forced to sell his estate and move to New York, dependent upon a son-in-law for support. Grant, back at his Wall Street firm and in grave health, was the first to write his memoirs in order to relieve financial difficulties (he received $450,000); Nixon was $600,000 in debt when he left office, which he immediately turned around through his memoirs and television appearances.

8. Films and ads—everything public—adds to this atmosphere; next to a news item that the Rosenbergs may fight their sentence are ads for pink cigarettes; there is a photo of a man "sweating behind bars in a B. Altman & Co. ad" with the caption: "Are you facing a 90-day sentence?" and a "floor-level peek up the skirt of a woman strapped into a chair" (for an airlines). The Beekman Theater has the double bill *Double Confesion* and *Murder without Crime*. Times Square features *High Treason, A Slight Case of Larceny, Three Sinners* and even *The Atomic City*. Rita Hayworth's *Salome* exploits both the execution and the sex angle.

5 *Pricksongs and Descants*: An Introduction to the Short Fictions

1. Gado, pp. 150–51.
2. The *"Dedicatoria y Prólogo a don Miguel de Cervantes Saavedra"* is in the *Pricksongs and Descants*, pp. 76–79; the essay on Beckett is discussed at length in chap. 1.
3. During the Inquisition, imaginative fictions were viewed with suspicion, for literature was supposed to exemplify and reinforce conventional morality. The sixteenth- and seventeenth-century writer, like Cervantes in his *Novelas ejemplares*, would have apologized, as Coover does here, for the "bad things" that follow, more than for the subtle and overly polished things people would say about him: *el mal que han de decir de mí más de cuatro sotiles y almidonados*.
4. These remarks are also discussed at length in chap. 1.
5. This is wonderfully ironic. Cervantes conceived his Quixote as a realistic answer to the fantastic Amadíses of traditional, chivalric romance, but he became so enamored of his "antihero," he transformed him into the figure we all know. Similarly, although Coover would demystify his reader and lead him to clarification and maturity with his own "barber's basin" on his head, he ultimately evokes a transcendent experience filled with magic, mystery, and mystification. His "bones" are the pillars of classical temples.
6. Coover has said these short, experimental fictions allowed him to exhaust a single metaphor in a limited space not permitted in the novels. Obviously, he exhausts much more than this.
7. See William H. Gass, *Fiction and the Figures of Life* (New York: Knopf, 1970), p. 105–6.

7 More Innovations: Old and New

1. This is a revision of "A Cat in the Hat for President," *New American Review*, no. 4 (New York: New American Library, 1968), pp. 7–45.
2. Beginning "Religion, sex, politics . . . " on pp. 4–5 here; on p. 30, in *Origin*.
3. "Oedipus in Argentina," *New York Times Book Review*, 26 July 1981, pp. 1, 25–26.

Selected Bibliography

Works by Robert Coover

"One Summer in Spain: Five Poems." *Fiddlehead* [Canada] (Autumn 1960): 18–19.

"Blackdamp." *Noble Savage* 4 (October 1961): 218–19.

"The Square Shooter and the Saint." *Evergreen Review* 25 (July–August 1962): 92–101.

"Dinner with the King of England." *Evergreen Review* 27 (November–December 1962): 110–18.

"D. D. Baby." *Cavalier* 13 (July 1963): 53–56, 93.

"The Second Son." *Evergreen Review* 31 (October–November 1963): 72–88.

"El caminante" [translation of Guillermo Putzeys Alvarez story]. *Cultura* [El Salvador] 30 (October–December 1963): n.p.

"Que la puerta estaba abierta" and "La espiral del leproso" [Spanish translation of "That Door was Open" and "The Leper's Helix"]. *Revista Universidad de San Carlos* [Guatemala] 65 (1963): 151–55.

"The Neighbors." *Argosy* [London], January 1965, n.p.

The Origin of the Brunists. New York: G. P. Putnam's Sons, 1966.

"The Mex Would Arrive in Gentry's Junction at 12:10." *Evergreen Review* 47 (June 1967): 63–65, 98–102.

"The Cat in the Hat for President." In *New American Review*. No. 4. New York: New American Library, 1968, pp. 7–45.

"The Osprey and the Sparrowhawk" [translation of Ricardo Estrada poem]. *Quarterly Review of Literature* 15 (1968): 259–62.

The Universal Baseball Association, Inc., J. Henry Waugh, Prop. New York: Random House, 1968.

"Incident in the Streets of the City." *Playboy* 16 (January 1969): 80–88, 238–39.

"Letter from Patmos" [poem]. *Quarterly Review of Literature* 16 (1969): 29–31.

Pricksongs and Descants. New York: E. P. Dutton, 1969.

"That the Door Opened." *Quarterly Review of Literature* 16 (1969): 311–17.

"The Reunion." *Iowa Review* 1 (Fall 1970): 64–69.

"Some Notes about Puff." *Iowa Review*, Winter 1970, pp. 29–31.

"Debris" [poem]. *Panache* 9 (1971): 7.

"McDuff on the Mound." *Iowa Review* 2 (Fall 1971): 111–20.

"The First Annual Congress of the High Church of Hard Core (Notes from the Underground)." *Evergreen Review* 89 (May 1971): 16, 74.

175

"The Last Quixote." In *New American Review*. No. 11. New York: Simon and Schuster, 1971, pp. 132–43.

A Theological Position. New York: E. P. Dutton, 1972.

"Beginnings." *Harper's* 244 (March 1972): 82–87.

"Lucky Pierre and the Music Lesson." In *New American Review*. No. 14. New York: Simon and Schuster, 1972, pp. 202–12.

"The Old Men" and "An Encounter." *The Little Magazine* 1 (1972): n.p.

The Water Pourer [an unpublished chapter from *The Origin of the Brunists*]. Bloomfield Hills, Mich., and Columbia, S. C.: Bruccoli Clark, 1972.

"The Dead Queen." *Quarterly Review of Literature* 18 (1973): 304–13.

"The Old Man" [poem]. *Panache* 12 (1973): 12–13.

"The Public Burning of Ethel and Julius Rosenberg: An Historical Romance. *TriQuarterly* 26 (Winter 1974): 262–81.

"Lucky Pierre and the Cunt Auction." *Antaeus*, Spring–Summer 1974, pp. 13–14.

"Whatever Happened to Gloomy Gus of the Chicago Bears?" *American Review* 22 (1975): 31–111.

"The Fallguy's Faith." *TriQuarterly* 35 (Winter 1976): 79–80.

"The Convention." *Panache* 18 (1977): 20–29.

"The Master's Voice." *American Review* 26 (November 1977): 361–88.

The Public Burning. New York: A Richard Seaver Book/Viking Press, 1977.

"The Tinkerer." *Antaeus* 24 (1977): 111–12.

Hair O' The Chine. Bloomfield Hills, Mich., and Columbia, S. C.: Bruccoli Clark, 1979.

"A Working Day" [an earlier version of *Spanking the Maid*]. *Iowa Review* 10 (Summer 1979): 1–27.

"In Bed One Night." *Playboy* 27 (January 1980): 150–51, 316.

A Political Fable. New York: Viking Press, 1980.

After Lazarus. Bloomfield Hills, Mich., and Columbia, S. C.: Bruccoli Clark, 1980.

Charlie in the House of Rue. Lincoln, Mass.: Penmaen Press, 1980.

Spanking the Maid. Bloomfield Hills, Mich., and Columbia, S. C.: Bruccoli Clark, 1981; New York: Grove Press, 1982.

Works about Robert Coover

Berman, Neil. "Coover's Universal Baseball Association: Play as Personalized Myth." *Modern Fiction Studies* 24 (1978): 209–22.

Bigsby, C. W. E., and Heide Ziegler. *The Radical Imagination and the Liberal Tradition*. London: Junction Books, 1982.

Blachowicz, Camille. "Bibliography: Robert Bly and Robert Coover." *Great Lakes Review* 3 (1976): 69–73.

Cope, Jackson I. "Robert Coover's Fictions." *Iowa Review* 2 (Fall 1971): 94–110.

Dillard, R. H. W. "Robert Coover." *Hollins Critic* 7 (1970): 1–11.

Durand, Régis. "The Exemplary Fictions of Robert Coover." In *Les Américanistes*. Ed. I. and C. Johnson. Port Washington, N. Y.: Kennikat Press, 1978.

Federman, Raymond. *Surfiction*. Chicago: Swallow Press, 1975.

Gabert, Charla, "The Metamorphisis of Charlie." *Chicago Review* 32 (Autumn 1980): 60–64.

Gado, Frank. "Robert Coover." In his *Conversations on Writers and Writing*. Schenectady: Union College Press, 1973.

Gass, William H. *Fiction and the Figures of Life*. New York: Knopf, 1970.

Hansen, Arlen J. "The Dice of God, Einstein, Heisenberg, and Robert Coover." *Novel* 10 (1976): 49–58.

Harris, Charles B. "The Morning After." In his *Contemporary Novelists of the Absurd*. New Haven: College and University Press, 1971.

Heckard, Margaret. "Robert Coover, Metafiction, and Freedom." *Twentieth Century Literature* 22 (1976): 219–27.

Hertzel, Leo J. "An Interview with Robert Coover." *Critique* 11 (1969): 25–29.

———. "What's Wrong with the Christians?" *Critique* 11 (1969): 11–24.

Hume, Kathryn. "Robert Coover's Fiction: The Naked and the Mythic." *Novel*, Winter 1979, pp. 127–48.

Johnson, R. E., Jr. "Structuralism and the Reading of Contemporary Fiction." *Soundings* 58 (Fall 1975): 299–306.

Kadragic, Alma. "An Interview with Robert Coover." *Shantih* 2 (Summer 1972): 57–60.

Kissel, Susan. "The Contemporary Artist and His Audience in the Short Stories of Robert Coover," *Studies in Short Fiction* 10 (Winter 1979): 49–54.

Klinkowitz, Jerome. *Literary Disruptions: The Making of a Post-Contemporary Fiction*. Urbana: University of Illinois Press, 1975.

McCaffery, Larry. "Donald Barthelme, Robert Coover, William H. Gass: Three Checklists." *Bulletin of Bibliography* 31 (July–September 1974): 101–6.

———. "Robert Coover." In *The Dictionary of Literary Biography*. Vol. 2. Eds. J. Helterman and R. Layman. Detroit: Bruccoli Clark/Gale Research, 1978, pp. 106–21.

———. "The Magic of Fiction-Making." *Fiction International* 4–5 (Winter 1975): 147–53.

Pearse, James A. "Beyond the Narrational Frame: Interpretation and Metafiction," *Quarterly Review of Speech* 66 (February 1980): 73–84.

Schmitz, Neil. "A Prisoner of Words." *Partisan Review* 40 (Winter 1973): 131–35.

———. "Robert Coover and the Hazards of Metafiction." *Novel* 7 (Spring 1974): 210–19.

Scholes, Robert. *Fabulation and Metafiction*. Urbana: University of Illinois Press, 1979.

Schultz, Max F. "Politics of Parody." In his *Black Humor Fiction of the Sixties*. Athens: Ohio University Press, 1973.

Shelton, Frank. "Humor and Balance in Coover's *The Universal Baseball Association*." *Critique* 15 (1975): 78–90.

Wineapple, Brenda. "Robert Coover's Playing Fields." *Iowa Review* 10 (1979): 66–74.

Woolf, Geoffrey. "An American Epic." *New Times* 9 (August 1977): 48–57.

Zavarzaden, Mas'ud. *The Mythopoeic Reality*. Urbana: University of Illinois Press, 1976.

Index

Lois Gordon is chairman and professor of English and comparative literature at Fairleigh Dickinson University, in Teaneck, New Jersey. She is the author of the earliest books on Harold Pinter (1969) and Donald Barthelme (1981) and has also published extensively on a wide variety of modern writers including T. S. Eliot, William Faulkner, Randall Jarrell, Arthur Miller, and Samuel Beckett. She is presently at work on a history of modernism and postmodernism.

DATE DUE

PRINTED IN U.S.A.